# PORSCHE

HAYNES CLASSIC MAKES SERIES

# PORSCHE

## ENGINEERING FOR EXCELLENCE

TONY DRON

First published in May 2008

A catalogue record for this book is available from the
British Library

ISBN 978 1 84425 882 1

Library of Congress control no: 2007943097

Published by Haynes Publishing, Sparkford,
Yeovil, Somerset BA22 7JJ, UK
Tel: 01963 442030 Fax: 01963 440001
Int. tel: +44 1963 442030   Int. fax: +44 1963 440001
E-mail: sales@haynes.co.uk
Website: www.haynes.co.uk

Haynes North America Inc.
861 Lawrence Drive, Newbury Park,
California 91320, USA

Printed and bound in Great Britain by
J. H. Haynes & Co. Ltd, Sparkford

# contents

# Preface

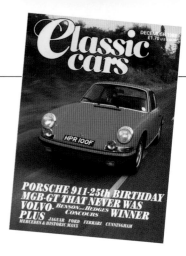

*Celebrating the 25th birthday of the 911 in Classic Cars, December 1988. As the then editor of the magazine, I am seen here driving David Cocker's 1967 2.0-litre 911S, a car so remarkably original that it had never had one panel resprayed. Twenty years on, David still owns HPR 100F and he tells me the original paint is retained to this day.*
(Mike Valente, Classic Cars)

At the heart of it, this book is about what Porsche cars are like to drive. There must be hundreds of books on Porsche cars but none appears to have tackled the subject from that angle. Many writers have traced the brilliant technical progress of Porsche car design and engineering through the decades, and Karl Ludvigsen, author of *Porsche, Excellence Was Expected*, is the king of them all. On the other hand, for pure dry facts the *Porsche Data Book*, published by Haynes in 2006, appears to be the definitive reference work, although I reckon I have found the odd error in it. To be fair, has there ever

been a book with no error in its pages?

Here, I hope, is something entirely different, in style at least. My ambition was to write a true story that can be read more like a novel than a list of facts. Many years have been spent trying to get it right. You won't find much about boardroom politics or personalities, nor does the book delve very deeply into technical detail, though that side of things has been included – I hope with a light touch – where it's essential to the thread, but that's as far as it goes. Every basic model from the earliest days has been covered and, while I cannot pretend that every obscure special example has

been catalogued, I hope you will find this a reasonably comprehensive story.

Each national market is different when it comes to buying new cars. The tradition in Germany, even for expensive cars, has been one of offering a base model with a vast menu of extra items from which the customer can choose what he wants. In the UK, customers have expected high-quality cars to come equipped with a vast array of extras as standard equipment. A base model in Britain has therefore tended to be a right-hand-drive car, ordered from the factory by the concessionaires, which has something between 20 and 50 extras from the German list, and judged by them to be required here 'as standard'. The luxury version will have had more 'extras' added and may have been given a different designation. Slight differences in model names exist, therefore, from one country to another, and it would be a huge bore to try to go into any detail over that. Far more importantly, I have attempted to give a thoughtful insight into Porsche cars from the start, as seen from our side of the English Channel – and it's a view strictly from the driver's seat. I leave you to decide how well or how badly I have achieved this.

My first Porsche driving experience was in a 356 in the late 1960s when my younger brother bought a used Super

90 Coupé. I was astonished by its
qualities, not least because it was then
ten years old yet still drove like a new
car. Since then I have driven hundreds
of Porsches – as a road test writer for
magazines and newspapers, as a
Porsche salesman for a brief time in
North-East England, as an instructor at
Porsche Driving Days over ten years, as
a professional race driver – and even
as an owner. I just happen to have
been around Porsche cars for a very
long time and, if I can be forgiven for
blowing my own trumpet briefly here,
it's perhaps worth mentioning that
since 1978 I have won dozens of races
in eight very different models of
Porsche, from the 924 to the 934. I
drove a works 924GT at Le Mans in
1980 and for many years raced a
variety of 911s and 928s both for
private owners and for Porsche Cars
Great Britain under the AFN banner.

But this book is not about me: it's all
about these great cars from Stuttgart,
from the early 356 to the latest
models. More often than not, they
have been outstandingly good. There
have been surprisingly few Porsche
cars that have not lived up to that
description, and I can't think of
another manufacturer who gets close
on that score. Obviously enough, the
wonderful 911, through all its
incarnations, has usually been the
mainstay of the company through thick
and thin over many decades now; it's
perhaps because of the 911's
extraordinary success that it took
Porsche so many years to devise other
models that their customers wanted to
buy in sufficient numbers.

It's one thing to be ingenious, to
appreciate how to design and
construct a motor car that is a superb
driving machine. It's quite another to
get your marketing policy correct right
across the board. It's probably fair to
suggest that Porsche did not pull off
that trick properly until the mid-1990s,
when the front-engined sports cars
were dropped and the new Boxster was
launched. Since then, the company
seems to have been very much on
track with all its new product launches.
The Cayenne, for example, has proved
an outstanding success.

In those extremely rare cases where I
feel that a Porsche model has fallen
short in some way, I have been honest
about it. More often, I have felt that
some very fine Porsche cars were
wrongly dismissed by a motoring
public that failed to appreciate a great
machine when it was staring us all in
the face from behind the showroom
windows. The curiously underrated 968
is very much a case in point.

My enthusiasm for Porsche cars is as
strong as ever: driving the latest models
remains an experience to savour. For 60
years, Porsche people have known
what real drivers want: a supreme road-
driving experience coupled with equally
supreme reliability. This is my modest
tribute to their fabulous products. I
hope you enjoy it.

*This one would have made a good caption
competition. In the pits at Le Mans, 1980,
from left: Jürgen Barth, the author, the back of
Porsche Cars Great Britain Ltd PR man Mike
Cotton, and Derek Bell. (Jeff Bloxham)*

*On the frozen lake at St Moritz in 1985 with
my 911S 2.2. We were there for the centenary
of the St Moritz Tobogganing Club and its
Cresta Run. The Sotheby's Cup was a rally for
Cresta members from London to St Moritz via
Moët et Chandon in Epernay, followed by races
on the lake. My false moustache and eyebrows
were intended to disguise me as Edgar Jessop.
Standing by the car is my friend and co-driver,
Jeremy Coulter, but it was Mike Salmon who
joined me as my passenger for the somewhat
furious races. The car went well until packed
snow jammed the throttles open.*
(Author's collection)

# Introduction

H ow did they do it? From the very start, the secret of Porsche's success has baffled some of the best brains in other parts of the motor industry. Throughout the past half-century there has been no shortage of people prepared to explain why the whole idea of a rear-engined sports car is wrong. Yet the enduring

triumph of the 911 has made such critics look foolish time and time again.

Revered by those who have discovered its qualities over the past 40 years and more, the 911 is the key to what Porsche is all about: serious high performance, superb quality, a supremely satisfying driving experience with the reliability of a Volkswagen

*The first true Porsche, the one-off Roadster of 1948, was built at Gmünd. Although this was a mid-engined design, the classic Porsche style was already clear. (LAT)*

Beetle. That last bit left the opposition scratching their heads even harder.

With the Cayenne selling so well today, Porsche appears at last to have cracked the problem of building a commercially successful motor vehicle that does not have its engine behind the driver. The front-engined Porsches, which began with the 928 and 924 in the late 1970s, are covered in detail later in this book but it's the 911 that has repeatedly saved the day for Porsche as a trading concern. It must be admitted, however, that the mid-engined Boxster did exactly this a decade ago.

There is a deep emotional commitment to the 911 both within the factory and among enthusiasts outside. Generations of Porsche engineers have devoted themselves to its constant development. At the same time the entire company has always been seriously committed to engineering excellence, to producing something more than a car that simply works well and goes very fast. A Porsche car has always had to be a fully serviceable product, fit for maximum effort and ideally with minimal mechanical attention.

Porsche may be uniquely famous today for its rear-engined 911 model but, since the industry began, countless others have placed the engine behind the back axle line. Take the Rover Scarab that was shown at the 1931 British Motor Show at Olympia. That small four-seater open car had a rear-mounted 839cc air-cooled engine driving the back wheels, with independent suspension all round. The concept was remarkably similar to Dr Porsche's VW of the 1930s and one wonders how different the British company's history might have been had the Scarab not been abandoned at a Rover board meeting at the end of 1931.

Two decades later, however, Porsche was the company that made the high-performance rear-engined car succeed. As is well known, it all began in a small former sawmill, tucked away in the mountain village of Gmünd, just south of Katschberg in Austria. They were there because the

German Ministry of Munitions had ordered them to relocate to a safe place when things started to get rather hot in Stuttgart in the autumn of 1944.

Dr Ferdinand Porsche died on 30 January 1951. Before the 356, he had never made a car in his own name. A proud and driven man, he had tackled dozens of major projects for other concerns. His Beetle, as it came to be known, has endured in popular legend. He remains revered for the awesome Auto Union Grand Prix cars of the 1930s and for much more besides in the earlier days of motoring and motor sport. Among fellow automotive engineers, his successes with torsion-bar springing, advanced steering geometry and trailing-arm independent front suspension were widely-noted achievements in a long career, dating back to the end of the 19th century and full of ingenious developments.

Dr Porsche had set up his own independent design office in 1930, working to contract for other

companies. His work lived on through his son, 'Ferry', who had long been his assistant and who probably deserved more credit than he ever got for Porsche's work in the 1930s.

That's the problem with growing up in the shadow of a famous father. Son Ferry seemed more relaxed than his father, undoubtedly more charming and socially at ease. His temperament was ideally suited to the modern, post-war world that wanted to get on and leave the hell of grim conflict in Europe behind.

Every bit as bright as his father, Ferry was a better businessman. He could see the path ahead for his company and had learnt how to find the

*Patented by Dr Porsche, the basic engineering layout of 'Hitler's Volkswagen' appeared in* The Motor *of 31 December 1935. The suspension and the engine/transmission positioning show the true origin of the Porsche car, a line of thought that would lead ultimately to the 911. (The Motor)*

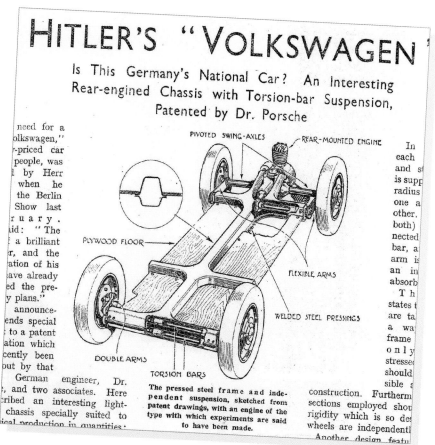

outstanding individuals to create a core team. He was able to delegate appropriately, too, without losing control. Soon after the Second World War, Ferry took up the reins and the original 356 sports car was very much his project. He was the man responsible for creating the Porsche company we know today.

Back in 1948, Porsche was very much a local business. Allied occupation forces were in control and had been rather surprised to find Porsche's small establishment tucked away in that remote Gmünd sawmill. Ferry's first prototype was an open, mid-engined car. In a remarkably prescient scoop, the first driving impressions of that car to be printed in

*'Please do not touch', it says on the old vee-windscreen. The remarkably original Roadster, the first Porsche car, is a treasured museum piece in Porsche's collection. Unusually well thought-out for its day, the interior reveals that driver comfort was always a strong point in Porsche design. (LAT)*

England appeared in *The Motor* of 21 July 1948, written by Max Troesch, then a freelance motoring journalist, who had previously been an engineer employed by Dr Porsche.

Ferry Porsche soon moved on to develop a more practical rear-engined coupé version, starting a line of development that is still with us today. The 356 was first shown formally to the world at the Geneva motor show in March 1949. It weighed 11.7cwt, was powered by a modestly tweaked VW engine producing 40bhp, and was tested independently at 84mph. It was the right place to launch the car: most early customers by far were Swiss, for in that neutral country there were enough discerning people who had not been financially ruined by the war.

Porsche cars had made a start but, to avoid his own ruin, Ferry could not afford one serious false step. The family was far from poor but he lacked the industrial might to forge ahead regardless of risk. At the same time, he was to be regularly tempted by offers to give it all up and take a well-paid

job with a bigger German car maker. He chose, despite all that, to stick to his own course, building the 356.

Carefully calculated risks had to be taken at key stages. In November 1949 he ordered 500 bodies from the Reutter coachworks in Stuttgart. Fourteen years later, Porsche would take control of all the shares of Reutter GmbH, thus assuming full responsibility for Porsche body production. From that point in 1963 the Reutter family retained the old Recaro factory in Stuttgart and continued to produce accessories, including Porsche's famous seats, but that move made Porsche a fully-fledged manufacturer in control of its own destiny.

Ferry was looking around the world from the start, appointing a Dutch agent in 1949 and aiming to sell cars in the US as early as possible. First, however, he had to get back into his factory in Stuttgart. This was no easy matter and had to be done in stages. For a start, the real life 'Sergeant Bilkos' were in the old Porsche works

in Stuttgart: the American First Motor Pool saw no need to vacate the place in a hurry for the sake of Porsche but, with patient negotiation and help from the city's mayor, Porsche did steadily return to its home city, bit by bit, around 1950. At first, Ferry rented production space from Reutter but eventually he was able to retrieve his old factory and began to expand.

The first Porsche built in Germany was on the road in spring 1950, and 300 cars were made that year. These Stuttgart production cars had all-steel bodies, unlike the cars previously constructed in Austria which had aluminium outer panels. All these early Porsche cars had cable brakes and lever-arm dampers, but the factory had adopted hydraulic braking and telescopic dampers by 1951.

Right from the start, Porsches were great sports cars for everyday use. They had long gearing and a slippery shape for extremely rapid cruising on long, level straights, yet anyone who took one into the mountains could not fail to be impressed by the handling and performance. They excelled at climbing hairpin bends and dedicated owners soon got the hang of sliding them sideways into corners and flicking them through ess-bends by controlling the natural pendulum effect of the engine's weight at the back.

As the years went by, some said that Porsche had changed the very meaning of the term sports car – which has always been hard to define satisfactorily, when you think about it. Others have claimed that Porsche actually invented the true GT car, a tag that is perhaps easier to pin down even though it was soon openly abused by other manufacturers looking for a bit of cheap glory by adding a GT badge to some pretty dull lumps of metal.

Whatever the truth of all that, Porsche ploughed its own furrow and gradually assumed a position of strength with a corner of the market where it had no true rivals. Of course, there has always been a choice for those looking for a fast car but the lack of direct imitators over the years still seems remarkable to me. Nothing else

looks like a Porsche, nothing else feels quite like a Porsche and nothing else that fast is so easily serviced – just like a family car.

Sports cars and sports-car racing have always been the very essence of Porsche. Porsches were phenomenally successful in the lower-capacity classes in rallies and races, notably at Le Mans, from the very early days. The company also made a serious effort in Formula 1, and works driver Dan Gurney did actually win the French GP at Rouen in 1962, even if tenacity and a bit of luck were very much involved in the result. Graham Hill (BRM), John Surtees (Lola) and Jim Clark (Lotus) had all led that GP before Gurney but they all dropped out.

To be honest, in those days Porsche had always looked the odd man out in F1, but in sports-car racing that was never the case. There Porsche was at home, in its element and it was seldom anything other than mighty impressive to see. Unlike those in most rival concerns, Porsche engineers always moved freely between the competition

side and the road-car business, taking the same company ethos into every discipline and every task attempted. There can be no doubt that this has played a large part in making the road cars such outstanding products.

It seems modest now but in 1961, a decade after returning to Stuttgart, Porsche produced a record 8,240 vehicles, of which 65.7 per cent were exported. Don't you love the typical precision of that figure? Production was planned to increase by ten per cent in 1962. The marque was firmly established and on the brink of producing the all-conquering 911. The story of driving all the cars follows in this book.

*Looks familiar. The speedometer and prominent tachometer of the unique Roadster will easily be recognised by owners of later Porsche cars. The green colouring was retained to 1967, white being used for the 1968 model year. The right-hand side of the oil temperature gauge, note, registers degrees Fahrenheit. Was Porsche already thinking of US and UK sales? (LAT)*

# The 356

In 1983, the Porsche Club Great Britain put on a superb three-day International 356 Meeting, attracting 95 cars from eight countries. The line-up on the grid at Donington Park race circuit included examples of most 356 models made. (Classic Cars)

The Porsche 12? The Porsche 60? Anyone heard of them? Porsche projects have always been given a number and it gives an idea of how much had gone before that the first car actually to carry the Porsche name had the number 356.

Occasionally the company altered its own rules, as in the 1970s with the 924 and 928, and once in the 1960s it was forced to do so in the case of the 901. All that came decades after the

Porsche Projects 12 and 60. Type 12 was in fact the original design for an inexpensive family car that Dr Porsche had tried to get into production in 1931. We know this because they took out a British patent and the drawing then appeared in *The Motor* magazine for 31 December 1935, attributed to Dr Porsche, Karl Rabe and Walter Boxan. This seems to represent the true origin of the Porsche car.

The basic elements are all there, the

only substantial differences being a plywood floor around the steel backbone chassis and a three-cylinder radial engine. Three prototypes were built by Zündapp, the bodies being constructed by Reutter of Stuttgart, a company that would later build the 356 and ultimately be taken over by Porsche in 1963. Unfortunately, those historic prototypes were destroyed in an air raid in 1944.

Back in 1933, by then with help from NSU, Porsche had persisted further with his 'people's car' project and it was taken up by the Hitler government. Following on from the Type 12, there were enough differences in the actual Volkswagen, as it came to be called, to justify a new Porsche drawing office project number, Type 60.

A further pointer to Porsche's future came with the three very special Type 60K10 race cars, capable of 90mph and completed in mid-1939 for the mythical Berlin–Rome 800-mile road race. Hitler's invasion of Poland put a stop to that far-fetched event, so Ferdinand Porsche regularly used one of his incredible but redundant race cars on the road during the war years. One imagines it attracted some attention.

In the tough conditions after the war, when VW was revived in an astonishing way under the British army, the Porsche people resolutely got back on track. The air-cooled horizontally-opposed four-cylinder engine and the basic suspension design of that original Porsche Type 60 were carried through into the post-war 356. Although the 356 was developed rapidly, the original Volkswagen engine formed the basis of Porsche's normal production power units throughout the 356 era, until the six-cylinder was launched with the 901(soon renamed 911) in 1963. It's hard to believe it now but the original standard post-war production VW engine, of 1,131cc, produced just 25bhp.

The first Porsches offered to the public actually had 1,086cc engines, in order to qualify for the under-1,100cc category of motor sport. This was done by narrowing the bores. At the start, only the cylinder heads were pure

Porsche products but the complete engine was redesigned in-house by Dr Fuhrmann in 1952 and by 1960 not one part in Porsche's engines was supplied by VW, even though a few components were still interchangeable.

Throughout its life the basic 356 range retained this pushrod engine in various stages of development. Later on, we'll get to the Spyder, the Speedster and the Carrera versions not to mention some very different overhead-cam Porsche engines of the 1950s. First, however, let's stick to the basic 356 through the early years.

Engines, gearboxes, brakes and countless small parts were improved, and the bodies were modernised. The split vee-screen had officially gone from the Coupé by 1952, replaced by a single panel of glass with a marked bend down the centre line, but a few other models retained split screens for some time and the more modern look of the 356A, with its evenly curved one-piece windscreen, did not arrive until 1955. Bumpers were fitted, mainly to satisfy overseas markets. Despite the air-cooled rear engine, an effective heater was developed, though in the early days some engine smells did still get through to the cabin.

Early 356s have been rare items for decades now but I was once lucky enough to get behind the wheel of a

*This rare shot shows Porsche personnel arriving at the Paris motor show in October 1951, with a heavily-badged early 356. (The Motor/LAT)*

truly venerable Cabriolet. Back in 1983, it was Britain's turn to host the International 356 Meeting. The Porsche Club of Great Britain put on a superb three-day event, attracting 95 cars from eight countries. Part of the meeting was a driving day at Donington Circuit and as I was then the Editor of *Classic Cars* magazine, and known to be something of a Porsche nut, I was invited to drive some of the early cars there.

The oldest car at Donington that day was a 1954 356 cabriolet 1500 that I was amazed to discover had never been restored. It was totally genuine, complete with that antique-looking vee-windscreen and its original engine, producing just 55bhp at 4000rpm. It was even still fitted with its first set of skinny 3.25J x 16in wheels and had been run from new with nothing more than regular servicing, a remarkable fact considering that in 1983 it was already 29 years old.

Its then owner, David Cleaver, allowed me to drive him round the circuit and this is what I noted at the time: 'To drive, and I hope I shall be

# Porsche 356
## (Stuttgart-built Pre-A)
### 1950–54

**ENGINE:**
Four-cylinder horizontally opposed, air-cooled; rear-mounted

| | |
|---|---|
| Bore x stroke | 73.5mm x 64.0mm |
| Capacity | 1,086cc |
| Valve actuation | pushrod ohv |
| Compression ratio | 7:1 |
| Induction | Twin Solex 32 PBI |
| Power | 40bhp at 4,200rpm |
| Maximum torque | 52lb ft at 2,800rpm |

*1.3-litre (from 1951)*
As 1.1-litre except:

| | |
|---|---|
| Bore x stroke | 80.0mm x 64.0mm |
| Capacity | 1,286cc |
| Compression ratio | 6.5:1 |
| Power | 44bhp at 4,200rpm |
| Maximum torque | 60lb ft at 2,800rpm |

*1500 (1952)*
As 1.3-litre except:

| | |
|---|---|
| Bore x stroke | 80.0mm x 74.0mm |
| Capacity | 1,488cc |
| Compression ratio | 7:1 |
| Induction | Twin Solex 40 PBIC (1953–55: Twin Solex 32 PBI) |
| Power | 60bhp at 5,000rpm (1953–55: 55bhp at 4,200rpm) |
| Maximum torque | 75lb ft at 3,000rpm (1953–55: 78lb ft at 2,800rpm) |

*1500 Super (1953–55)*
As 1500 except:

| | |
|---|---|
| Compression ratio | 8.2:1 |
| Induction | Twin Solex 40 PBIC |
| Power | 70bhp at 5,000rpm |
| Maximum torque | 80lb ft at 3,600rpm |

*1300 Super (1954–55)*
As 1.3-litre except:

| | |
|---|---|
| Bore x stroke | 74.5mm x 74.0mm |
| Capacity | 1,290cc |
| Compression ratio | 8.2:1 |
| Induction | 1955: Twin Solex 32 PBIC or 40PCIB |
| Power | 60bhp at 5,500rpm |
| Maximum torque | 65lb ft at 3,600rpm |

**TRANSMISSION:**
Rear-wheel drive; four-speed manual gearbox (all-synchromesh from 1952)

**SUSPENSION:**
*Front:* Independent by transverse laminated torsion bars, trailing arms; telescopic dampers; anti-roll bar
*Rear:* Independent by transverse torsion bars, swing axles; lever-arm dampers (double-acting telescopic dampers from 1952)

**STEERING:**
Worm-and-peg with divided track-rod

**BRAKES:**
Hydraulic; light-alloy drums with cast-iron inserts
*Front:* Drum (11in), twin-leading-shoe
*Rear:* Drum (11in)
Earliest models have 9in drums all-round
No servo

**WHEELS/TYRES:**
Steel wheels
Tyres (according to model) 3.00 to 5.00 x 16in (5.25 x 16in on some roadsters and Speedsters)

**BODYWORK:**
Monocoque construction with body welded to steel box-section chassis
Coupé, Cabriolet, Speedster

**DIMENSIONS:**

| | |
|---|---|
| Length | 12ft 11.5in |
| Wheelbase | 6ft 10.7in |
| Track, front | 4ft 2.8in |
| Track, rear | 4ft 1.2in |
| Width | 5ft 5.4in |
| Height | 4ft 3.2in |

*These figures refer to a typical Coupé or Cabriolet throughout the 356 era; Speedsters and Convertibles were 3in lower*

**WEIGHT:**
11.9cwt–16.3cwt (605–830kg), *according to model: Coupés rose from 770kg to 830kg in 1950–55*

**PERFORMANCE:**
(Source: *The Autocar*)
(1500 Coupé)

| | |
|---|---|
| Max speed | 87mph |
| 0–60mph | 17.0sec |
| Standing quarter-mile | 20.1sec |

*Figures for other models can be found but are not regarded as reliable*

forgiven for this, it's the nearest thing to a hovercraft on wheels. Discernibly a Porsche, it has to be said they advanced pretty rapidly after this model. More to the point, this machine has been all over Europe in the five years or so that David has owned it... David says he paid £500 for the car; it has been 'round the clock' two or three times and it has never broken down on him once... It's a very remarkable possession.'

To be fair to the car, I think it was

*Snapped by the author at the PCGB's 'Porsches at the Castle' at Hedingham Castle in 2007, this superb pre-A split-screen, left-hand-drive 356 1.3-litre, dating from 1951, was imported to the UK in 1957. It was there by invitation of local Porsche specialist Andy Prill. (Author)*

**PRICE IN UK INCLUDING TAX WHEN NEW:**
1.3 Coupé: £1,842 (January 1953)
1500 Super convertible: £2,378 (idem)

**NUMBER BUILT ('Pre-A' types only):**

| | |
|---|---|
| Coupé | 6,252 |
| Cabriolet | 1,593 |
| Speedster | 1,234 |

Additionally one 356/1 mid-engined prototype and 52 rear-engined 356/2 production cars were handbuilt at Gmünd, Austria, in 1948–50 before the company returned to Stuttgart and proper production began

# Porsche 356A
## 1956–59

As earlier 356s except:

**ENGINE:**

*1300 (1956–57)*

| | |
|---|---|
| Bore x stroke | 74.5mm x 74.0mm |
| Capacity | 1,290cc |
| Compression ratio | 6.5:1 |
| Power | 44bhp at 4,200rpm |
| Maximum torque | 60lb ft at 2,800rpm |

*1300 Super (1956–57)*
As 1300 except:

| | |
|---|---|
| Compression ratio | 7.5:1 |
| Power | 60bhp at 5,500rpm |
| Maximum torque | 65lb ft at 3,600rpm |

*1600*
As 1300 except:

| | |
|---|---|
| Bore x stroke | 82.5mm x 74.0mm |

| | |
|---|---|
| Capacity | 1,582cc |
| Compression ratio | 7.5:1 |
| Power | 60bhp at 4,500rpm |
| Maximum torque | 81lb ft at 2,800rpm |

*1600 Super*
As 1600 except:

| | |
|---|---|
| Compression ratio | 8.5:1 |
| Induction | Twin Solex 40 PBIC (1958–59: Zenith 32 NDIX) |
| Power | 75bhp at 5,000rpm |
| Maximum torque | 86lb ft at 3,700rpm |

*1500 GS Carrera (1956–58)*
As 1600 except:

Porsche Type 547 engine with aluminium blocks and heads, crankshaft roller bearings, dry sump – all-new, famously designed in-house by Dr Ernst Fuhrmann

| | |
|---|---|
| Bore x stroke | 85.0mm x 66.0mm |
| Capacity | 1,498cc |
| Valve actuation | dohc per bank |
| Compression ratio | 9.0:1 |
| Induction | Twin Solex 40 PII |
| Power | 100bhp at 6,200rpm |
| Maximum torque | 88lb ft at 5,200rpm |

*1500 GS Carrera GT (1957–58)*
As 1956–57 GS Carrera except:

| | |
|---|---|
| Induction | Twin Solex 40 PII-4 |
| Power | 110bhp at 6,400rpm |
| Maximum torque | 91lb ft at 5,200rpm |

**WHEELS/TYRES:**
Tyres 5.60 x 15in (Some later models 5.90 x 15in)

**BODYWORK:**
Improved monocoque steel structure, visibly notable for change from 'bent' windscreen to single-curve 'panorama' style
Coupé, Cabriolet, Speedster

**WEIGHT:**
Typical Coupé/Cabriolet: 16.7cwt (850kg)
Speedster 1600: 15.0cwt (760kg)

**PERFORMANCE:**
(Source: Porsche)
1600 Coupé/1500 GS Carrera GT Coupé

| | |
|---|---|
| Max speed | 99mph/124mph |
| 0–62mph | 16.5sec/11.0sec |

**PRICE IN UK INCLUDING TAX WHEN NEW:**
(January 1956)

| | |
|---|---|
| 1600 Coupé | £1,891 |
| 1600 Super Coupé | £2,071 |
| 1600 Cabriolet | £2,071 |
| 1600 Super Cabriolet | £2,251 |
| Carrera Coupé | £2,799 |

**NUMBER BUILT:**

| | |
|---|---|
| 356A Coupé | 13,016 |
| 356A Cabriolet | 3,285 (all 1300 and 1600 engines) |
| 356A Speedster | 2,910 (all versions) |
| 356A Convertible D | 1,330 (all versions) |
| 356A 1500 GS | 447 |
| 356A Speedster GS/GT | 167 |
| GS Carrera GT Coupé | 35 |

Additionally 204 356A Carrera 1600s with plain-bearing engines built in 1959 ▶

---

somewhat overdue for a suspension and steering overhaul but it still got round the circuit respectably quickly even if it was hard to make a mental connection between the car's steering wheel and its attitude through the corners.

I like to think I can maintain an open mind and make an accurate assessment of any car, but it probably didn't help that I had driven to Donington that day in the latest 1983 911SC Cabriolet. It's sobering to think that if that car has survived, then it in its turn is now most definitely a classic in its own right.

As for the hovercraft reference, I did have experience of such a device, having been given a trip in a two-seater model off Skegness beach and round the pier by a brave chap called Lord Hotham. On the move, the

hovercraft was marginally more alarming than that 1954 356 cabrio, but only because the sea was a bit choppy at the time.

Another thing I do remember from that 1983 356 Meeting was the PCGB quiz that ran through the three days. One of the questions was 'How many 356 models were made?' The answer, I was surprised to learn, was 52. I shall do my best to sort through them in the following pages.

First, though, let's spool back to the 1951 British Motor Show, the first at which the 356 was present. Some have claimed that the Porsche was the star of the event. Not so. Perhaps we could argue that it deserved to be, but let's be honest: the unique qualities of the small Porsche sports car were understood only by a tiny minority at first.

The headlines from that 1951 Show went to the many completely new British cars, some of which were deserving of attention in their way. The truth is that Austin's A30, a worthy little family car at a good price, grabbed most of the attention at Earl's Court that year. And you didn't need to be that clever to know that success for the A30 and its kind was vital to Britain's chances of post-war recovery. That's where the attention was bound to be focused.

British press reaction to the 356 was mixed. Some commented on the characteristically blunt German styling of the convertible, with one adding that although a small car, the Porsche recalled the massive pre-war Mercedes convertibles in its looks.

What a very odd comment that is. What on earth was that journalist

# Porsche 550 1500 RS Spyder
## 1954–56

**ENGINE:**
Four-cylinder horizontally opposed, air-cooled, roller crankshaft bearings, dry sump; mid-mounted. Again, this was the Porsche Type 547 engine

| | |
|---|---|
| Bore x stroke | 85.0mm x 66.0.0mm |
| Capacity | 1,498cc |
| Valve actuation | dohc per bank |
| Compression ratio | 9.5:1 |
| Induction | Twin Solex 40 PII or twin Weber 40 DCM |
| Power | 110bhp at 6,200rpm |
| Maximum torque | 95lb ft at 5,300rpm |

*Note: First factory cars were fitted with race-modified push-rod ohv engines*

**TRANSMISSION:**
Rear-wheel drive; four-speed manual (all-synchromesh) gearbox; limited-slip differential

**SUSPENSION:**
*Front:* Independent by transverse laminated torsion bars, trailing arms; double-acting telescopic dampers; adjustable anti-roll bar
*Rear:* Independent by transverse torsion bars, swing axles with trailing arms, compensating spring; double-acting telescopic dampers

**STEERING:**
Worm-and-peg with divided track-rod

**BRAKES:**
Hydraulic; light-alloy drums with cast-iron inserts
*Front:* Drum (11in); twin-leading-shoe
*Rear:* Drum (11in)
No servo

**WHEELS/TYRES:**
Steel wheels
Tyres 5.00 x 16in front; 5.25 x 16in rear

**BODYWORK:**
Open racing two-seater
Aluminium over steel-tube spaceframe, based on prototype's ladder-style chassis and reinforced with steel panels
For 1956, much-improved and stiffer spaceframe introduced for the 550A

**DIMENSIONS:**

| | |
|---|---|
| Length | 11ft 9.7in |
| Wheelbase | 6ft 10.7in |
| Track, front | 4ft 2.8in |
| Track, rear | 4ft 1.2in |
| Width | 5ft 1.0in |
| Height | 3ft 4.0in |

**WEIGHT:**
13.5cwt (686kg)

**PERFORMANCE:**
(Source: Porsche)
*1954 1500 RS Spyder*

| | |
|---|---|
| Max speed | 137mph |
| 0–62mph | 10sec approx |

**PRICE IN UK INCLUDING TAX WHEN NEW:**
Type 550/1500 Spyder £3,847 (October 1955)

**NUMBER BUILT:**
90

# Porsche 356B
## 1959–63

As 356A except:
*1962 Super 75*

**ENGINE:**
Four-cylinder horizontally-opposed, air-cooled; rear-mounted

| | |
|---|---|
| Bore x stroke | 82.5mm x 74.0mm |
| Capacity | 1,582cc |
| Valve actuation | Pushrod |
| Compression ratio | 8.5:1 |
| Induction | Twin Zenith 32 NDIX double-choke downdraught |
| Power | 75bhp at 5,000rpm* |
| Maximum torque | Not quoted |

*Also offered in standard (60bhp) and Super 90 (90bhp) form

**STEERING:**
As 356A but with addition of hydraulic damper

**BRAKES:**
As 356A except for new cooling fins; a few late 356Bs had 356C disc brakes

**WHEELS/TYRES:**
165-15 radial-ply tyres optional

**BODYWORK:**
Largely as 356A 'T5' at first; body styles included Coupé, Cabriolet, Hardtop/Cabriolet, Hardtop-Coupé, Roadster. From September, 1961, improved 'T6' body was distinguished by bigger glass area

**WEIGHT:**
17.5cwt (889kg)

**PERFORMANCE:**
(Source: *The Motor*)

| | |
|---|---|
| Max speed | 106.6mph |
| 0–60mph | 13.5sec |
| Standing quarter-mile | 18.8sec |

*Left: Competing at Wiscombe Park hillclimb in about 1960, Denis Jenkinson has his 356 nicely lined up on the approach to the gate. A great 356 enthusiast, 'Jenks' had his 1500 uprated to 1600 Super specification for competition purposes. He remained faithful to Porsche until the end of the 356 era, when he switched to a new Jaguar E-type.
(Denis Jenkinson collection)*

*Right: As Motor Sport magazine's top race reporter, 'Jenks' covered countless miles all over Europe in early Porsches. His 356 is seen here in 1955 behind the similar car of F1 driver, Wolfgang Graf Berghe von Trips. The location is Castle Hemmersbach, the von Trips family home at Horrem in Germany's Rhineland.
(Denis Jenkinson collection)*

PRICE IN UK INCLUDING TAX WHEN NEW:
Super 75 £2,348 (May 1962, as part of nine-model range, from standard Coupé at £2,163 to Super 90 Cabriolet at £2,876)

NUMBER BUILT:

| | |
|---|---|
| Coupé T5 body | 8,559 |
| Coupé T6 body | 12,038 |
| Cabriolet T5 | 3,094 |
| Cabriolet T6 | 3,100 |
| Hardtop-Coupé T5 | 1,048 |
| Hardtop-Coupé T6 | 699 |
| 1600 Roadster T5 | 2,653 |
| 1600 Roadster T6 | 249 (all engine versions) |

# 356B 2000 GS Carrera 2
### 1962–63

As 356B except:

ENGINE:
Enlarged version of the Type 547 engine

| | |
|---|---|
| Bore x stroke | 92.0mm x 74.0mm |
| Capacity | 1,966cc |
| Valve actuation | dohc per bank |
| Compression ratio | 9.5:1 (9.8:1) |
| Induction | Twin Solex 40 PII-4 double-choke downdraught (Weber 46 IDM 2) |
| Power | 130bhp (140bhp in GS-GT) at 6,200rpm |
| Maximum torque | 119lb ft at 4,600rpm (GS-GT: 128lb ft at 4,700rpm) |

WHEELS/TYRES:
Tyres 165-15 radial-ply (GS-GT: 165R15)

BODYWORK
Aluminium doors, bonnet, engine lid; Plexiglas side and rear windows and ultra-lightweight competition versions were available

WEIGHT:
GS 19.9cwt (1,010kg); GS-GT 16.7cwt (850kg)

PERFORMANCE:
(Source: Porsche)

| | |
|---|---|
| Max speed | 124mph (GS-GT: 130mph) |
| 0–60mph | 9.0sec (GS-GT: 8.0sec approx) |

PRICE IN UK INCLUDING TAX WHEN NEW:
Not officially listed in UK

NUMBER BUILT:
310 (all types)

# Porsche 356C 1600/1600SC
### 1964–65

As 356B except:

ENGINE:

| | |
|---|---|
| Power | 75bhp at 5,200rpm/ 95bhp at 5,800rpm |
| Maximum torque | 91lb ft at 3,600rpm/ 91lb ft at 4,200rpm |

*The 1600SC had aluminium cylinders with a ferrous coating*

BRAKES:
*Front:* 10.8in discs
*Rear:* 11.2in discs

WHEELS/TYRES:
Tyres 5.60-15 Sport/165-15 radial-ply

WEIGHT:
18.4cwt (935kg)

PERFORMANCE:
(Source: Porsche/*Motor*)

| | |
|---|---|
| Max speed | 108.5mph/ 112.5mph |
| 0–62mph | 14.0sec/13.2sec |
| Standing quarter-mile | 18.8sec/18.7sec |

PRICE IN UK INCLUDING TAX WHEN NEW:
(January 1964)

| | |
|---|---|
| 1600C Coupé | £2,063 |
| 1600C Cabriolet | £2,313 |
| 1600SC Coupé | £2,277 |
| 1600SC Cabriolet | £2,527 |

NUMBER BUILT:

| | |
|---|---|
| 356C/SC Coupé | 13,510 |
| 356C/SC Cabriolet | 3,175 |

# 356C 2000 GS Carrera 2
### 1964

As 356B 2000 GS Carrera 2 except:

WEIGHT:
19.9cwt (1,010kg)

PERFORMANCE:
(Source: Porsche)

| | |
|---|---|
| Max speed | 124mph |
| 0–62mph | 9.0sec |

PRICE IN UK INCLUDING TAX WHEN NEW:

| | |
|---|---|
| 2-litre Carrera | £3,734 (January 1964) |

NUMBER BUILT:
126

trying to say? It remains a puzzle, I must admit. In fact I struggled to find any reaction at all to Porsche's first official appearance in Britain. One writer did call it 'beautifully streamlined': at least that observation made sense.

The first two Porsches to be shown formally in the metal to the British public were a brand new Coupé and a Cabriolet, displayed on a stand at that 1951 British Motor Show. Incredibly enough, both survived at least into the 1990s. The Cabriolet was found in a barn in Sussex, with only 56,000 miles covered. It was bought by David Mills, an aesthete with a deep understanding of what that car was all about. He had

*Possibly the only surviving perfect Pre-A 356 1500 with right-hand drive, this superb machine, first registered in May 1955, belongs to Richard Green, a great Porsche connoisseur who also owns some of the fastest recent 911s. Richard, at the wheel here, is as enthusiastic about this 55bhp model as he is when discussing his recent GT 2s. (Classic Cars)*

it perfectly restored in 1988, back at the factory in Stuttgart. The Coupé was restored in Britain in the early 1990s.

Although I never drove David's car, he described the driving experience to me enthusiastically and he was a person whose opinion deserved respect: a light car with a stiff frame that did not shake, light and direct steering, plus an amazingly smooth ride for a car of those times when many sports cars were still real bone-shakers. His car, having been faithfully restored to its original state, still had the non-synchromesh VW gearbox that needed skilled double-declutching, both up and down, to avoid crunching the gears.

Even so, the essential Porsche qualities mentioned above were well in evidence.

These two Porsches were in fact the first German cars of any kind to be shown in England since the Second World War and the importer was Connaught Engineering, a garage on the Portsmouth Road at Send, Surrey. Connaught was already famous among

enthusiasts for the fine racing cars it made while operating on a modest budget. Indeed, Connaught was a very small outfit but Porsche was keeping the right company in England. No doubt about that.

Acting for Connaught, the enterprising Charles Meisl was behind these earliest Porsches in Britain and he had arranged for *The Autocar* magazine to get a brief impression of the very first Porsche to come to the UK, a Coupé that had arrived in March 1951.

The tester was surprised at the comfort and generous accommodation once he got down inside and was seated close to the uncluttered flat floor. He was impressed by the acceleration above 50mph that was obviously much helped by the 'well-streamlined' body. Then there was the low wind noise, and the fact that engine noise was left behind at speed.

The importance of his next point is easy to miss today. Back in 1951, few cars could cruise at 70mph, yet the Porsche with its small engine could

manage this with ease, and still turn in an incredible 35–40mpg. The claimed maximum of 85mph, said *The Autocar*, seemed honest. And then the writer hit the nail on the head, suggesting that the Porsche's designer had clearly gone all-out for certain truly great qualities while accepting some unimportant disadvantages. Porsche had avoided any compromise that might have led to a sort of well-intentioned mediocrity, he said.

The car was not perfect. It had that noisy VW gearbox and it wasn't easy to change gear. It was easy, however, to provoke pronounced oversteer, and in a straight line the aerodynamics and rear engine made it sensitive to side winds. This meant that the driver had to give 'some concentration' – weren't they polite, the road-testers of 50 years ago? – to steering at high speeds, especially on a windy day.

Despite his good manners, that unnamed *The Autocar* journalist got it all right, concluding that the new Porsche car offered a unique combination of comfort, performance and economy. The weight of that first car to reach British soil was just 13.75cwt, a mere 699kg.

In Britain, few people then knew anything about any German cars, but earlier in 1951 the German motor show in Frankfurt had revealed a renascent and surprisingly vigorous car industry. *The Motor* magazine had mentioned that 'the Porsche is now in production with a modified cylinder head and 1,286cc, which results in 42bhp'. Although it's accepted today that those early 1300s produced 44bhp, it's more interesting to note that no fewer than 86 cars had been made in February, 88 were turned out in March and 1951 production had exceeded a total of 1,000 by the end of August.

Reporting from Frankfurt, *The Motor* referred to the Porsche as 'handbuilt and handsome' but still described it as 'a modification of the German Volkswagen' (which, as mentioned earlier, produced 25bhp from 1,131cc and had a top speed of 57.3mph).

By the end of 1951, Porsche production was up to 130 cars per month. There were about 100

*The Pre-A dashboard was remarkably similar to the well-designed arrangement of the original Roadster. The two-spoke steering wheel and column indicator stalk were introduced in late 1952. (LAT)*

employees, nearly all under 40, and the engine builders were still stamping their personal initials on each crankcase. In retrospect, that surely must have set Porsche products apart from 'modified VWs' but this rather posh practice was later abandoned because it was causing friction between Porsche's 'ordinary' workers and the exalted élite, the engine builders.

Although the original car had a 40bhp 1100 engine, the 44bhp 1300 was soon added as an option and already, in 1951, there was a race-tuned prototype 1500, developing 75bhp at 7,000rpm. It was used by Walter Gloeckler in the Freiburg hillclimb.

The clutch, gearbox, differential, front and rear axle assemblies and the laminated torsion bars were still derived from those of the standard VW but this was an acceptable detail. At the heart of the Porsche was a stiff, semi-self-supporting bodyframe in a short-wheelbase car with a low centre of gravity.

The Porsche was effective. Its makers knew that, as did the early customers and, as we have seen, at least a couple of discerning British motoring journalists. Porsche needed to prove the value of its car to a wider audience, so in September 1951 it went to Montlhéry, near Paris, and took speed records for 1,100cc and 1,500cc cars.

The 500-mile 1,100cc record was pushed above 100mph, to 100.56mph to be exact. Mind you, they only just beat the existing and rather remarkable record of 98.18mph set by Eyston and Denly in a British Riley 20 years before. The Porsche was obviously specially prepared for that feat but one suspects it was far closer to a production model than the racing Riley had been.

Racing mattered, too, and before long Porsche had begun its long and deeply rewarding affair with the Le Mans 24 Hrs, far and away the world's most important sports-car race. Any chance of outright victory there was out of the question at that stage, but the efficient Porsches were immediately successful in the classes for cars with smaller engines.

All the while, much of Ferry Porsche's concentration was firmly fixed on the export market for road cars, especially on the far side of the Atlantic. By the end of 1951, Porsche had exported a modest 30 cars to the US through the Hoffman Motor Car Corporation of New York, but it was an important start. Many small manufacturers, and some quite big ones, have got out of their depth in the vastness of the United States and failed to make a mark. Porsche did not fail.

Ferry Porsche himself visited the USA late in 1951 to research that promising market further. Within a year, annual sales there were running at 600 cars. Porsche had a good product and it had begun to sell cars ever further from home. It was vital to iron out the perceived faults, one of which was that rather grim standard VW gearbox. No time was wasted. In 1952, Porsche was able to announce at the Paris show that in future all its cars would have full synchromesh on all four forward speeds.

This ingenious Porsche synchromesh system was reliable, enabled extremely

*A stylish couple admiring the current Porsche 356 Cabriolet at the Paris motor show, September 1954. This 1955 model year example is one of the last of the Pre-A cars, still with the 'bent' windscreen. By then all Porsche engines featured the company's own three-piece crankcases, the VW castings used previously having been replaced. (The Motor/LAT)*

fast noiseless changes, and was also so compact that it could fit into the original VW gearbox case. Developed from Porsche's design for the Cisitalia racing car, a special project of 1946–47, it had no connection with VW's own synchromesh system introduced at about the same time.

Better brakes and a wider range of engines were announced at this stage, a new 1.5-litre engine, developing 55bhp or 60bhp, joining the existing 1.1-litre and 1.3-litre units. Intended for competition use, there was also a 1.5-litre Super, developing 69bhp. Porsche was on the march, already a serious player, and with that came all the problems and hard decisions of what had rapidly become a fairly big business. Exports mattered very much but it wasn't enough simply to make the cars desirable to foreign buyers.

In some cases, notably the important British market, they had to secure government permission to sell the cars in any appreciable numbers. Even then, more than seven years after the war, when such foreign cars were imported to Britain they were still denied to British buyers. They could be sold only to US servicemen, or to diplomats, or else to overseas visitors

who were required to re-export them fairly promptly. The occasional personal import sold through a small, alert garage in Surrey was one thing, but bigger numbers were sought by Porsche and that meant red tape and negotiations with officialdom.

At the end of May, 1953 a reciprocal arrangement was announced between the UK and West Germany that would enable the limited import/export of each other's cars. Under this deal, up to £2.7m worth of German cars would be permitted to enter Britain.

A week later, the first announcement of prices for a German make of car in Britain was followed by the partial lifting by the Board of Trade's import restrictions. Connaught simply had not been big enough to tackle the long haul of introducing Porsche to Britain, so since January 1953 Charles Meisl had been representing the German company's UK interests via the Colborne Garage Ltd at Ripley in Surrey. Quoted Porsche prices in Britain ranged from the 1.3 Coupé at £1,842 to the 1500 Super convertible at £2,378 (both including Import Duty and Purchase Tax).

British Import Duty loaded a heavy penalty on foreign cars. At the time a Jaguar XK120, which was without question the sexiest new supercar in the public mind, cost a few pounds over £1,600. What chance did this curious small-engined device from Germany hope to stand in the UK against that sort of opposition? Even so, other markets were growing fast for Porsche at that stage and 356 production was running at 4,000 cars a year, over three times the rate of just two years before.

One way to generate excitement was to put out rumours of a sensational new product, just around the corner. It began to get around that a new Porsche model, a replica of the latest Le Mans car, would become available for sale, even in Britain, with twin overhead cams, a mid-mounted engine and performance in the 150mph bracket. That probably seemed beyond belief to most Brits at the time.

In fact the real Porsche news for Britain at the very end of 1953 was the

appointment of AFN Ltd, of Isleworth in West London, as the new concessionaire. Charles Meisl, who had been heavily involved in bringing Porsche to Britain, moved from Colborne to AFN but he did not remain long and was still bitter over his treatment many decades later; he went on to enjoy a successful career, mainly as the British importer of Cibié lights.

AFN, named after the initials of founder Archie Frazer-Nash, had been in the capable hands of the Aldington family since the late 1920s, back in the days when the company was still producing Frazer-Nash's idiosyncratic chain-transmission sports cars. The Isleworth firm's appointment to the Porsche franchise was the start of a serious effort by the Porsche factory to sell the cars in the UK. AFN Ltd was well up to the task and made an enduring success of this relationship. British prices for Porsche cars were reduced, briefly, in September 1954 but every car in the Porsche range still remained more expensive than an XK120. It was also announced that Porsche's 550 Spyder would indeed become available in Britain at some point in the future.

The interiors of Porsche cars probably mystified the uninitiated at the time. They looked spartan at first glance but everything was of the highest quality, right down to the superbly-designed seats. These days we'd be horrified at the lack of head restraints but such safety issues were not understood then. In 1953 and 1954, respectively, Porsche introduced the 1500 Super and the 1300 Super: these were high-performance models that indicated Porsche's growing desire to create its own very special engines. Crankshaft roller bearings by Hirth were a feature but I suspect that these were extremely rare cars even then. Maybe I shall see one some day, but it hasn't happened yet.

All these early Porsches were cars that appealed to successful, intelligent, energetic young individuals who knew how to drive. In a distinctly club-like atmosphere, AFN began to draw a group of such people as regular Porsche customers. Once they had owned a 356 for a short time, most of them were permanently hooked.

Once such was a young dentist, Colin Dexter. He and his father had heard of a 356 that was possibly for sale, second-hand in Surrey. They went to see it at a motorcycle dealership and when the car's owner appeared from the workshops, wiping oil from

*On the left, Denis Jenkinson's Pre-A, acquired in 1955, is badged 'Continental' – a name then reserved usually for cars exported to the USA. Alongside is the 356A model that superseded it from late 1955 – giving a good illustration of the altered styling, especially the more modern windscreen of the later car. (Denis Jenkinson collection)*

his hands, they realised it was John Surtees, already a World Champion on two wheels. Surtees said he had decided not to sell but he would be delighted to take them out. Colin was allowed a short drive.

That was enough. As soon as he could he ordered a new car from AFN who, very decently, explained that the 356A would be arriving soon, powered by a new a 1.6-litre engine. He was offered a new 1500 and was told that if he bought it AFN would swap the 1500 for a new bigger engine, free of any charge, as soon as they started to come through.

'You'd never do that today, of course,' Colin told me in 2005. 'You'd keep it original. But I took them up on the deal and they were as good as their word.'

When he retired in the mid-1990s, Colin found himself thinking wistfully

*Marked in the archive only as a 1956 356A 1600, this example has a sunroof but, more interesting, the note-taking figure on the right is none other than celebrated* Motor Sport *Editor Bill Boddy, then famously a VW Beetle fan.* (LAT)

back to that 1955 356 1500 so frequently that he went out and bought another. He kept it for about ten years before selling it to another, much younger Porsche enthusiast, Richard Green. Shortly before this book went to press, Richard was kind enough to let me drive it for a feature in *Classic Cars* magazine.

'What grabs you immediately with the 356,' I wrote, 'is that fabulous Porsche steering. The wheel feels alive, telling you so much, and then the car itself seems to glide effortlessly over any bumps and dips. It's light and responsive…and there's no problem with these drum brakes. It's ready to slide the tail whenever you like, for sure, but you can flick it around to advantage with a little practice.

'What an incredibly modern car it must have seemed back in 1955,' I continued. 'Porsche had thought out its own future for high performance driving, and it worked. Despite small engines and modest power outputs, Porsches like this were already winning major European rallies.

'Porsche's vision embraced the whole package, including driving comfort for human beings of all sizes. It's a tiny car, this old 356, a mere 13ft long; once during our test I noticed how much more bulky a modern Ford Escort looked beside it, yet the Porsche isn't cramped. I am 6ft 5in tall but, for comfort alone, I'd rather spend a day driving it than many a modern car. Somebody, probably Ferry Porsche himself, designed that bit properly; it's just great and the cabin is more like an old aircraft than a car. The one strange bit is the wand-like gear lever, which, in right-hand drive, is rather under one's left leg. The Reutter (later Recaro) seats, the other controls and the driving position are still superb, astonishingly so, enabling

fatigue-free long journeys at high speed. In this area alone, Porsche was decades ahead.'

The top speed of the pre-A 1500 was a mere 87mph but that was quick enough in the early 1950s. Today Richard sees it as a rare work of art that he has come to appreciate to the full alongside more modern Porsches: his garage includes several 911 GT2s of more recent times.

Away from the factory, the core values of the 356 were soon appreciated by small bands of intelligent, well-informed enthusiasts in Germany and in all Porsche's early export markets. The efficiency of the design gave surprising speed, good acceleration and superior traction when climbing slippery hills. All that, and it still delivered excellent fuel consumption.

Owners also admired the quality of construction, the smooth ride over rough surfaces, the uniquely responsive steering feel, the lack of body-roll in corners, and Porsche's deep understanding of what made for a modern, comfortable driving position in a sports car. In our admiration for classic cars in general these days it's easy to forget how shockingly uncomfortable most of them were, even those that were very expensive. A driver should feel comfortable after a day at the wheel and should not develop back trouble after a few months with a car. Porsche was a lone pioneer in this field.

Inherent problems of other kinds would be tackled relentlessly in the years to come. These included the finer points of handling with a rear-engined car through fast, open corners, the ease with which the 356 could spin when driven badly, and the difficulty of braking and steering the car at speed downhill on slippery mountain roads.

While the little Porsches were soon achieving amazing overall results in major European rallies, it had to be admitted that even the best drivers often got to the finish with battered front wings as evidence of exciting Alpine descents. Even so, the 356 was making its mark in a big way and it was already a very rewarding road car for the skilled, if rather wealthy, road driver.

It was simply to mark a host of rapidly-introduced improvements that the model name was changed to 356A in September 1955. Continuous development has been a policy pursued energetically by Porsche from the very start. A front anti-roll bar, later combined with softer springing all round and needle-roller bearings in the front suspension, had certainly helped make the 356 more controllable some time before that, but such a huge number of changes to the engine, chassis and other details had mounted up that the change in name was more than justified.

The 356A didn't look that different, but in fact a comprehensive reworking and modernising of the whole car had taken place, including the introduction of a 1.6-litre version. Even the monocoque was redesigned and rationalised, yet externally the bodywork was hardly changed. This is part of the charm of Porsche. Other

A 1956 356A 1600 Super, also with sunroof. The 'Super' specification raised power from 60bhp to 75bhp, pushing top speed up from 99mph to 108.5mph. By March of that year, a total of 10,000 356s had been built. (LAT)

manufacturers, even then, were altering styling details simply to 'facelift', as we came to say later, a tired old model. Instead of resorting to that cynical ploy, Porsche improved the car itself.

Throughout the engines the move was towards stronger components of Porsche's own specification, enabling progressive increases in power and capacity as well as improving reliability: for example a thermostatically-controlled supply of warm air to the carburettors brought smoother running. According to that doyen of 356 enthusiasts, the late Denis Jenkinson, a significant change was in the gearbox front mounting, curing a then well-known niggling weakness. 'Jenks' recalled that fast driving over rough roads tended to break the bonded steel-and-rubber sandwich plate, making the car feel pretty rough, but as he recorded in his Porsche 356 book it was easy enough to replace these mountings quickly in a hotel car park. A fundamental rethink over that mounting apparently made

the 356 smoother to drive at all times as well as being more durable. I believe he called at the factory once and this precise repair/modification was carried out but I'm afraid the details of that story are now lost in the mists of time.

The 356A was stronger than its predecessors and it was also a much safer car for inexperienced drivers to handle. This big change, in my view, marked the start of a kind of dialogue between the engineers at Porsche and the enthusiasts who drove the cars. It would go on for decades.

It goes like this. Keen drivers love a rear-engined Porsche but critics say that the car doesn't handle properly because it's too easy to spin. The 356A was a first attempt to answer those critics. It understeered more at first and was more stable. The engineers

*Right*: The Motor *magazine gave driving impressions of this 356A 1600 in January 1956, commenting favourably on the low wind noise in a 100mph car. It seems the testers parked it on a cobbled autobahn in Germany to get this picture. Different times!* (The Motor/LAT)

had done a good job and the informed enthusiasts still liked it because the cars had become quicker through corners. A few, those rather dimwittedly hooked on instant oversteer, I suspect, didn't like it. I reckon the 356A retained all the great virtues and moved the model up several notches: it was more robust, and overall was undoubtedly faster thanks to its improved balance in the faster corners.

Going further, I would argue strongly that much later, many years into the 911 programme, there came a time when roadgoing Porsches did become so idiot-proof that the essential driving pleasure was lost, but the factory corrected that problem reasonably quickly: we shall get into that later in the book. Sticking to the 356A for now, in my personal view all the points went to the engineers that time. It was a greatly improved motor car.

Cast iron was retained for the standard engine's cylinder barrels but in the overhead-cam power unit, and in all Super-series models, aluminium alloy was introduced, with chromium-plated bores. The quality was unquestionable but the price this implied was always a sensitive issue for Porsche with the 356, especially in the British market.

In 1954, the concessionaires at AFN Ltd could point out the superior design, the build quality, the performance, the driving experience and the overall style of the 356. No doubt that enabled some customers to justify the £1,842 British market price tag for a bottom of the range 1300 Coupé, even when an Austin-Healey 100 cost only £1,063. That was all fair enough, but British Porsche salesmen must have been keen to keep one fact dead quiet: Swiss buyers in those days were offered the Austin-Healey at £1,208 and the Porsche 1300 cost just £1,217 over there. International variations in tax rules were largely to blame for such confusing anomalies.

In September 1954, Porsche prices in Britain were reduced, dropping the standard 1500 Coupé from £1,971 to £1,786 after tax and duty. By the Motor Show the following month, however, the prices had been smartly put back up to their old levels. Perhaps it was thought no-one would notice that neat little trick while the sensational 550 Spyder was making its first UK show appearance alongside the regular rear-engined road cars.

Sure, Porsches have always been expensive, especially in the UK, but I think we all knew that. The point is that they were always desirable because they were great to drive and, equally important, great to own because they were so reliable and, apart from a few extreme competition-

type models, utterly fuss-free.

There were signs that Porsches were already becoming Americanised but such touches were usually carried out tastefully and, after all, the US had quickly become half of Porsche's total market. The one serious lapse in good taste, perhaps, was the Speedster, to be covered in more depth later on. Oddly enough, that weird-looking thing still creates great excitement for certain enthusiasts.

Styling changes were at the heart of the 356B of 1959, the most obvious being that the headlights were mounted higher. This was necessary to retain the right appearance while meeting the latest US bumper-height regulations. Of all the 356 models, only the B had two body styles in its lifetime. It started with the 'T5', basically an updated 356A, but moved on to the 'T6' body with more glass area, a reshaped bonnet and a twin-grille engine lid.

As the smaller engines were no longer appropriate to Porsche's market, they were then dropped and the 1600 became the norm. The new look was well received but Porsche's devotion to drum brakes, albeit of high quality, was beginning to attract adverse comment.

The first Porsche I ever drove was a nine-year-old 1960 356B Super 90 Coupé that my brother bought as a

Left: This superb 356A 1600 Cabriolet is an outstanding survivor from 1957. Only 3,285 were made in a four-year production run to 1959, the Cabriolet being outsold by the Coupé by nearly four to one. At £2,139 in the UK, tax paid when new, it cost £180 more than a contemporary Coupé. Right-hand-drive examples of this model are extremely rare today. (LAT)

Opposite top: This early 356B 1600 Cabriolet dates from 1959. Bumpers, headlights and front wings were higher than they had been on the 356A. The inlets under the bumper provided improved cooling for the front brakes. (LAT)

Opposite bottom left: Imported to the UK privately in 1990, this left-hand-drive 356B 1600 Super Cabriolet is another very rare car today. The single grille over the engine denotes an early 'T5' example, made in the 1960 and 1961 model years. The many bodywork revisions of the 1962–63 'T6' included a double grille over the engine. (LAT)

Opposite bottom right: A 356B 1600 Super engine of the 1960–63 model years, producing 75bhp at 5,000rpm. The standard 1600 gave 60bhp at that time and a Super 90 version was also available, producing 90bhp at 5,500rpm. (LAT)

used car with about 69,000 miles on the clock. That was in 1969, before I had become a journalist, but I was an established Formula Ford race driver by then, with a varied experience of driving all sorts of cars. My brother brought his newly-acquired Super 90 home one night and suggested I had a go. When new, this model had been the fastest Porsche road car available to date, excluding the extremes of expensive race-based engines. Introduced for the 1960 model year, the 356B Super 90 produced 90bhp and had a top speed of 112mph. It was still a comparatively fast road car in 1969.

Knowing little or nothing about Porsches then, I had no idea of what a 356B was, let alone the Super 90 version of it. A few miles down the road, I asked if the car been totally

A 356B 1600 *Super Coupé* with legendary
Californian motoring journalist *Pete Coltrin*
*about to take the wheel. Coltrin settled in*
*Modena in the late 1950s and made his name*
*with outstanding articles on the European*
*scene in the American magazine* Road &
Track. *This snap was taken by fellow*
*journalist Denis Jenkinson.* (Denis
Jenkinson collection)

rebuilt. 'No – just properly serviced,'
replied its proud new owner. 'Amazing,'
I muttered back, while pressing on
hard. 'It feels brand-new.' It did, too. I
had been given my introduction to
Porsche motoring.

The feel of the door as I had closed
it, the sound of the engine, the
performance, the steering, the driving
position and pedal design, even the
appearance of the instruments and the
panel lighting – all these things left a
deep impression. I knew I was driving a
most superior motor car.

An interesting feature of the 356B
Super 90 was its rear suspension,
which had a helper spring as standard.
That useful device, which further
improved the roadholding and the
handling balance of the 356, became
an option on the slower models.

With the 356C, unveiled in Britain in
August 1963, disc brakes became
standard on all 356s. These brakes
were specially developed by Porsche
and ATE, from Dunlop patents; those
at the rear contained a drum to ensure
an efficient parking brake, that
previously having been a problem with
some disc systems. As things turned
out, however, Porsche also had a few
problems with the transition to
discs on production cars, as we shall
see later.

As 356C production began, the
60bhp engine option was dropped,
making the Super 75 the standard unit.
New cylinder heads improved torque,
which made the engines more flexible.
The Super 90 was retained but the top
of the range became the 1600SC, its
power having been raised to 95bhp at
5,800rpm. Details included a quick-
action heater control handle,
apparently a trivial matter but an
improvement appreciated by those
who had been twirling a rather slow

screw control for years. As for the
handling, initial understeer was further
increased by yet softer rear suspension
and an even stiffer front anti-roll bar.
Externally, however, despite these
modifications the 356C was almost
indistinguishable from the 'B'.

Although the 901, which soon had its
name changed to 911, began to
appear at shows in 1963, the intention
was to go on producing the 356 for a
long time to come. No right-hand-drive
901/911 models were expected in
Britain before spring 1965, in any case,
and in fact only began arriving in
August that year. Indeed, the 356
remained in British price lists until
February 1966, being briefly sold
alongside the 911 and 912 models,
which had also been listed since
the Earl's Court Motor Show of
October, 1965.

So far I've hardly mentioned one of
the most sought-after of 356s, the
Speedster. Many people seem to think
that James Dean was killed in a 356
Speedster. He wasn't, but it's an
understandable mistake, as Porsche's
outrageously-styled roadster brought a

Above: Registered new in October 1963, this 356C Coupé, with the 75bhp 1600 engine and badged on its engine lid simply as a 'Porsche C', is a fine example of the 356 as it was in the final years before being replaced by the 911. A 95bhp SC model was also available but the 60bhp engine was dropped for the 356C. To look at, flatter hubcaps distinguish the 356C from the 'B'. Featured in Classic Cars magazine in December 2006, this car was owned by Steven Sterlacchini. (Classic Cars)

Right: Rear view of another very fine-looking red 356C Coupé, this one being a 1965 car. (LAT)

Below: A good place to be. Despite its age, it's comfortable for hours on end at the wheel of a 356. This is the well-designed interior of the 1963 356C 1600 Coupé. (Classic Cars)

Left: This archive picture I found was simply dated '1964' but something about it drew me in. The scene is clearly Woodcote Corner on Goodwood circuit and closer inspection revealed Autocar's Stuart Bladon, looking very relaxed as he presses on hard in this 356C. Stuart firmly denies being tuned to the BBC's Home Service whilst hammering round at the Guild of Motoring Writers' Test Day, but adds 'I would have made a bee-line for any Porsche. [I see I was] wearing collar and tie at a test day, and that was my rule in the more formal days before jeans and anoraks.' A proper gent, indeed. (Autocar/LAT)

Below: Cutaway drawing of the Porsche-ATE rear disc brake of the type used in the last 356 models and first 901/911 models. This appeared in the press in August 1963, when it was announced that all-round disc brakes would be standard on Porsche cars. Note the integral drum for the handbrake. (LAT)

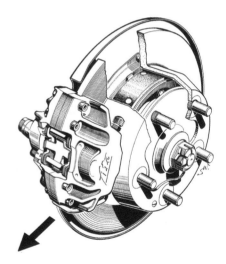

bit of dubious racy glamour to the marque in 1954. Dean, the screen-idol star of *Rebel Without a Cause* and just two other films, did own and race one, often being photographed in it. In fact he met his end on the road at the wheel of his new Porsche 550, in September 1955, within hours of taking delivery. The 550 was a real racer, and would be right outside the scope of this book except that some were used on the road. The Speedster, contemporary with the 550, was not a real racer but it was dressed up to look the part, to American eyes at least.

Not everybody liked it. With its slit-like, low windscreen and consequently very low roof, it was impossible for tall drivers to get inside it with the hood raised. Anyone even six feet tall found his head was touching the roof. Maybe I'm prejudiced against it because I am 6ft 5in, but I don't think so. There's more to my objections than that.

The Speedster's addition to the range was inspired by Max Hoffman, the go-ahead US Porsche importer at the time, who virtually insisted on it. Hoffman knew his business: sales went up and the Speedster was an attention-grabber for Porsche cars generally. All that didn't stop a large number of devoted Porsche enthusiasts, notably in Britain, from

regarding it as nothing more than a novelty item. If it was good for Porsche, that was fine by them because they were loyal, but it wasn't a car that the serious Porsche driver lusted after. And, let's be honest, it was always a rather odd-looking thing.

The Speedster was such an extreme version of the existing cabriolet theme it was almost a new design in its own right. Mainly to keep costs down it had a lightweight, simple interior and the simplest of soft tops. Porsche has said in recent times that the first examples were powered by the 1100 engine with either 60bhp or 75bhp. That may well have been so in Europe but the first production models were sold in the US and they were powered by 1500 and 1500S engines. Hoffman did not believe it was worth offering any Porsche model under 1.5 litres for sale in the States, and his judgement as a born salesman seems to have been predictably sound all along.

Being some 60kg – a hundredweight or so – lighter than the Coupé, the Speedster 1500S was undeniably lively on acceleration, with 0–60mph covered in close to ten seconds: in top, it could just pass the 100mph barrier. Later on, the 1600 engine became available in the Speedster.

A few months before the Speedster

first appeared, the 5,000th Porsche car had been built. That major landmark was passed in the middle of March, 1954, by which time the Porsche phenomenon was expanding worldwide with some strength. The Speedster, however, launched in the US in September 1954, was not available in other markets at first.

Getting on for 5,000 356 Speedsters were sold over the following years, and this despite the fact that it was a special model designed for a special market, and set apart from the mainstream production cars that sold in larger numbers. Although nearly all Speedsters were sold in the US, as originally planned, Porsche did begin to release it in small numbers to other markets in 1955, despite doubts within the factory that European Porsche drivers would be willing to return to old-fashioned sidescreens.

Perhaps because it looked so different, and was not as practical as a normal 356, the Speedster acquired a cult status that it has retained. Decades later, they went on to become highly-valued classics. Of the entire 356 range, only the Carrera models are worth more these days.

Don't forget that the real idea behind the original Speedster was to produce the cheapest possible version of the 356. In the years following the Second World War, the US became a happy hunting ground for British

sports car makers. Returning servicemen bought them and took them home, making names like MG, Austin-Healey and Triumph familiar to US drivers. The big manufacturers in the States began to respond with their own interpretation of the sports car theme.

Porsche meanwhile was engaged in redefining the very meaning of the term sports car and Porsche cars, being built to an unusually high standard, remained relatively expensive. The rise in Porsche sales in the US, having grown rapidly to nearly 600 cars a year, began to level off in the face of this cheaper competition.

Responding to Hoffman's request for a visually arresting basic car that he could sell for under $3,000 in the US, Porsche had worked with its coachbuilder, Reutter, to produce the

Speedster. The same quality of construction went into the new car but it was somewhat basic inside and, with the simple hood raised, visibility through the soft sidescreens was poor. A hardtop became available for the Speedster in 1955. Built by a company in California, it was soon approved by

*The visually-arresting 356 Speedster still attracts plenty of attention, and high values. The idea behind it, however, was to simplify the 356 and produce a cut-price model which could be sold in the USA for under $3,000 in 1954. Ace US Porsche importer Max Hoffman, worried by cheaper European sports cars, almost insisted on it. He was proved right and the Speedster was produced in Pre-A and, as shown, 356A forms. It must be said, however, that Coupé enthusiasts, rather stuffily, saw it as a lapse of good taste. (LAT)*

Above: An impressive array of 356 Speedsters lined up in the sunshine for 'Porsches at the Castle', Castle Hedingham 2007. (Author)

Left: Another snap from Hedingham Castle in 2007: the glamorous interior of this 356 Speedster perhaps reflects the fact that originally it was intended solely for the US market. Speedster 356s were later sold in limited numbers in Europe, however, satisfying a small demand for this special model. (Author)

the factory and sold through official Porsche dealers worldwide.

Throughout its production life, the Speedster benefited from the engine and chassis improvements applied to the 356 range generally, getting better instrumentation when the 356A appeared, for example. A more comprehensive range of improvements, specifically designed to improve the Speedster, arrived in the summer of 1958.

These changes all made sense: the basic look was retained but a new windscreen made slightly increased headroom possible, and there were better seats plus what some people called 'proper' wind-up side windows and large boxes for odd items built into the doors.

A new coachbuilder was engaged in 1958 to build these revised Speedster bodies. For the first time, it was then reported, Porsche offered a 356A with non-Reutter bodywork but that wasn't strictly true. Convertibles had been built by Gläser and others before that.

Known as the D-Type convertible, these new Speedster bodies were built by Drauz of Heilbronn. The design followed the Porsche house style closely but it was nearly as heavy as the 356C, which seemed to miss the point of the Speedster concept to some extent. It appears to have been an attempt to produce a fairly civilised roadster.

Oddly enough, and I am sure the weight had nothing to do with it, most American Porsche enthusiasts rejected the new version, known there as the 356 Convertible D, even though it had been designed, with Porsche's typical attention to the details, to answer all their criticisms of the original Speedster. American Porsche salesmen could only conclude that the customer is always right and there's no accounting for his taste.

In contrast to the Speedster, which was more for 'show' than for 'go', the Carrera was emphatically the performance 356 variant. Carrera is the Spanish word for 'race' and Porsche adopted it as a model name after remarkable early successes in the heroic Carrera Pan-Americana. Two

1.5-litre Porsche Spyders ran third and fourth overall in that gruelling event in 1954, winning their class and finishing ahead of cars three times their engine size.

Of all the 356 range, the Carreras are seen as the most desirable gems: collectors will pay the highest prices for a Carrera and their judgement is sound. Powered by Porsche's renowned four-cam engine, they are fabulous machines but, be warned, this engine was intended first and foremost for competition. Although the idea of adapting it for road use had existed in the mind of at least one senior engineer from the start, that actually came later and, when it went into the 356, the result was a car that was better suited to competition than shopping trips. Most drivers, even enthusiasts, will find one of the less valuable 356 models a more realistic, and probably more enjoyable, proposition for regular road use. These early Carreras feel flexible at low revs but such use is damaging to them, while constant use of more than 6,500rpm simply wears them out that bit quicker. Those who understood kept them between 3,000rpm and 6,500rpm most of the time. All this held true when they were new and so it remains.

Carreras are indeed much quicker than an 'ordinary' 356, once you get on a track, but they are noisier and considerably more expensive to maintain. When they first came out, only the engines and transmissions differentiated the Carreras from other models. They were even probably a fraction slower in the 0–60mph stakes than the cheaper 1600 Super model. At higher speeds, however, the Carrera had much quicker acceleration and was more than 10mph faster on top speed. Once it had really got moving it had the potential to leave a 356 Super well in its wake but only when driven by someone who was prepared to revel in taking it close to 7,000rpm every time and indulge in a great deal more gearchanging.

The race-based engines of those early Carreras were also very good at cooling themselves, so on cold winter

nights they could get quite chilly inside. Supplementary heating systems, by means of an alarming-sounding, electrically fired, petrol-burning heat exchanger, were not that effective either. Just bear in mind that the easier torque characteristics at low revs and the rather more effective heating systems make the cheaper cars far more comfortable to live with on a regular basis. To be sure, if you want the ultimate 356 you have to look seriously at the Carreras, but only in full knowledge of what they really represent.

The 356 Carrera first appeared at the Frankfurt show in September 1955 and was powered by a 100bhp version of Porsche's own flat-four 1.5-litre four-cam engine, complete with roller-bearing crankshaft. Basically the same unit as that in the racing 550, the overhead camshafts were shaft-driven, two Solex downdraught carburettors were used and there was twin-plug ignition from two separate coils and distributors. This engine had its own Porsche type number, 547, and it was designed by Dr Ernst Fuhrmann, who later became the company's Chief Executive. A top speed of 121mph was claimed for the Carrera Coupé in 1955 and the new model was to be available in all the 356 body variations. Unlike some manufacturers in those days, by the way, Porsche's claimed figures could always be believed.

Development was as rapid as ever. By the time the 356A/1500GS Carrera was shown at the British Motor Show at Earl's Court in October, 1956, the race-based engine was giving 110bhp at 6,200rpm and Carreras came with a guaranteed top speed of 125mph. By then there were no Carrera Cabriolets, only Coupés or Speedsters.

This 1500GS Carrera engine provided superb performance from the start, giving considerable extra speed and the characteristics of a genuine, top-class racing engine, both of which qualities were much appreciated by enthusiasts. It was admittedly noisy, not so much to the occupants as to anyone else in its vicinity as it flashed past. Porsche 356 Carreras were devastatingly successful in

*The 356A 1500 GS Carrera Speedster of 1956–57 was an extremely rare car in its day, only a tiny number being built. With at least 100bhp from its four-cam engine, and a top speed of 124mph, it was a much more potent machine than the 1600 Super. It was also, of course, much more expensive and the silver metallic paint would have increased the price. (LAT)*

competition, particularly in major European rallies. The French pairing of Storez and Buchet, for example, simply left the field standing in the 1957 Liège–Rome–Liège marathon, winning by a huge margin.

That result echoed Helmut Polensky's earlier achievements. He won that same event in 1952 and, navigated by works mechanic Herbert Linge – himself an accomplished driver – repeated that victory in 1954. There were countless similar successes notched up by Porsche rally and race drivers, both professional and amateur, in those days.

By 1957, Porsche was beginning to recognise that some of the wealthiest customers wanted the top of the range model for reasons of status alone. These owners had no intention of competing in anything. Thus in 1957 the Carrera became available either as the more comfortable 100bhp, 882kg (17.4cwt) 'Deluxe' or as the 110bhp, 811kg (16cwt) GT, the latter retaining the original competition-car character.

Weight and power crept up a little when Carrera engines were enlarged to 1,600cc in 1959. The Speedster version of the Carrera was then discontinued, so it was Coupés only for the Carrera from then on. The factory also altered the engine specification at that time, dropping the crankshaft roller bearings in favour of more durable plain bearings. That surely helped to increase engine life in road use but all these early Carrera engines were precision-built pieces of thoroughbred machinery and were always expensive to maintain in the long run, regardless of the type of bearings used for the crankshaft.

By late 1959, Porsche was sensibly much more keen to sell the pushrod-engined Super 90 to roadgoing customers, generally reserving the Carreras for known customers who intended to compete and who were good enough to achieve decent results. The reduced numbers of Carreras leaving the factory from that time were more extreme than ever, with lightweight bodies, plastic side windows and other fittings appropriate to serious circuit racing.

A very small number of special alloy-bodied Carreras, with a sleeker body style, were constructed for Porsche by Abarth in Italy at this time but these were purely racing machines, intended to extend the competition life of the 356 Carrera. They were successful in that respect.

Maybe I'm wrong on this but I sense that it took Porsche some time really to accept that there were rich customers out there, even then, who simply wanted to be seen in what they saw as 'the best Porsche', the most expensive

A great driving experience, the 356A 1500 GS
Carrera Speedster required expert skill to get
the best from such a race-based machine in
terms of performance and especially when it
came to maximising engine life. Not a car for
everyday use, it's a top collectors' item. (LAT)

It was rare for such valuable machinery as this
356 Carrera 2 to be loaned to magazines in
1963. At £3,754, twice the price of a 356C,
they were precious machines but I came across
this shot, clearly showing Charles Bulmer, then
Technical Editor of The Motor. He remembers
it and even recognises the road, a favourite test
route. The 2-litre engine gave 130bhp at
6,200rpm. (The Motor/LAT)

*Above: The engine in this 356A 1500 GS Carrera Speedster of the late 1950s hints at its exotic nature with those impressive intake trumpets. The power output would have been 100–110bhp, depending on the chosen specification. (LAT)*

*Above right: Caught on the author's camera in the workshops of Maxted-Page and Prill Ltd in 2007, with a sign over it saying 'Do not touch, on pain of death!' You just don't scrap a 356 2-litre four-cam Carrera engine, even when someone has blown it wide open, as this one was. Only a highly skilled specialist can tackle such a complex job. (Author)*

top-of-the-range model, regardless of its suitability to their personal motoring requirements. Porsche was essentially logical and perhaps the company took time to appreciate the illogical motives of some customers.

Apparently bowing to such customers (and accepting their money) once again, the factory announced a new 356 Carrera 2 road car in October 1961, powered by a 2-litre version of the 547 engine. Just too late for the British show, it was unveiled at Frankfurt very shortly after that. Based on the 356B Coupé body, it was more 'civilised' for road use than previous Carreras had been. The weight of this production model grew to over 1,100kg, or roughly 22cwt, making it heavier than earlier Carreras, too, but the performance of the 2-litre engine more than compensated for the increased weight.

This enlarged production version of the engine raised maximum power to

130bhp at 6,200rpm, and the 7,000rpm rev limit was unchanged. Up to 130mph was claimed for the lightweight GS-GT version, which was tuned to give 140bhp. Other major benefits also came with this increase in capacity: in this form the Carrera was more flexible thanks to improved torque at lower revs, it was smoother and quieter for those inside the car, and the exhaust was also far less raucous as far as the outside world was concerned.

Without doubt the best 356 Carrera I have been in was one of these later Carrera 2s, owned at the time by Armin Baumann of Switzerland. In partnership with Marco Marinelli, Baumann was recognised as a top 356 specialist restorer and his 1962 GS 2-litre had just been rebuilt in their Zurich workshops to the ultimate 1962 competition specification when he brought it over to England for the 1983 International 356 meeting at Donington.

I could hardly blame him for refusing to let anyone else except his business partner, Marco, drive his precious machine. Marco turned out to be an expert circuit driver with a relaxed style and I was happy to be his passenger for several entertaining and very fast laps of Donington circuit. He had the 356 technique taped: slightly sideways into all the corners, he planted his foot on the throttle each time and the little car shot away under perfect control.

Armin's car was like new and the attention to detail was superb: it had the proper original type of Porsche racing seats, plastic side widows and even the drop-straps instead of door window winders. The bonnet, doors

and windows were in aluminium, and the 1962 racing filler was correctly cut into the centre of the bonnet. There were no back seats and the original rollcage was still fitted.

As you might guess, this car was perfection itself and by far the quickest 356 of many I saw on the circuit that day. It sounded great, too, and it's hardly surprising that a car like this is worth perhaps three times the value of a contemporary pushrod-engined 356. But I still say that the standard car is the thing to get for normal road use and just as much fun to drive in its way. The Carrera is simply the 356 connoisseur collector's ultimate machine.

Porsche had not been swift to jump at the fashionable new disc brakes in the 1950s. One reason was that the drum brakes they used were extremely good; another was the difficulty at that time of designing a really effective parking brake to work with discs. An even better reason was the company's reluctance to pay royalties on this new braking technology. Once the handbrake problem was overcome to Porsche's satisfaction, by means of separate small drums at the rear, disc brakes of a unique type were fitted to 2-litre 356 Carreras from late 1962. These were supplied by ATE, who it seems had signed a disc-brake agreement with Girling, that company holding certain patents.

Despite Porsche's best efforts, however, on this occasion both these new parking brakes and the new disc-brake system gave some trouble in service. Other cars in the range remained on drums for some months to come and the last few 356 Carreras, based on the 356C, had disc brakes of a more conventional pattern. Porsche had felt that its own system was essentially superior to all others but, lacking the industrial clout to make all others follow their lead, the company was forced to fall in line with the rest of the world on that issue. Such minor problems were soon sorted out, however and in the summer of 1963 the company was able to state that all Porsche cars would have discs.

On 23–24 March 1963 a new and very special version of the Carrera made its first appearance at the Alle-sur-Semois hillclimb in Belgium. This was the 2-litre Carrera GTL, and had a race-tuned engine, on Webers and with a special exhaust system, that delivered a beefy 165bhp.

Radically lightened from 19.9cwt to 14.6cwt by the use of racing seats, plastic windows, light alloy doors, bonnet, engine lid and other panels, it also had a rollcage and a 22-gallon fuel tank. Top speed was rumoured to be 150mph at 7,200rpm.

A few competition examples of the 547 engine were said to have produced 180bhp by the end of their development. Porsche was getting close to the ultimate expression of the 356 theme and the day of the bigger six-cylinder 911 was dawning. Meanwhile on the circuits the 904, still powered by the latest version of the 547 competition engine, was taking the extreme path demanded by modern motor racing. Mid-engined, with a plastic body on a strong platform frame, it represented the start of a new era in motor sport. Race cars had ceased to be specially-prepared production models and had become a separate breed, and later 904s were powered by an even more evolved 692 version of the engine.

The question of how many 356 Carreras were built remains unanswered, as precise records of such things were not kept in those days. Official estimates today suggest there were 310 356B 2-litre Carreras of all types, plus 126 based on the 356C. For sure, unexpectedly high demand for this outstanding car resulted in far more

sales than Porsche ever anticipated at that launch in 1955 and some suggest that more were made than the company ever claimed. In motor industry production terms, however, it was a relatively low volume model. The fact is that only a few hundred were made and thus the 356 Carrera, in any style of body, remains an extremely rare item.

*Early in 1960, Carlo Abarth of Turin built 21 special lightweight race cars for Porsche. This was the 356B Carrera GTL-Abarth, or Porsche Type 756. Long, low and aerodynamically efficient for its day, it was powered by the 1.6-litre Carrera engine which in full-race form produced 135bhp at 7,400rpm. Top speed was said to be over 137mph. (Classic & Sports Car/LAT)*

# Buying hints

**1.** All 356s made prior to the 356A are so rare these days that we hardly need to discuss the prospect of finding one. In fact, getting your hands on any good 356 today isn't so easy because they don't often come up for sale.

**2.** Cabriolets fetch a considerable premium even though, in the eyes of the traditionally minded purist, the Coupé is the true classic 356. For me, the Coupé is also preferable by far as a car to drive.

**3.** Every 356 was beautifully made but many were lost to corrosion decades ago, rust prevention being not so well understood then. When buying one, it's advisable to jack it up, remove the wheels and examine the metal deep within the structure for signs of rot.

**4.** Checking for rust is relatively easy in theory, but more expertise is called for when inspecting a 356

that's up for sale. All versions had a very subtle shape and potential buyers should be aware that some restorers in the past didn't manage to reproduce the curves correctly. It's important to watch out for poor work of that kind as it's very hard to do anything to correct it later.

**5.** Most 356s at some stage suffered from poor maintenance and bodged repairs, so before buying one it's wise first to join Porsche Club Great Britain or your national club. Then find the best example you can and get a recognised expert to check it before you buy. You should take your time before you even think of parting with money.

**6.** Take your time, too, getting to understand the 356's handling. These are cars from another age, and unlike a modern hot hatch they can recognise a bad pair of hands and bite back. Once you know them, however, they are supremely rewarding to drive.

# The fabulous 550

It was inevitable that Porsche would have to start making purpose-built race cars sooner rather than later. This was necessary to avoid being outpaced by a growing number of rivals. The 356 had proved successful in competition but it was essentially a road car. Although it could still be used as a (somewhat phenomenal) road car, the 550 of 1953 was an inspired step towards a pure racing design and, thanks to good engineering and wise management, Porsche continued to make a profitable business out of motor

sport with it. Porsche is also famous for using its design type numbers as model names but some freedom of action has been exercised over the years: the weight target for the 550 is now conveniently said to have been 550kg – or 10.8cwt – when in fact the actual car came out at 686kg.

Inspiration for the 550 went back to Porsche's co-operation with Walter Gloeckler, a successful VW dealer in Frankfurt and also a talented race driver of considerable vision. His attitude and the results achieved with his Porsche-powered specials, the most

notable of which were mid-engined, impressed the Porsche people and a productive relationship sprang up between the factory and Gloeckler.

When they came to design the 550 for 1953, Porsche engineers based the new car very closely on Gloeckler's mid-engined developments. The earliest 550s had race-modified pushrod-ohv engines but a brand new engine of pure Porsche design was also on the way and the 550 was conceived with this in mind.

A strong pointer to the future was seen on the Porsche stand at the Geneva show early in 1953. This car, built it was said as a one-off for a Swiss customer, was powered by a '1500' engine giving a claimed 100bhp. An open two-seater, it had a low-cut, racing style screen and the car weighed a claimed 9.4cwt, in other words a mere 477kg.

These power and weight figures, one suspects, are highly unreliable. They did not come from the factory: probably they were put to the press by a well-meaning outsider who chose to shoot a very big line. What could be seen plainly on that car, however, was a special tubular chassis and, most interesting of all, the mid-engined layout.

Putting the engine ahead of the rear axle in that way meant a reversal of the 356 rear axle links from trailing to leading. That in turn meant that the rear wheels toed out on roll instead of toeing in and the short truth of that was that it made for a faster car that was likely to go into snap oversteer on fast corners. To put it mildly, these cars required the skill of a top professional racer to get the best from them.

This book is really about Porsche road cars but motor sport, and especially the Le Mans 24-hours, has been at the very core of all that this company has striven for over the years. The competition and normal production sides of Porsche have always been genuinely interwoven, so motor sport cannot be ignored completely here.

*Above: The property of Porsche Cars Great Britain Ltd, this superb early 550 1500 RS Spyder is truly at the heart of Porsche's heritage. Through 1954–56, just 90 of these pure racing machines were made. Mid-engined, with ladder frames and aluminium bodies, they were fitted with the four-cam Carrera engine. Extremely successful in competition, early examples were prone to snap into oversteer, demanding extreme driving skill. (Author)*

*Right: The welded aluminium dash was a load-bearing chassis component of the 550 1500RS Spyder racing car of 1954–56. The lack of trim indicates the serious purpose behind the design. (Author)*

Anyway, the 550 just couldn't be left out of this book. As early as 1953, Porsche's effort at Le Mans had started to look very special indeed. The purpose-built mid-engined 550 racing prototypes entered by the factory had coupé bodies that were a mere 30in high. The officially claimed power output of the 1,488cc Le Mans team works engines at that time was 80bhp at 6,000rpm, which tells us that that Swiss chap back in Geneva really had been talking rubbish.

The factory was still going for modest class wins but it was done in style, with the beautifully-designed and beautifully-built little cars finishing first and second in the 1,500cc class at Le Mans in 1953, and 15th and 16th overall. The Porsche 550 programme had got off to an impressive start.

Following the 1953 Le Mans 24 Hrs, word began to get around in Britain that replicas of Porsche's Le Mans cars might become available for sale. These special road cars, it was suggested, might have dohc heads and be capable of something approaching 150mph. They would be expensive and there would be quite a wait to get one, it was said. That sounds like more PR hype, this time from the British agent, but at least there was a strong element of truth in the story that time.

In 1953 Porsche had indeed begun to experiment with an open competition prototype based on the Le Mans coupé layout. When the Paris show opened that September, there indeed was the very special new Porsche two-seater that had been promised to the public. The body featured rear 'stabilising fins' that were then believed to offer an aerodynamic advantage even if, looking back, they seem to have been inspired more by fashion than physics.

Porsche's latest model was mid-engined and powered by the four-cam unit then producing 110bhp. There was one very important difference under the skin. Unlike the 1953 Le Mans cars,

this new model had trailing radius arms to locate the rear swing-axle independent suspension, maintaining much more satisfactory geometry on roll and thus making them more controllable when driven at speed by ordinary mortals. I suspect that the professional race drivers, too, were somewhat relieved by this change.

The chassis was a mixture of platform and tubular frame, helping to keep the weight down to 13cwt, or 662kg. It was based on a ladder-type construction but the subsequent 550A of 1956 was constructed around a proper spaceframe that was naturally much stiffer. Performance figures and price were presumably matters of discretion to be discussed privately with each customer, for these cars were at first strictly to special order only.

The Porsche 550/1500RS, dubbed the Spyder, had arrived, even if none would actually be delivered to customers for about a year. Indeed, the model would not appear in the official British price lists under that name until later in 1955 – and at a price of £3,847. Stunningly expensive, it cost the British buyer even more than the £3,684 a new Aston Martin DB3S Competition Model commanded. Just to put this in perspective, the new MGA cost £844 at the time.

But the 550 Spyder was a new kind of car, bearing no relationship to the Volkswagen whatsoever. It was a thoroughbred Porsche racing car. There were people within Porsche, without question, who had a deep-seated desire to get ahead with their own high-tech developments, to escape from the VW connection completely, and to concentrate on the 550, with their own design of four-cam, light-alloy engines, incorporating advanced Hirth roller-bearing crankshafts and all the other special parts they had developed or were working on at the time. Those Hirth crankshafts served the company well in advanced engines intended for competition; but being multi-part assemblies requiring abnormally precise machining, they were expensive and unsuited to series production for standard road cars. Later in the 1950s, for the

*Late in 1955, young Cambridge graduate Dick Bensted-Smith is about to climb aboard the latest 550 Spyder for a fast trip down the autobahn. Bensted-Smith was later to edit* The Motor *magazine (but has no memory of this 550 Spyder). Only the factory test driver (wearing helmet) was then allowed to drive the 137mph competition model seen here. Parked behind it is the contemporary 356A 1.6-litre. (The Motor/ LAT)*

# The fabulous 550 (continued)

*Above: The Technical Editor of The Motor, Joe Lowrey, takes his turn alongside the factory test driver for a ride on the open autobahn in the 137mph 550 Spyder in 1955. Without a screen for the passenger, it was apparently a genuinely breathtaking experience. (The Motor/ LAT)*

*Above right: Note the 550 Spyder's mid-engined layout. With 110bhp from the four-cam 1500 Carrera engine, this lightweight racer was easily the fastest Porsche car yet made in 1955. (The Motor/ LAT)*

Carrera, as mentioned earlier, Porsche developed simpler crankshafts, with plain bearings. These were equally effective but had the special advantage of being far more practical in the hands of average owners who did not understand how to use and care for such complicated machinery.

In January 1954, an alternative version of the 550, with raised rear decking and a high padded headrest was unveiled at the Brussels show. It was rather less attractive than the original, in my opinion. For the 1954 Le Mans race, Porsche entered three of the latest 550 Spyders, two of which were sidelined long before the finish, but one survived to win the 1500 class and take 12th overall. The following year, the company fielded another strong team of updated open 550s, still aiming for class success. Not only did they succeed gloriously

in that respect but they managed to finish fourth and fifth overall. But 1955, of course, was the year of the great Le Mans tragedy and that somewhat overshadowed Porsche's truly outstanding achievement.

The 550s may have been pure race cars, with no luggage space and a cockpit designed only for the track, but over the years a few people have used these rare cars on the road. In September of 1955, as mentioned already, James Dean had his notorious fatal road accident in his own 550, hitting another car at high speed when driving to a motor race. This ghastly tragedy was not Porsche's fault in any way, of course, but the stark truth was that Dean's loss was a nightmare in marketing terms. American people did associate the Porsche name with what had happened and it took some years for that unfair negative image to wear off.

Back on the circuits, Porsches had got nearer to the front of the field every year, especially at Le Mans. This consistently rising pattern of success proved that Porsche was on the right track. People even began to suggest that the impossible could happen: one of these unusual small cars could actually win the race outright, on a combination of fundamental merit and reliability.

By 1956, a more realistic top speed of 137mph was claimed for the 550 Spyder production car. Journalist Joe Lowrey got a fast autobahn ride in one from the Stuttgart factory. From the

passenger's seat, without even an aeroscreen for protection, he conceded that it was quick but said that scientific observation was impossible. The factory's test driver only complained that Joe's head and shoulders were slowing the car down.

Now, it would be great to say I have driven a perfect 550 myself. I can't quite claim that but, about 20 years ago, I did get a go at Donington in a 1955 RS Spyder, fitted with a race-tuned 1,600cc pushrod engine instead of the four-cam unit it would have had originally, and this is what I wrote in *Classic Cars* magazine afterwards:

'This was Edgar (father of Jürgen) Barth's hillclimb car when new and spent some time in Jo Siffert's museum. Now owned by Crispin Manners, and brought to the meeting by John Lucas, this car is currently being used in HSCC events with some success. Really, it needs a rebuild, but it was interesting to drive despite its faults.

'Through the Craner Curves, it popped out of top gear when I lifted off on the first lap. Second time around I took those corners flat out with my hand on the lever and, as we dropped down the hill towards the apex, the rear suspension literally jacked itself up even though I had not lifted off. The car is very light and not very powerful (about 110bhp) and I realised it was playing its joker on me. It was actually trying to spin! Before it had us sideways, this fairly innocuous attempt at murder was countered by an armful of opposite lock and a reduction in throttle opening. We stuttered down the right hand side of the track, off line but laughing contentedly at the naughty little machine. I am sure that properly sorted, and with the right engine and gearbox, it would be terrific fun to drive. It must have been marvellous on those spectacular European hillclimbs.'

Yes, indeed, it must. And, sorry, but that's as close as I have ever got to the true 550 driving experience.

Before closing this glorious chapter of Porsche history we should also note the very special new Porsche entered for Maglioli, for 1957's Le Mans. This development of the 550 racer was lower, lighter and had a new chassis frame. In qualifying, this car recorded 142mph on the straight. Most unfortunately, he was taken out of the race when he came across Tony Brooks and his crashed Aston Martin on the track at Tertre Rouge corner.

Some say that Maglioli managed to miss Brooks, who was lying in the road, but wrecked his Porsche when he hit the Aston. The version that I believe to be true has Brooks trapped and unconscious under the upside down Aston, exactly on the racing line, just as the unfortunate Maglioli arrived. Maglioli hit the Aston, neatly flipping it off Brooks who was released and left lying on the road, essentially unhurt but still 'out for the count'. By some miracle, neither driver was seriously hurt.

Through the 1950s, Porsche's racing machinery had been steadily progressing further away from the road cars, the 1958 racing model having coil springs and a Watt linkage for the rear suspension. Properly speaking, this was a Type 718 and it was a rather different animal when seen alongside the road cars of its day. In fact one of them was specially modified for the new Formula 2, with a central single seat, and it won the supporting race to the 1958 French GP at Rheims. In a clever promotional move, Porsche selected French ace Jean Behra to drive it: he took pole and led all the way, beating a high-class field that included Peter Collins in a works Ferrari.

No doubt the slippery, all-enveloping body helped the Porsche on that ultra-fast circuit in the French champagne country. Porsche persisted with top single-seater racing but their cars looked and sounded very different from the mainstream of F1 and F2 cars at the time. They seemed a bit out of place in that company but they nevertheless did achieve considerable success. Yet, all the while, Porsche's natural home in motor racing was clearly in sports-car events.

It's worth remembering that Porsche broke the might of Ferrari in the 1959 Targa Florio, taking the top four places in that race with a variety of models, headed by a 1500RS – a pure racing model that had been developed into a formidably competitive machine over the previous couple of years. That model was a sign of things to come, showing that Porsche was a rapidly growing force. The essential point is that the link between road and competition machinery, however tenuous at times, was never broken – certainly not in the minds of the engineers who created them.

*A beautifully restored 550 RS Spyder, photographed at the old Bridgehampton Race Circuit in Long Island, New York State. Several different designs of headrest fairings and fins, as seen here, were tried on these cars.* (Classic & Sports Car/ LAT)

# The 'small-bumper' 911

A close family atmosphere had been built up around those who made, sold, bought and drove Porsche cars during the 356 era. This small, intimate cult had grown naturally and its members were intelligent, capable, well-educated people with a modern outlook. In fact, fairly strong remnants of that spirit lasted for decades, right up to the 'funny money' boom at the end of the 1980s, when a very different type of owner began to buy Porsches in the UK. That would be a painful time for traditional Porsche enthusiasts but there's no need to go into that here.

Back in the early 1960s, production of the 356 was in full swing but it was obvious that a new model would soon be needed for a changing world. In

*Clean lines of the original Typ 901 2-litre Coupé of 1963. The name was soon changed to 911, following a challenge from Peugeot over the right to use zero in that way. (Porsche)*

short, a bigger, faster Porsche was required. The answer was to introduce the concept and the look of that new model well before the 356 era came to an end. Such launches, with information carefully leaked in controlled stages, are common enough now but they were rare 40 years ago. It seems likely that Porsche was genuinely concerned about the risks involved in replacing the deservedly sacred 356 that had served the company so well. Over 73,000 356s had by then been made since the company had got going in 1948.

Whatever the reason for the long-drawn-out launch of the 911, the specification of the original new model was an open secret long before it was unveiled. American journalist Jesse Alexander, a fully signed-up Porsche cult member from the early days, had owned three 356s and was able to 'predict' the new Porsche in 1962.

He claimed he was merely guessing but when he forecast a bigger, rear-engined, air-cooled car with more cylinders it seems clear enough that he had been given inside information ahead of the pack. That was natural enough in those days of that pleasant clubby atmosphere at Porsche. The factory guarded its image and reputation carefully, for sure, but exactly the right information could be released early to a trusted enthusiast, such as Alexander, who had bothered to keep in touch. He was accepted as a friend of Porsche, in the best possible sense.

It has always fascinated me that the 911 was eased into the public eye in this discreet way just a couple of years after the Jaguar E-type coupé had come in with such a huge bang at the 1961 Geneva show. In comparison, the 911's entrance, at Frankfurt in September 1963, was a comparatively low-key affair.

Although it was on the show stand, the world was told the new model was still a long way off. And, as everybody knows, it was called the 901 at first, at least until Peugeot got legally-minded about numbers with a zero in the middle. Porsche backed down promptly, the new Porsche became the 911, and no great upset was caused.

*Getting close: what appears to be a very mildly disguised 901 is in fact the Typ 7 prototype of Ferdinand 'Butzi' Porsche's new design, built by Reutter and out on road test from the factory on 10 July 1963. (Porsche)*

Few of these very early 911s are left now and those that do remain are really collectors' curiosities. It's hardly a secret that the 911 was improved rapidly in the early days and, over the decades since, there has been a long string of models – usually faster, often less thirsty, and better to drive than those that went before.

By today's standards the original 911 was quite a modest performer. The new six-cylinder engines, still mounted in the rear in classic Porsche style, produced 130bhp from two litres, giving a top speed of just over 130mph and 0–60mph in 8.3 seconds. In other words, the first 911s were virtually identical in performance to the recent VW Golf FSi, but it's interesting that the 2005 VW needed more power, 150bhp in fact, to achieve this, whilst using only about half the fuel of the 40-year-old Porsche. Some current Golf GTis, of course, produce nearly 200bhp and are much quicker than the first 911s, but we live in a different world today.

The production version of the original 911 Coupé went on sale in September 1964. It was joined by the innovative open-topped Targa version two years later. The wide-based metal hoop over the passenger area kept the new Targa body admirably stiff and gave decent rollover protection. Perhaps because it lacked the pure, flowing curve of the Coupé's roofline, the Targa attracted buyers who had never thought of buying a Porsche before. It was soon noted, however, that a large percentage of those Targa-buying newcomers switched to a 911 Coupé when buying their second Porsche.

Although the early 911 doesn't sound that fast now, and it was a long way short of the slightly unrealistic 150mph claimed for Jaguar's E-type, a car that could do 130mph in 1965 was likely to outpace almost anything else it met on the road. To keep faith with

# Porsche 911/911T/911S
## 1964–68/1967–68/1966–68

**ENGINE:**
Six-cylinder horizontally opposed, air-cooled; aluminium-alloy crankcase and cylinders; rear-mounted*

| | |
|---|---|
| Bore x stroke | 80.0 x 66.0mm |
| Capacity | 1,991cc |
| Valve actuation | sohc per bank |
| Compression ratio | 9.0:1/9.8:1 |
| Induction | two triple-choke Weber** |
| Power | 130bhp at 6,100rpm |
| | 110bhp at 5,800rpm |
| | 160bhp at 6,600rpm |
| Maximum torque | 130lb ft at 4,300rpm |
| | 115lb ft at 4,200rpm |
| | 133lb ft at 5,200rpm |

*cast-iron cylinders on 911T
**Until February 1966, six Solex single-choke carbs on 911

**TRANSMISSION:**
Rear-wheel drive; manual five-speed gearbox. Four-speed 'Sportomatic' option from late 1967

**SUSPENSION:**
*Front:* Independent by MacPherson struts, lower wishbones and longitudinal torsion bars; anti-roll bar standard on 'S', optional on most other models
*Rear:* Independent by trailing arms and transverse torsion bars; telescopic dampers; anti-roll bar standard on 'S', optional on most other models

**STEERING:**
Rack-and-pinion

**BRAKES:**
*Front:* Disc (11.1in), ventilated on 911S
*Rear:* Disc (11.2in), ventilated on 911S

**WHEELS/TYRES:**
Steel wheels, 4.5J x 15in (911) or 5.5J x 15in (911T); alloy wheels, 5J x 15in, on 911S
Tyres 165 HR 15

**BODYWORK:**
Steel monocoque
Coupé 2+2 or Targa (from early 1967)

**DIMENSIONS:**

| | |
|---|---|
| Length | 13ft 8in |
| Wheelbase | 7ft 3in |
| Track, front | 4ft 5in |
| Track, rear | 4ft 4.25in |
| Width | 5ft 3.25in |
| Height | 4ft 3.5in |

**WEIGHT:**
20.4cwt (1,034kg)

**PERFORMANCE:**
(Source: *Motor*/Porsche/Porsche)

| | |
|---|---|
| Max speed | 129.8mph/124mph/140mph |
| 0–60mph | 8.3sec/10.0sec*/7.6sec* |
| Standing quarter-mile | 16.1sec/not quoted/not quoted |

*0–62mph

**PRICE IN UK INCLUDING TAX WHEN NEW:**
911: £2,996 (December 1966)
911T: £3,105 (February 1968)
911S: £3,556 (February 1967)

**NUMBER BUILT:**
911 Coupé: 6,607
911 Targa: 236
911T Coupé: 1,611
911T Targa: 789
911S Coupé: 3,573
911S Targa: 925

Additionally 82 '901' coupés before name changed to 911

# Porsche 912
## 1964–68

As original 911 except:

**ENGINE:**
Four-cylinder horizontally opposed, air-cooled; rear-mounted

| | |
|---|---|
| Bore x stroke | 82.5mm x 74.0mm |
| Capacity | 1,582cc |
| Valve actuation | pushrod ohv |
| Compression ratio | 9.3:1 |
| Induction | Two Solex 40 PJJ-4 carburettors |
| Power | 90bhp at 5,800rpm |
| Maximum torque | 90lb ft at 3,500rpm |

**TRANSMISSION:**
Rear-wheel drive; manual four-speed gearbox; five-speed optional 1965–66, but later standard

**BRAKES:**
*Front:* Disc (10.6in)
*Rear:* Disc (11.0in)

**WHEELS/TYRES:**
Tyres Dunlop SP 165-15s

**BODYWORK:**
Targa option from late 1966

**DIMENSIONS:**

| | |
|---|---|
| Track, front | 4ft 4.5in |
| Track, rear | 4ft 3.75in |
| Height | 4ft 4in |

**WEIGHT:**
18.8cwt (955kg)

**PERFORMANCE:**
(Source: *Motor*)

| | |
|---|---|
| Max speed | 116.6mph |
| 0–60mph | 11.7sec |
| Standing quarter-mile | 18.2sec |

**PRICE IN UK INCLUDING TAX WHEN NEW:**
£2,467 (October 1965)

the fans of the 356, some of whom felt they could not afford a new 911, a new 912 model was released in 1965. Briefly, because it's covered in its own separate section, the 912 had 911 looks but was powered by the old four-cylinder 1,600cc engine, giving 90bhp; it was also considerably lighter than a 911, and top speed was 118mph.

In both Coupé and Targa forms the new 911, being larger and more practical than the 356, gave Porsche an opportunity to appeal to a wider customer base. But although the old 'Porsche fraternity' feeling was still very much alive, some of these new owners, unfamiliar with the concept,

**NUMBER BUILT:**
Coupé: 28,333
Targa: 2,562

# Porsche 911T/911E/911S (2-litre)
### 1968–69

As earlier 911 except:

**ENGINE:**
Magnesium-alloy crankcase on all models; 911T retains cast-iron cylinders

| | |
|---|---|
| Compression ratio | 8.6:1/9.1:1/9.9:1 |
| Induction | two Weber triple-choke carburettors/ Bosch injection/idem |
| Power | 110bhp at 5,800rpm 140bhp at 6,500rpm 170bhp at 6,800rpm |
| Maximum torque | 115lb ft at 4,200rpm 130lb ft at 4,500rpm 135lb ft at 5,500rpm |

**TRANSMISSION:**
Sport-o-matic no longer available on 911S

**SUSPENSION:**
*Front:* Independent by wishbones; hydropneumatic struts standard on 2.0 and 2.2 'E' models from 1969 model year. This was optional on 'S' and 'T' models

**BRAKES:**
Ventilated discs on 911T Targa and 911E/911S

**WHEELS/TYRES:**
Alloy 5.5J x 15in (911T) or forged alloy 6J x 15in (911E/911S)
Tyres 165-15/185/70 HR 15/185/70 VR 15

**DIMENSIONS:**

| | |
|---|---|
| Wheelbase | 7ft 5.3in |
| Track, front | 4ft 5.5in |
| Track, rear | 4ft 4.75in |

**WEIGHT:**
22.5cwt (1,142kg)/22.5cwt (1,142kg)/ 21.3cwt (1,080kg)

**PERFORMANCE:**
(Source: Porsche/*Autocar/Motor*)

| | |
|---|---|
| Max speed | 124mph/130mph/ 136.5mph |
| 0–60mph | 10.0sec*/9.8sec/7.3sec |
| Standing quarter-mile | not quoted/17.0sec/ 15.8sec |

* 0–62mph
911E figures are for Sport-o-matic

**PRICE IN UK INCLUDING TAX WHEN NEW:**
911T: £3,228 (October 1968)
911E: £3,993 (October 1968)
911S: £4,385 (October 1968)

**NUMBER BUILT:**
911T Coupé: 1,611
911T Targa: 789
911E Coupé: 1,968
911E Targa: 858
911S Coupé: 1,492
911S Targa: 614

# Porsche 911L
### 1967–68

The 911L was almost identical to the early 911, except for altered cam profiles. Power was unchanged.

As for early 911 except:

**PERFORMANCE**
(Source: *Motor*. *Note: Porsche Cars only claimed a modest 121mph for this model)

| | |
|---|---|
| Max speed | 124mph |
| 0–62mph | 10.0sec |

(Source: Porsche Cars)
Sport-o-matic 911L

| | |
|---|---|
| Max speed | 127.0mph* |
| 0–60mph | 9.8sec |
| Standing quarter-mile | 17.1sec |

**PRICE IN UK INCLUDING TAX WHEN NEW**
£3,450 (February 1968)
Note: by then the 911S had risen to £3,965

**NUMBER BUILT**
Coupé: 1,169
Targa: 444

# Porsche 911T/911E/911S (2.2-litre)
### 1969–71

As 911 2-litre except:

**ENGINE**

| | |
|---|---|
| Bore x stroke | 84.0 x 66.0mm |
| Capacity | 2,195cc |
| Compression ratio | unchanged/9.1:1/9.8:1 |
| Induction | two Solex carburettors/ Bosch injection/idem |
| Power | 125bhp at 5,800rpm 155bhp at 6,200rpm 180bhp at 6,500rpm |
| Maximum torque | 131lb ft at 4,200rpm 141lb ft at 4,500rpm 147lb ft at 5,500rpm |

**BRAKES:**
*Front:* Disc, ventilated (11.1in)
*Rear:* Disc, ventilated (11.4in)

**WEIGHT:**
20.7cwt/(1,050kg)/20.6cwt (1,047kg)/ 20.4cwt (1,034kg)

▶

*Opposite: Ferdinand Alexander 'Butzi' Porsche, the eldest son of Dr 'Ferry' Porsche, with his original design triumph, unveiled to the world in the autumn of 1963. (Porsche)*

*Right: Displayed for the first time, the new Porsche 901 on the company's stand at the Frankfurt show in September 1963. The Motor called it 'the most notable car for the enthusiast' at the show. British reporters, however, were told that production would not begin 'for some time' and that the car was intended only for limited production in the German home market, for a price there of around £2,000. Nobody guessed its true long-term potential then, not even its creators. (The Motor/LAT)*

► **PERFORMANCE:**
(Source: *Autocar*/*Motor*/Porsche)

| | |
|---|---|
| Max speed | 129mph/137mph/ |
| | 143mph |
| 0–60mph | 8.1sec/7.0sec/7.5sec |
| Standing quarter-mile | 16.0sec/15.4sec/ |
| | not quoted |

**PRICE IN UK INCLUDING TAX WHEN NEW:**
911T: £3,397 (October 1969)
911E: £4,215 (October 1969)
911S: £4,766 (October 1969)

**NUMBER BUILT:**
911T Coupé: 11,019
911T Targa: 6,000
911E Coupé: 3,028
911E Targa: 1,848
911S Coupé: 3,154
911S Targa: 1,496

# Porsche 911T/911E/911S (2.4-litre)
## 1971–73

As 911 2.2-litre except:

**ENGINE:**

| | |
|---|---|
| Bore x stroke | 84.0 x 70.4mm |
| Capacity | 2,341cc |
| Compression ratio | 7.5:1/8.0:1/8.5:1 |
| Power | 130bhp at 5,600rpm |
| | 165bhp at 6,200rpm |
| | 190bhp at 6,500rpm |
| Maximum torque | 145lb ft at 4,000rpm |
| | 152lb ft at 4,500rpm |
| | 159lb ft at 5,200rpm |

(From 1972 model year onwards, US versions of 911T 2.4 produced 140bhp at 5,600rpm)

**WHEELS/TYRES:**
911E wheels now pressure-cast alloy

**DIMENSIONS:**

| | |
|---|---|
| Wheelbase | 7ft 5.4in |
| Track, front | 4ft 6.25in (911E/911S) |
| Track, rear | 4ft 5.5in (911E/911S) |

**WEIGHT:**
20.1cwt (1,020kg)/21.4cwt (1,086kg)/
21.8cwt (1,105kg)

**PERFORMANCE:**
(Source: *Motor*/*Autocar*/*Motor*)

| | |
|---|---|
| Max speed | 127mph/139mph/ |
| | 145.3mph |
| 0–60mph | 7.6sec/6.4sec/6.2sec |
| Standing quarter-mile | 15.7sec/14.4sec/14.7sec |

**PRICE IN UK INCLUDING TAX WHEN NEW:**
911T: £3,971 (October 1971)
911E: £4,827 (October 1971)
911S: £5,402 (October 1971)

**NUMBER BUILT:**
911T Coupé: 10,173
911T Targa: 7,147
911E Coupé: 2,470
911E Targa: 1,896
911S Coupé: 3,160
911S Targa: 1,894

# Porsche 911 Carrera RS
## 1972–73

As 911S 2.4-litre except:

**ENGINE:**

| | |
|---|---|
| Bore x stroke | 90.0mm x 70.4mm |
| Capacity | 2,687cc |
| Power | 210bhp at 6,300rpm |
| Maximum torque | 188lb ft at 5,100rpm |

**SUSPENSION:**
Uprated to competition specification;
Bilstein dampers

**WHEELS/TYRES:**
Forged alloy wheels, 6J front and 7J rear
Tyres Pirelli CN36 185/70 x 15in front and
215/60 x 15in rear

**BODYWORK:**
Many lightweight panels; lightweight glass;
glassfibre engine lid with 'duck's tail' rear spoiler
and slightly widened rear arches

**DIMENSIONS:**

| | |
|---|---|
| Track, rear | 4ft 6.9in |

**WEIGHT:**
Sports (lightweight): 18.9cwt–20.4cwt
(960kg–1,036kg)
Touring: 21.2cwt (1,075kg)
Homologated racing weight: 17.7cwt (900kg)

**PERFORMANCE:**
Sports/Touring
(Source: Porsche/*Autocar*)

| | |
|---|---|
| Max speed | 152mph/149mph |
| 0–62mph/0–60mph | 5.8sec/5.5sec |
| Standing quarter-mile | not quoted/14.1sec |

**PRICE IN UK INCLUDING TAX WHEN NEW:**
Sport (lightweight): £6,112 (May 1973)
Touring: £7,193 (idem)

**NUMBER BUILT:**
Numbers are disputed: some say 1,590, of which
1,036 were Sports (lightweight)

The factory now says 1,308 Touring, 200 Sports
(lightweight) plus 17 homologation models

Additionally 49 examples of the RSR were built
for circuit racing, not road use; producing over
300bhp, they had 917-type brakes and were
radically stripped-out for pure racing

---

started getting into trouble with the car's handling.

Even dedicated fans had to admit that there was a bit of a problem. The essence of it was soon narrowed down to the short wheelbase and light front end. The stopgap answer was crude but simple and it was kept a fairly closely guarded secret. When cars came in for service they were treated to the latest factory tweak, free of charge. This actually involved fitting two 11kg (24lb) cast-iron weights (not lead as some people maintain), concealed within the outer corners of the front bumpers.

It seems to have worked, reducing the number of incidents in which customers lost control. In the showrooms, many dealers were able to dismiss the technical details of the procedure with mysterious talk of high-tech development, no doubt accompanied by a nod and a wink. Fair enough: they couldn't really say anything else, could they?

The first 911S, introduced in September 1966, gave 160bhp, good enough for 0–60mph in 8.0 seconds and 137mph. There was also a very rare lightweight racing version, the 911R, of which a mere 20 were made after four prototypes had been constructed. No performance figures were ever issued for the 911R but it was capable of at least 145mph. Weighing only a little over 800kg (about 16cwt) and powered by a full-race 2-litre engine that produced 210bhp at 8,000rpm, the acceleration was pretty remarkable.

The 911R project was a pet scheme of Dr Ferdinand Piëch, Dr Porsche's grandson and Ferry Porsche's nephew. At the age of 29, Piëch was promoted to head Research & Development at the Zuffenhausen factory in 1966 and his place in the company was no act of idle nepotism, as his subsequent glittering career would prove. A brilliant engineer, he rose many years later to be the overall head of the entire VW Group and his many pet projects along the way have included such highlights as the Porsche 917, the all-aluminium Audis, and the recent utterly dominant Audi Le Mans winners.

As today's aluminium Audi road cars suggest, Piëch had a big thing about weight reduction and that's how the 911R came about. He went through the

Above: Keeping to tradition, the new engine for the 1963 901 was horizontally opposed, air-cooled and rear-mounted. It was a short-stroke 1,991cc design giving 130bhp at 6,200rpm on a 9:1 compression ratio. The departure from Porsche tradition was the use of six cylinders instead of four, thereby improving smoothness and allowing ample development potential. (Porsche)

Above right: The 901's interior had a deceptively simple appearance. Driver comfort had long been a hallmark of Porsche design and the 901 was no exception. Some minor controls were still not so good but the fundamentally vital issue of correct driver positioning was properly addressed. The 901 was nearly 5in longer than the 356, permitting a useful increase in cabin space. (Porsche)

Right: Road testers Roger Bell (driving) and Michael Bowler (operating the stopwatches) at speed on the banked circuit at MIRA in 1966. Top speed was measured at 129.8mph for this standard 2-litre Coupé, undergoing Motor magazine's first 911 road test. The second-generation Porsche retained the family resemblance, they said, and the new 911 was 'designed for hard driving'. This car was raced by Vic Elford in 1967. (Motor/LAT)

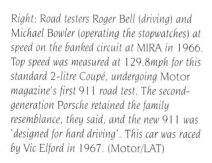

*Early 911 Targa: the original design for the 1967 model year had a standard 2-litre engine and a flexible rear window that could be unzipped and folded down. The Targa body opened up an expanding Porsche market even further and was also offered in 912 and 911S specification. Many first-time 911 Targa buyers later bought new Coupés. (Porsche)*

911 late in 1966, reducing the weight of every component to the bare minimum and then installing that full-race engine.

The whole idea was to go racing with this 911 supercar and blast the opposition into the weeds, which the 911R would surely have done. Piëch and the Porsche racing boss, Huschke von Hanstein, wanted to make 400 of them and get them homologated for international motor sport but the project was halted when the

company's sales and marketing people got cold feet. They reckoned they couldn't sell 40 examples of such a special car, let alone 400. Later events suggest they were wrong, but they had their way at the time.

Running as prototypes, the few 911Rs that were made did get into races and rallies, performing extremely well. In one most unlikely event in 1967, the third of the prototype 911Rs was used to test and promote Porsche's then-new semi-automatic transmission, the Sport-o-matic. For a single event in August that year, the car was fitted with this gearbox and a roadgoing 175bhp Sport version of the standard engine, and entered in the Marathon de la Route, a long-forgotten contest that replaced the old Liège Rally.

The Marathon de la Route involved a flat-out blast round the old

Nürburgring for three and a half days, non-stop. Drivers Vic Elford, Hans Herrmann and Jochen Neerpasch shared this unique 911R and won outright quite comfortably. Porsche's engineering chief, Helmuth Bott, was delighted to see that the Sport-o-matic gearbox gave no trouble at all. Apparently the result helped sales of the new gearbox no end but I doubt whether the customers had any real idea of just what a gruelling test it had withstood.

While writing this book, I was lucky enough to drive that very car on the old Nürburgring. It had just been restored to its proper original 911R specification, producing 210bhp and driving through a manual five-speed gearbox. Although the suspension needed a bit of sorting – the ride height was certainly too high, especially at the back – this superbly

# The misunderstood 912

There is not much interest in the modest 912 these days, to tell the truth, and that's a shame. Even in its day it was largely overlooked by most Porsche fans and that too was a pity because, although it was no road rocket, it always had a particular charm of its own. It's one of those understated cars that you don't appreciate properly until you've tried it, as I found when I tested a used example in the early 1970s.

Created to offer an affordable Porsche that 356 owners could move up to when the old model finally went out of production, it was a 911-lookalike entry-level Porsche, powered by a 90bhp flat-four engine. Made from the start of 1965, it came to the UK during that year and remained on sale until the end of the 1960s.

On acceleration, with 0–60mph in a rather leisurely 11.7 seconds, it was still very much a match for popular British sports cars such as the contemporary Triumph TR4A or a sports saloon such as the Ford Lotus-Cortina and, thanks to superior aerodynamics, it was considerably quicker on top speed than either of them, at about 118mph. The snag was that it cost over two and a half times as much as the TR or the Lotus-Cortina.

Those who bought a 912, however, got a beautifully made car that looked exactly the same as a 911, inside and out, but that was rather different to drive. Being about 82kg (180lb) lighter than the 911, it was more softly sprung. Most of the weight reduction was right at the back of the car, thanks to its smaller four-cylinder engine, and the truth was that the 912 felt supremely well balanced, easy to drive, and extremely safe. It had that distinctive and delightfully informative Porsche feel in the steering, though road testers at the time did comment that they could sense all too well its somewhat excessive tendency to aquaplane in the wet.

Just slightly faster than the £2,278 356 1600SC it replaced, the 912 was originally offered on the UK market at £2,467 including tax. As the new 911 was coming in at the same time at about £1,000 more than that, the marketing logic behind the 912 was clear enough. With fuel consumption in the 23–30mpg range, and an easy all-day 100mph cruising ability, the agile and well-built 912 had some strong points in its favour even if outright performance was not its strongest suit. Nearly 31,000 were sold in five years of production so perhaps it was better loved in its day than we sometimes think now. A final version of the 912, sold in the US just for the 1976 model year as the 912E, was a stopgap before the 924 was launched. It had a fuel-injected engine derived from that of the 914 and is highly prized by discerning collectors.

*The original 912, here on test with Motor in 1966. With a light, four-cylinder engine and modest performance from just 90bhp, the magazine said that the whole car 'feels supremely well balanced'. The 912's quality was undeniable and it had enormous charm, but it did cost quite a lot more than a 150mph E-type fixed-head coupé...*
*(Motor/LAT)*

*Opposite: A 911R, fitted with a 'cooking' engine and the new Sport-o-matic transmission, en route to a dominant victory in the 1967 Marathon de la Route, a three-and-a-half day event on the old Nürburgring. Vic Elford drove all the night sessions single-handed, often in thick fog. Seen here leaving Metzgesfeld, with the castle of Nürburg in the background, this beautiful image of the winning machine captures the spirit of another age. (LAT)*

*Above: The 1967 Marathon de la Route winner returned to the Nürburgring in 2005, and is seen here entering the Karussell banking with the author at the wheel. One of 20 original 911R racing lightweights, it was briefly converted when new to Sport-o-matic specification for the Marathon. Owner Andrew Horsell had just had the car restored to its proper, original 911R configuration when this track test took place. (Classic Cars)*

restored car would have delighted any 911 fan. With a small engine and maximum torque occurring as high as 6,000rpm, standing starts are not its strongest point but once on the move

it's a different matter: it flies. The scream of a race-tuned 2-litre Porsche flat-six at high revs is alone enough to get the blood moving, and the little lightweight Coupé got round the 'Ring very quickly indeed even though I was not prepared to take too many liberties with the handling as it was on that day. I got the feeling that if I had stuck the tail out, in classic 911 style, it probably would not have wanted to come back. As these cars are now worth getting on for £300,000, and this beautiful example has such an outstanding history, I exercised a degree of respectful caution.

Talking to Vic Elford about it later, he insists that it can be tamed with the right adjustments and I have no doubt that he's right. Vic, don't forget, was an exceptional driver who won many events, including the 1968 Monte Carlo Rally, in a works 911. His description of how to handle a 1960s 911 in those circumstances appears here in a separate panel, and it's worth reading closely. As I have suggested, Vic's driving then was something beyond the reach of ordinary mortals.

Another starring rôle turned up for the 911R in October 1967 – completely unexpectedly. Some Swiss drivers had booked Monza for a few days to take some 2-litre world records with a 904 racer but its dampers failed terminally after a few hours. The factory instantly packed a 911R with spares and drove it across the Alps to Monza as a replacement. No problem: it covered more than 12,000 miles at an average of just over 130mph, and took all the records going.

Meanwhile, for 1968 Porsche offered the 911 as a fully-fledged range comprising the T, the L and the S, in ascending order of performance. It's worth reminding ourselves, too, that a genuine link between the road cars and at least some of the competition machinery has been an enduring feature of the way Porsche has gone about its business. In fact, the existence of that ethos has been an invaluable characteristic of the factory from the start. Few of those very early 911s survive now, however. It was not so much accidents that removed them from our roads, as the 911's misguided

enemies might like to suggest. By modern standards, few were made in the first place and it was simple old age and the dreaded rust that claimed most of them in due course.

In launching the 911, Porsche had made the transition from 356 to a new generation of car that retained the most attractive elements of the traditional product. With its greater size and larger six-cylinder engine, there was scope for endless development. In terms of performance, handling and general refinement – and, indeed, rustproofing – even better things were to come, and soon.

At the very end of 1970 I was lucky enough to join *Motor*, then one of

*This 1968 2-litre five-speed manual 911L appeared in a 1970* Motor *group test when it was already two and a half years old and had done 24,000 miles. The verdict – 'it felt and behaved virtually as new' – will come as no surprise to Porsche owners. The driver here is the late Jim Tosen. (Motor/LAT)*

# The Sport-o-matic

This was Porsche's attempt, probably commercially very successful, to widen the 911 market – but most enthusiasts loathed it. The Sport-o-matic introduced in late 1967 gave a clutchless gearchange but it was not strictly an automatic. A torque converter was built into the transmission so that it was possible to stop and pull away again without disengaging anything. There was a clutch that was automatically operated via a microswitch in the gear knob, making this one car in which lazy drivers could not trundle about with one hand resting on the gear lever.

A normal type of gearbox was retained but the lever could be used to select L, D, D3 or D4. For relaxed driving, D gave a high ratio and great deal of torque-converter thrashing as the engine revved away and the transmission caught up.

All very ingenious, the result was a car that was easy to drive but not at all pleasing to most enthusiasts. The name Sport-o-matic was an odd choice because in this form the 911 was neither a true automatic nor a truly sporting machine. Perhaps it gave access to 911 ownership for a large number of Californian girlie types. But, honestly, was that really a good thing?

I had always thought that Sport-o-matics were aimed mainly at the important US market and used to believe that it had been very well received there. However, I was delighted recently to discover a 1968 911 Sport-o-matic Road Test in the highly respected US *Car & Driver* magazine. Not taken in for one second, they panned it in no uncertain terms.

Many years ago a Porsche specialist told me that Sport-o-matic spare parts were becoming difficult to

obtain. There was little demand for them because most of the cars that had started off with that stain on their characters had been converted to normal transmission. And a good job, too, if you ask me, notwithstanding that impressive victory it achieved in the 1967 Marathon de la Route.

Having gone on about what a load of rubbish the Sport-o-matic was, I have to balance that view with a completely different attitude from an unexpected quarter. After his Marathon de la Route outright win with one of them, that bravest and most accomplished of 911 works drivers, Vic Elford, ordered a Sport-o-matic road car for 1968. He says he used it to tow the fastest caravan on the road to race meetings all over Europe. And he adds that it was great. Whatever else we might feel about it, that transmission was obviously even tougher than we realised.

Britain's two top weekly magazines, as a road-test team member. As I had run out of money in motor racing back in 1969, this was a supreme stroke of good fortune. In fact, becoming a *Motor* road-tester was beyond my wildest hopes. It was a fabulous job, an education in itself as to what constitutes a good road car and I soon came to an inevitable conclusion. Driving virtually every new car on the market for months on end brought me to the firm conviction that Porsche cars were the business.

In fact, my introduction to professional journalism was no gentle matter. The first couple of months were easy enough but suddenly the job changed completely. Tragically, two young members of our fairly small specialist team died unexpectedly that summer, both from causes that had nothing to do with motoring. Suddenly, I found myself thrust into unexpected responsibilities and a workload that kept us hard at it seven days a week for six months until the editorial team was back up to full strength. Working on a top motoring weekly has always been a stressful occupation at the best of times, but it's exciting.

At *Motor*, among hundreds of cars tested, I soon got to drive half a dozen capable of around 150mph. The original Aston Martin DBS V8 stands out in my memory, as does the little Ferrari Dino 246GT. But the Lamborghini Jarama that passed through our hands has left no lasting mark in my head at all. That sounds terrible, but I just cannot remember it: perhaps I didn't drive it much, maybe not at all, but that's unlikely.

Driving hard in every new car as they come up, week in and week out, gives you a very clear idea of how they match up. It's a privileged position that money cannot buy. I was impressed early in the summer of 1971 by the Porsche 911E 2.2: as usual, we all had our turn in that test car. I think Roger Bell wrote the road test, saying that it was worth the high price because it did exactly what was wanted of it. It behaved like a real sports car and it was fast, strong and solid; above all, it felt as though it

*Above: Registered new in April 1970, this 2.2 911S is seen here in the early 1980s when it was my daily transport. The discreet front spoiler, absent on this model, came in with the following 2.4-litre 911S, improving stability enormously, but this car was always kept to its original specification. (Classic Cars)*

*Below: As an incurable Nürburgring addict, I have made frequent visits to the place since 1965, both as a tourist and as a race driver. This was one of my touring visits in the early 1980s, prompted by curiosity to see the new circuit under construction. My 2.2 911S is parked in the snow on the main straight and the old grandstand can still be seen on the right. Winter tyres were essential for such trips in a 911. (Author)*

*Above: A 2.4-litre 911T Targa on test with Autocar in 1973. Writer Geoff Howard said that, ten years on, the 911 seemed as young as ever, probably more so. The 'T', with 130bhp, was the least powerful of the range but still capable of 127mph and 0–60mph in 7.6sec. The more satisfactory fixed safety-glass rear window for the Targa had been introduced for 1968, at first as an option but standard from the 1969 model year. (Autocar/ LAT)*

*Below: The occasional rear seats are cleverly designed: when folded down they provide a useful flat surface for extra luggage. Here's the interior of a 1973 911T Targa – almost all 911s are much the same. (LAT)*

would carry on forever. The top speed was 137mph, and we measured a 0–60mph time of 7.0 seconds. It gave me my first brief experience of 911 driving, and I liked it very much.

Porsche had revised the chassis back in 1969, lengthening the wheelbase and improving stability. Frightening stories of unexpected spins in the pre-1969 cars still did the rounds in the pubs but those days were rapidly becoming a distant memory even then.

At the very end of the year it was time to test the latest Porsche, the 911S 2.4 for the 1972 model year. After nearly 12 months on the Road Test Team, I had done enough to be entrusted with writing that important road test. Any starry-eyed nonsense had long since been knocked out of my head and by then I felt part of a serious professional team. We tried to make our road tests concise, interesting and entertaining but above all they had to be consistently objective, matching the high standards that a national authority such as *Motor* then represented.

This is how I started that test report: 'Fantasy, it often seems to us, features as strongly in the minds of many designers of expensive GT cars as it

does in the daydreams of a blindly admiring public. The fact is that many costly motor cars do not live up to their exalted reputations; perhaps they cannot cruise for long periods at high speed without giving trouble, possibly an ordinary Mini is quicker round corners, or in some cases they are simply unreliable. One of the few exceptions to this rule is the Porsche 911...'

Even then, that was a simple fact. Having driven most of the opposition, I realised that this car was something quite out of the ordinary. Part of our 2,019-mile test involved a trip across France and back to measure the 911's top speed: it came out at a mean 145.3mph with a best one way of exactly 150.0mph. When we arrived at the hotel after several hundred miles of hard driving that day, I got out from the driving seat, walked across the road and looked back at the Porsche for some minutes.

'That's what one bloody fine GT car really looks like,' I remarked quietly to my colleague, Road Test Editor Anthony Curtis; incredibly enough, the basic 911 design was then already getting on for a decade old. With its understated dignity, the German car was far less flashy than some rivals but few of them could get anywhere near it as a machine to drive. The styling of cars has been relatively unimportant to me ever since. Sure, a car's looks do matter but how the vehicle performs is the real test. In that 911S, I had found 'The Machine' at that point in time and from that moment I began to appreciate the subtlety of its styling in a deeper way.

A minor fault of the 911E 2.2 the previous summer had been some aerodynamic lift that made the steering feel light at high speeds. This new 1972 2.4S came as standard with a new spoiler below the front bumper. Although it didn't look like much of a thing, that spoiler transformed the high-speed stability and I reported honestly that the car felt 'very stable at 150mph'. That tiny change really did make a huge difference.

Although *Motor* road tests were written by an individual team member, we were quite rightly obliged to incorporate the collective view of the whole department. That produced the consistent, considered and balanced opinion of every car tested that was so important to us. It meant, however, that I had to include the fair point that it was possible to lose the tail end, and in some circumstances the 911 2.4S was not a very forgiving car.

While I respected my expert colleagues, I was able to state my own firmly held conviction thus: 'Any strong critics of the handling of a 911S have either not driven an up-to-date model or else simply have not the experience to take advantage of a first-class rear-engined sports car.'

Perhaps that sounds a bit high-handed now but many of my colleagues agreed enthusiastically with that view. I am pleased to get it in print again because it is, quite simply, the truth. Typical of the 911 was that ultimately reassuring feeling of the steering wheel being alive in your hands: 'Most other cars feel quite dead by comparison,' I wrote. Porsche had adopted rack-and-pinion for the 911, but the steering box of the previous 356 communicated a similarly superb feel.

*Above: At the controls – a 2.4-litre 911E from the early 1970s. At first, some aspects of classic Porsche driving, like the unusual pedals, could seem strange but before long most owners preferred 911s to more conventional cars. To my mind, that instrument layout remains exceptionally good but some people did express minor complaints. Forget that, I say, and revel in the feel of a great car. (LAT)*

*Below: Engine bay of a 1972 2.4 911E. Testing this car in November 1971, Autocar commented on the staggering acceleration – 0–60mph in 6.4sec – and mentioned that the 911 was homologated as a four-seat saloon for competition. This prompted author/race driver Paul Frère to write a letter. It had been true until the end of 1969 but after that date 911s were categorised as Group 3 GT cars, 'which makes sense', said Frère. (Autocar/LAT)*

# Vic Elford on driving the early 911 in competition

While writing this book I asked Vic for an exclusive insight into how he won all those major rallies. In particular, how did he manage to be so bloody quick in a 911, downhill on ice and snow? It's best, I think, in his own words:

'People often ask me how come Porsche came after me to drive the 911. They didn't! On the contrary, I was largely responsible for Porsche getting into rallies. You may remember that 1966 was an awful season for me with Ford. On the

*The great Vic Elford about to plunge down from the mountains, defying ice and snow on that descent in the dark, to a dominant and famous victory in the 1968 Monte Carlo Rally. In these early 911s, Vic was supreme, especially in such difficult conditions – nobody else was close. (Motor/LAT)*

Monte, after the first mountain circuit there were only two cars in the hunt, Timo Makinen in a Mini and me in a Lotus Cortina. On the way up the Levens hill climb my fuel pump failed and that was that. As it happens, that was purely academic since all the Minis and Fords were disqualified because of the lighting nonsense, so that Citroën could win.

I won the Rallye des Fleurs (later to become the San Remo) then was disqualified because Ford had got the homologation papers wrong! In Greece I drove about three quarters of the rally with no clutch. I won but was disqualified for taking an unintentional short cut.

On the Coupe des Alpes I led all the way. Not only the Touring category but the GT category overall as well (ie Porsches, Ferraris, etc.). All the way, that is, until the very last, easy, up and over, special stage. It was so

inconsequential that the factory teams didn't even bother to have Service at the end – we were only an hour from the finish in Cannes. My distributor broke on the way up! (You might have noticed that both breakages occurred in parts labelled 'Lucas'.)

In Cannes, even though I knew him only very vaguely, I called Huschke von Hanstein and asked if I could see him. We had lunch beside the pool at the Hotel Martinez and I told him I had started to see 911s and was persuaded they were going to be good. Could I drive one?

'But my boy, we don't have a rally programme. We only give a little help to people like Gunther Klass.' (From then on, Huschke always called me 'My boy' or 'Vicki'.) I asked him to simply lend me a car for Corsica so I could prove to him how good I thought the car could be in my hands.

After a couple of weeks he called me

to say 'yes'. No recce car, no money, just basic service, which as it turned out was just two mechanics and a van with a jack and a few wheels and tyres in it. I did a great recce with David Stone – in a rental car at my expense – and decided the rally was going to be strictly about learning how to drive the car: the notorious rear engine, only 5.5in wheels, and it was *big* compared to the little R8 Gordinis and Alpines. We finished third and Huschke, and Stuttgart, were over the moon.

He offered me the Monte Carlo, but no contract – just one rally at a time. I accepted and we led Monte all the way till I got caught with the wrong tyres when it snowed as we went over the Turini for the last time. Again we finished third, but went on from there to three wins and the European Championship.

On the Monte the following year we were leading as we headed out onto the last mountain section, the 600km up in the Alpes Maritimes. On the first special stage I was really tense and nervous and my Porsche team-mate Pauli Toivonen beat me – which *never* happened. Over the Turini the first time saw no improvement. I just couldn't settle down and go fast. Then we had a long liaison section up to St Sauveur and the start of the Col de la Couillole. We had been out to see it the night before and my notes, which I really believe were the absolute best, gave me total confidence in the road conditions.

On the way to St Sauveur, David gave me a lecture. 'Remember you are the best in the mountains. Forget last year, forget this is the Monte. *Nobody* can beat you in the mountains!'

By the time we got to St Sauveur I felt relaxed and comfortable. Over a quick sandwich and coffee, we checked with Huschke and decided to go with racing tyres. David said, 'Don't worry, we were out last night and we know where all the ice and snow is. There might be less tonight, but there certainly isn't more.'

The Couillole is tight and twisty on the way up, very fast on the way down, where at times we were reaching speeds of 120mph, planing over the top of the occasional patch of ice and snow. On the 26km, 17-minute test, we took a minute off the next car, Gérard Larrousse in an Alpine.

At the end it took me about four goes to light a cigarette – and you know how dramatic that was for me. On the way back to the main road I asked David how many corners he thought I could have taken quicker. He said three. I thought it was two. How to go so fast downhill on ice and snow in a 911? The real secret of driving a 911 in its early days was *balance*.

In Corsica, and then on the first Monte, where we had a good long recce, I had plenty of time to learn. The first thing I learnt was that with all that weight at the rear (weight distribution in those days was about 40/60) the balance could be changed by the tiniest throttle or steering adjustment. The 911 already had a pretty fearsome reputation for spinning out. It was probably justified, because if the back started to get out of line most drivers would then simply lift off the throttle. The sudden lift would unload the rear wheels, load up the front ones, thus giving them more grip and a spin was inevitable.

With the 'rotation point' of a 911 being literally between the front wheels, by the time most drivers realise the rear end is sliding out, it's too late. And once it starts sliding, the slide *accelerates*. By then it's usually too late to catch it.

Once I understood the balance and dynamics of a 911 I found it to be the most manoeuvrable, predictable and *safe* car under extreme conditions.

Going downhill on ice and snow you have to realise that with only 5.5in wheels it's not going to stop very well in a straight line. So the best way to slow down is to put the car sideways, thus giving a footprint twice as big on the roadway. Approaching a downhill

left hairpin, you put the car sideways, but pointing to the *right*. With a little discreet caressing of the steering wheel, the throttle and the brake, you keep the car balanced until you get close to the corner. With the car sideways you already have the advantage of starting to slow down *much* later than if it were going straight. And believe it or not, you still have *total* control of the car for what is coming. On the final approach you *over-correct* on the steering, which has the effect of causing the car to start to spin. At the appropriate moment, before the car goes off the road backwards, you get back on the throttle *hard* (you *must* have a limited slip final drive) which keeps the car pushed back onto the road and keeps it in the corner where you can start accelerating as soon as you are pointing the right way, even though you are still in the corner.

All that comes from the basic 'Triangle of Forces', fully explained in my book *Porsche High-Performance Driving Handbook*.

If there is one single expression that counts, it's '*balance* and *extreme sensitivity*'.

On the Tulip rally we were number 1 and running first on the road. Coming out of a tunnel in the French Alps on the first night we hit sheet ice all over the road. We crashed into the rock face and pushed the front wing back onto the tyre. Using the towrope and a convenient telegraph pole, we managed to get it out enough to get to the next Control and Service. Somehow David managed to check in without anyone knowing we had lost three minutes. Which meant three minutes I needed to make up on the special stages. We did it by setting fastest time on every single stage, including breaking the outright hillclimb record up the Col de la Fauçille and even beating Timo on a *downhill* test on the Ballon d'Alsace.

Then there was the 2,341cc engine, producing 190bhp at 6,500rpm, which revved so willingly to the 7,300rpm limit and sounded so wonderful doing it. Although the original 2-litre had been slightly at a loss in hilly country, the extra torque of the 2.4 meant that high performance was available at all times. And it felt indestructible. That one-way maximum of a genuine 150mph was held for 4km in our test and the Porsche was totally unfussed, as always. It could run flat-out all day, to tell the truth.

Here was a car that had been thoroughly thought out and properly built to do the job. There was a very faint drizzle when we did our maximum speed run, for example, and I noticed that the wipers were calmly doing their job, without a trace of lift. The speedo needle gave an accurate reading at 150mph, too. Other cars, even expensive ones, just weren't like that. As I say, I didn't have stars in my eyes: I simply noted such things and loved the car all the more for them.

Admittedly, the fuel consumption was a rather heavy 13.3mpg, but that was not such an issue then, and it did run on two-star (91 octane) petrol. Porsche engineers, however, were well aware of an impending need for improved fuel economy and from then on, usually year by year, we saw marked improvements in mpg figures.

Early in 1972, therefore, the ranks of confirmed Porsche enthusiasts had gained a new recruit in me, and with good reason. I had driven the pick of new European cars that year, and I had driven them fast as part of my job. Working with the experienced team on that magazine had taught me much, and entirely thanks to my colleagues I did know what I was talking about – eventually! After driving the Porsche hard all day, you just switched off and it was ready to start again fresh the next day. Indeed, it was true: the Porsche 911 was the business.

Shortly after the road test appeared in print, in January 1972, I was taken aside for one of his quiet little chats by John Aldington, then the boss of Porsche Cars Great Britain Ltd. He berated me for stating that the 911 had its roots way back in the VW Beetle. It was true enough but he wasn't very pleased that I had said it.

Looking back at that road test today, I recall being distressed not by John Aldington's stern words so much as by the Art Editor's choice of a photograph of the car at speed on a wet MIRA test track: only one headlight was working. Having gone on about the car's unbelievable reliability, I still feel a bit silly about that. I know it didn't really matter: headlamp bulbs do fail from time to time, and it was far from unusual

in those days. So what? But I wasn't happy.

A dozen years later I ran a 2.2S as my everyday classic car. One winter's morning, high in the Swiss mountains, the temperature was minus 30C and the car had been outside all night. Taking care not to allow my hand to stick to the frozen handle, I unlocked the door. The engine started first time. Out of mechanical sympathy I gave it a few minutes to warm up and get the oil moving properly, then off we went on the snow-covered roads. No problem. What a great car.

The 2.4-litre 911E was in the same league as a driving experience, but less powerful at 165bhp. On the road it felt more relaxed, more torquey and it still had a respectable top speed of 137mph. The nose spoiler of the 'S' was an option that well-informed 911E customers chose.

Before leaving the 2.4-litre 911s, we should take a passing glance at the other end of the range, the more modest 911T. While the 'S' version seemed almost incomparable at the time, by 1973 the 911T was beginning to look a bit sad as well as being rather overpriced, in the UK market at least.

It had many of the great features of the S such as the roadholding and handling, excellent brakes and outstanding build quality but its performance, from a modest 130bhp,

was similar to that of some stylish and exciting machinery that was half its price, such as the Datsun 240Z, the Lotus Elan Sprint, the Lotus Europa and the Lotus +2S 130.

That nose spoiler was also optional on the 'T' for a time, though it did eventually become a standard fitting across the 911 range. Without it, the 911T lacked the superb high-speed steering stability of the 'S', and without the breathtaking performance of its faster brother, other things began to be noticed. The long clutch pedal travel with its over-centre feel and the dated heating controls and relatively poor ventilation come to mind, while compared to rivals the fuel consumption of less than 16mpg was a further demerit. In short, for that money the 911T wasn't good enough. At this relatively modest end of the Porsche product range, a bit of fresh thinking was already overdue.

But whatever engine you chose, every Porsche salesman in Britain, back in the early 1970s, came to know that a majority of first-time 911 buyers in Britain ordered a Targa, but an equally large proportion of people buying their second new 911 would insist on a Coupé. Statistics also showed that anyone who had bought one new 911 was extremely likely to replace it with another.

The deeper qualities of Porsche's unique 911 fostered that kind of customer loyalty. Once you had used one on a daily basis, it was hard to accept anything else and somehow one came to understand that the coupé style of body was at the heart of what Porsche motoring was all about. Even back in the 356 days, when fairly large numbers of open cars were made, the coupé brigade regarded themselves as slightly superior, the true connoisseurs, the élite of real Porsche drivers. It's an opinion with which I soon agreed one hundred per cent and I have not changed my mind. Years later, when we started seeing four-wheel-drive cabriolets in the showrooms, the very idea of such a combination seemed mildly bizarre.

In 1973, the original Porsche coupé concept was brought to its ultimate expression in the 2.7-litre Carrera RS. Here the mix of suspension development, low weight and engine enlargement produced an all-time classic, a sublime machine to drive. Porsche called it the Carrera RS 2.7, and advertised it in the M471 Sport and M472 Touring versions, both of which were derived from the base 'RSH' homologation version. The term 'Lightweight' was always colloquial, not official – though for decades we have all known exactly what 'RSL' means.

After that peak of achievement for Porsche, engineers throughout the motor industry were faced with a mounting number of other problems involving impact bumpers and every aspect of passenger protection in accidents, not to mention emissions reductions and a host of other stuff. As a result, all cars became vastly more complicated, and heavier. Over the decades since then, the brains at Porsche have fought this battle with extraordinary skill and, often, they have achieved truly great success: if I could afford it, I'd grab my cheque book right now and rush off to order a brand new 911GT 3. So don't accuse me of being a nostalgic old fool who thinks that a 1973 2.7 RSL is a better car than the latest model. It isn't, but it has always been something very special indeed to drive, a perfect expression of the art of automobile engineering before the world got complicated. Nobody is allowed to build cars that way any more.

The classic RS was, of course, built primarily as a good old homologation special. Back in 1967, as mentioned already, a similar project had been killed off at birth when the company's sales and marketing people had said that they could not possibly sell enough of the special 911R model to ordinary road users.

In 1972, the sales experts put forward exactly the same argument against the 2.7 RS. But a great engineer, Dr

*Opposite: The Carrera RS 2.7 of the 1973 model year was the ultimate expression of the 911 road car before things like impact-bumper legislation changed our world. Intended as an homologation special, twice the 500 required were instantly sold. That odd-looking spoiler reduced lift at maximum speed from 320lb to 93lb. The prominent 'Carrera' side stripes seen in this* Autocar *picture were a delete option.* (Autocar/LAT)

*Right: The superb balance of the Carrera RS 2.7 is demonstrated by owner and former* Motor *road tester Gordon Bruce. His car was made in late 1972 and first registered in February 1973.* (Gordon Bruce)

The author racing Chester Wedgewood's 1973 Carrera RS 2.7 to a win at Thruxton in the mid-1980s. The car's excellent handling is obvious here, as is the high level of grip from the BFGoodrich tyres on a greasy surface. Sponsored by Giroflex, the car was prepared by Neil Bainbridge Racing and won the top class in the British championship in both years contested. (Chris Harvey)

Fuhrmann, was at the head of the company by then and he insisted that they would jolly well have to sell them, all 500 of them in this case, whether they liked it or not. The company should be racing identifiable products, he felt, not just exotic machinery such as the incredibly expensive 917. The 911 had to be raced properly and the 2.7 RS was the way forward.

A desperate secret sales campaign went ahead behind closed doors, persuading every known close friend to place an order for a 2.7 RS. The company went into the Paris salon in autumn 1972 with an RS on the stand and 51 orders already taken but a week after the show the allocated 500 were all spoken for and suddenly all those close friends were being told that it might not be so easy, after all, to find them a car. Orders poured in at an astonishing rate, the production run was doubled and Porsche delivered the thousandth 2.7 RS in April 1973, more than satisfying the requirements of the relevant motor-sport authorities. It does make you wonder whether the

911R might not have sold equally well back in 1967.

That number, of over a thousand made, qualified the 911RS for production car competition, as well as the more obscure and rarified categories of motor sport that the company had in mind originally. In fact, so many were appearing on the road in Germany that Porsche was suddenly faced with an homologation problem in reverse: to satisfy an obscure domestic law, dealers had to fit many of the special rear spoilers after the cars had been registered, making them officially after-market extras.

So, what exactly was this remarkably desirable 911? The engine, producing 210bhp at 6,300rpm, had been enlarged to 2,687cc by means of innovative Nikasil-coated cylinder-lining that permitted a larger bore than had previously been considered possible with those blocks; additionally the engine was built from the lightest materials available. Even more impressive was the increase in torque, up from the 159lb ft of the 2.4S to a mighty 188lb ft at 5,100rpm, and it was a good, flattish curve that meant there was plenty of urge from quite low revs. The engine revved to 7,300rpm, still ran on two-star fuel and was no trouble in heavy traffic.

Stiffer suspension, with 911S-type anti-roll bars and Bilstein dampers, was complemented by 7in wheels at the rear and 6in rims at the front. Many of the body panels on the first 500 cars

were made from thinner steel than that used in normal 911s but the lower sections were still galvanised, a process that Porsche had adopted during 1970. Some of the RS production cars, called Touring models, retained certain de luxe items of trim and were about eight per cent more expensive to buy. For the ultimate performer, the so-called RSL ('L' standing for lightweight), everything was done to keep the weight down. There were no back seats, there was minimal soundproofing and underseal, a thin paint covering, rubber mats instead of carpets, racing seats, lightweight glass, door pull-straps instead of handles, a combined engine cover and rear spoiler in glassfibre on a metal frame – and certainly no electric windows and no passenger's sunvisor. Even the little coathooks were deleted. The prominent 'Carrera' wording along the lower sides of the bodies was a 'delete option' for owners who did not wish to attract too much attention.

That odd-looking rear spoiler was noticeable, however, but it made a huge difference, reducing quite substantial high-speed lift at the rear to a negligible level. At 152mph, lift fell from 320lb to 93lb. The benefit was very obvious as soon as the car was put through a fast corner at speed, for the Carrera RS with that spoiler was a beautifully balanced machine even when cornering hard at well over 100mph. Yet, when it came to top speed (152mph), far from holding it back that strange little upturned lip on the tail actually reduced drag very slightly.

But, more than 30 years ago, it has to be said that it did look somewhat bizarre, that funny bit tacked onto the engine lid. Later on in this book, I'm afraid I shall insult all those idiots who regard spoilers as mere styling – that has never been the case with Porsche, for whom such items are included in order to do a job – but for now it's enough to say that this machine could be driven to the limit on a circuit with supreme confidence. Putting the tail out and applying the power did not involve the slightest worry that the car might spin. It was simply a delight to wring every last fraction of a second out of its high potential.

All that effort to reduce weight did the trick in no uncertain terms: the homologated weight came out at 920kg, or 18.1cwt, a very handy figure for racing purposes. Even so, it was amazing when an American team won the 1973 Daytona 24-hours race in a 2.8 911RSR. I'm pretty sure, however, that the RSL I used to race weighed about 980kg. Top British Porsche expert Josh Sadler agrees: 'I'm sure you're right. The 920kg Homologation 'RSH' version was seriously and impractically minimal, with skinny wheels and tyres. That was the specification in which the cars were weighed for homologation purposes. They were then built up to their sales specification and an odd process that must have been. If you take the original carpet out of an early RS Touring, there'll be traces of the very dark blue lightweight carpet fibres still in the glue on the bodyshell! I just can't believe, however, that they did that with all of the first thousand.'

*Although this book is really about Porsche road cars, occasional reference to the racing is essential. In this Geoff Goddard photograph, we see the works 904 GTS of Herbert Linge and Gianni Balzarini on its way to second overall in the 1964 Targa Florio, which was won by the similar car of Colin Davis and Comte Antonio Pucci. Taking the fastest lap in the race, Davis emphasised Porsche's growing strength in top-level international racing. (Geoff Goddard collection)*

# Buying hints

**1.** Are you in that élite band of connoisseur collectors? If you want an everyday 911, which you can treat as a used car rather than a treasured museum piece which might do 13mpg, get a later model and forget these early cars.

**2.** Any serious buyer of a chrome-bumper 911 is probably already an expert who needs no tips from me. If you're not in that group but are still determined to get a 911 that's around 40 years old, these comments might be useful.

**3.** Recorded mileage is now completely irrelevant. Having chosen the model you want, bearing in mind that some of them were not only very thirsty but also not that fast by today's standards, it's the history and condition of the car that matter.

**4.** The golden rule before buying any car of this age is to do your homework first. It's always a good idea to join the appropriate club but it's essential in the case of a Porsche. The Porsche Club Great Britain is an excellent outfit, ready with helpful information. Through such contacts, you can form a close link with one of several first-class specialists in early

911s. Your relationship with that company will not be like dealing with a normal service garage. It's a much more personal thing. Some of these people have been mentioned elsewhere in the book, as you must have noticed, but you will find the right one for you by word of mouth after getting to know other members of the club.

**5.** So far you haven't even started to look for a car. That's the right way to do it but let's suppose that by pure chance you have just come across a car for sale and you're consumed by a passion to buy it. Well, don't, not unless you're sure you know what you're doing. Instead, work fast, find that genuine specialist and get his advice. Don't rely on an old mate who says he knows about classic cars. Get the right people behind you to avoid buying something that will cost you thousands more than it's worth to restore.

**6.** Know what you're getting into. Beyond normal servicing, you will need occasional engine rebuilds, gearbox rebuilds, suspension work, major repairs to brakes – and you will have to keep on top in the war against rust.

# The VW-Porsche 914 and 914/6

*Launched in late 1969 and built in collaboration with VW, the mid-engined 914 was a clever design but its inadequate performance, controversial looks and very high price always held back sales. In the UK, too, it didn't help that it was left-hand drive but there was a very good Crayford conversion to right-hand drive available at a hefty £600. (LAT)*

Was it going backwards or forwards? Those indicators/sidelights beside the pop-up headlights looked just like the back of a car. Despite being the product of a partnership between old friends, Volkswagen and Porsche, there was some vexed anxiety about the looks of the mid-engined, affordable sports car they intended to produce. The VW board didn't want it to look like a Beetle and the people at Porsche were equally anxious that it should not resemble a 911.

For that reason, it seems, the styling was put out to Gugelot Design GmbH in Neu-Ulm, not far from Stuttgart. The result was indeed original, cleanly bold and innovative but it was also undeniably a bit odd, the 914, even back in 1969, and that's probably one reason why it was less successful than it might have been. With its clean look resembling a 1970s toaster, vacuum cleaner or electric shaver, the 914's styling appeared to have been conceived by talented exponents of trendy industrial design, which is exactly

*Above left: Inside, the original 914 looked as a Porsche should. Note the nearly flat floor and the dashboard: it was all the proper stuff – pity about the price. (LAT)*

*Above: This 914 was featured in* Classic & Sports Car *in November 1990. Access to the mid-positioned engine was awkward in some ways, but mechanics could get at the vital bits and it did allow generous luggage accommodation front and rear. (Classic & Sports Car/LAT)*

the case, as it happened: Gugelot was famous in Germany for precisely that. But was this look right for a car?

There were other problems. The fact that there was rather too much wind noise inside probably didn't lose many sales. Far more important, the association with VW undoubtedly discouraged some snooty types from taking to it, despite Porsche's historic and very respectable link with the Wolfsburg marque.

Then there was the price, which was the most serious snag of the lot. The 914 was extremely expensive for its performance, which came from a modified VW 411 flat-four, and for its perceived position in the market. In Britain, indeed, the 914 was well over twice the price of the popular MGB, although in Germany, in fairness, the Porsche was slightly less expensive than the 'B'.

To raise the 914's profile, a 914/6 version was also presented from the start in 1969, using the six-cylinder 1,991cc engine from the old 911T. In that form, giving 110bhp, it was a quicker car but it was without any doubt far too costly for what it was and the model was dropped after a couple of years, leaving the four-cylinder version to soldier on until 1976.

Despite being considerably slower than an MGB in acceleration and only marginally better on top speed, the original 1,679cc 914 sold reasonably well in the US – without any VW badging, which must have helped at first. Notwithstanding the addition of a

1,971cc model later on, which gave a very welcome improvement to performance, the entire 914 project faded away in 1975/76.

For all that, which does sound rather like a disaster story, the 914 deserves a closer look. It was a very decent attempt at a theme to which Porsche would return with consummate success many years later – a mid-engined sports car that was cheaper than the classic rear-engined 911. But the Boxster of the 1990s, a 'pure' Porsche at a relatively attractive price, was unimaginable in 1969 when the 914 appeared.

The mid-engined layout adopted for the 914 was already almost universal in modern race cars by those days but it was a rare and exciting novelty in a road car. This added some considerable fascination, at a time when the motoring world was beginning to discover the superb ride quality and superior roadholding that this layout could offer. That said, the ride of the 914 was never quite as good as expected. In compensation, Porsche as usual did better than most in overcoming the inherent handling snags of mid-engined road cars, then seen as quite an intellectual puzzle. The theory was great, most of us agreed, but the widely-held fear was that mid-engined cars tended to let go with no warning and spin very quickly.

In designing the 914's suspension, Porsche took a sensible approach by choosing MacPherson struts, lower wishbones and torsion bars at the front, derived from the 911, with semi-

trailing arms and coil springs at the rear. The new rear suspension allowed for the installation of the four-cylinder and six-cylinder engines mounted ahead of the rear axle line but, despite being a novel layout for a road car, it was based on race-proven geometry. Anti-roll bars were not fitted to the original 914. This entire package was a very respectable arrangement at the time and, while not especially adventurous in its detail, it seemed a century ahead of many rivals, including the veteran MGB which, hard as it is to believe now, still had leaf springs and a live axle at the back.

The 914's chassis specification was undoubtedly an advantage for the German car but any such plus-point was wiped out in the UK because all 914s left the factory with left-hand drive. Crayford Engineering, a small but well-respected company just south of London, offered a good right-hand-drive changeover but that added a further 25 per cent to the price of an

*Above: Testers Roger Bell and Tony Curtis of Motor magazine play for the camera at Snetterton during their test of the 914/6 in company with a contemporary 911. This road test appeared in August 1970, and the basic message was that six cylinders delivered the required performance to the desirable 914 but the very high price was a big problem. (Motor/LAT)*

*Below: In the paddock at Snetterton circuit in 1970, Tony Curtis of Motor demonstrates how to stow the Targa top of the new 914/6. Unlike many mid-engined cars, even today, 914s offered good luggage accommodation – and at both ends of the car. (Motor/LAT)*

already incredibly expensive car. Driving one of those converted cars for a *Motor* road test back in 1971, I remember all of us being suitably impressed by its strong points. The conversion was well done even though Crayford could not overcome one oddity: the driver had what was obviously a passenger's door, complete with grab handle.

If that was of little account, the uncomfortable truth had to be told: 'The performance of the 914S is not the most nerve-racking treat that life holds in store but it's certainly adequate,' I wrote in that magazine, 37 years ago.

The 914 did have a fabulous feel to its rack-and-pinion steering, a feel that any Porsche enthusiast could recognise straight away, but there were serious faults elsewhere that had to be admitted. It had good pedals but an uncomfortably long clutch travel, brakes that were sharp at first but tended to fade with hard use, unsporting gear ratios – with that big gap between second and third – and a gearchange that was unacceptably vague even when brand-new. It was horribly easy to get second instead of fourth when changing up from third, for example. 'Most people could probably come to accept the gearchange but nobody is likely to

enthuse about it,' I commented. These days, I suggest, only skilled classic car enthusiasts could come to accept it. I think it's fair to say that your average Boxster driver would be struck dumb by the weird and wobbly feel of the 914's gearlever.

Devoted fans still rave about the handling of the 914 and that Crayford car was indeed delightful to drive in some respects, despite all the faults. A relaxed cruiser at speed, it also offered cornering forces that were in a new league for the average sports car enthusiast at the time; plus, the grip was astonishingly good in the wet.

That's fine, but I have to say that driving it absolutely on the limit was not such a laugh. Far from it. When the tail did come out, it happened very rapidly: it can't have been that bad because I did always catch it, but I never found it quite as reassuring a car to drive all-out as I felt it should have been. The Lotus Europa, a rare mid-engined rival of those days, felt much more comfortable at speed to me. It's a personal thing perhaps, but a 911, being far less nervous and unpredictable, felt miles better near and at the limit than either of them as far as I was concerned. The 914 might have had more grip but the 911 remained more confidence-inspiring, whatever the critics of rear-engined cars might say.

Even if you could feel sure of retaining control of a 914, the fact that you could not always tell whether it would understeer or oversteer at speed on real roads, as opposed to the clinical environment of a test track, made it a less than satisfying driving experience for some people, myself included, though I must admit that not everybody agreed with this analysis. I did wonder how hard those enthusiastic writers were really pushing them, I must say.

What the 914 did have that was distinctly lacking in the Lotus Europa was some luggage space. What's more, you could lift the Targa top off the VW-Porsche and stow it in the rear luggage compartment without losing much of the space there. That was pretty neat; and the 914 had a decent front 'boot' too.

# Porsche 914/6
## 1969–72

**ENGINE:**
Six-cylinder horizontally opposed, air-cooled; magnesium-alloy crankcase with cast-iron cylinders, alloy jackets and alloy heads; mid-mounted

| | |
|---|---|
| Bore x stroke | 80.0mm x 66mm |
| Capacity | 1,991cc |
| Valve actuation | sohc per bank |
| Compression ratio | 8.6:1 |
| Induction | Twin Weber 40 IDTPI carburettors |
| Power | 110bhp at 5,800rpm |
| Maximum torque | 115.5lb ft at 4,200rpm |

**TRANSMISSION:**
Rear-wheel drive; five-speed manual gearbox (four-speed Sport-o-matic optional in some markets)

**SUSPENSION:**
*Front:* Independent by MacPherson struts, lower wishbones and longitudinal torsion bars; double-acting telescopic dampers; anti-roll bar on later models
*Rear:* Independent by semi-trailing arms and coil springs, with supplementary hollow rubber springs; telescopic dampers

**STEERING:**
Rack-and-pinion

**BRAKES:**
*Front:* Disc, ventilated (11.12in)
*Rear:* Disc, solid (11.26in )

**WHEELS/TYRES:**
Alloy wheels, 5.5J x 15in
Tyres 165 HR 15

**BODYWORK:**
Steel monocoque
Coupé two-seater with detachable Targa top

**DIMENSIONS:**
| | |
|---|---|
| Length | 13ft 1in |
| Wheelbase | 8ft 0.5in |
| Track, front | 4ft 4.25in |
| Track, rear | 4ft 6.75in |
| Width | 5ft 5.5in (excluding mirrors) |
| Height | 4ft 0.25in |

**WEIGHT:**
18.9cwt (960kg)

**PERFORMANCE:**
(Source: *Motor*)
| | |
|---|---|
| Max speed | 120mph* |
| 0–60mph | 8.8sec |
| Standing quarter-mile | 16.1sec |

*Banked track: Porsche's claimed 125mph is realistic

**PRICE IN UK INCLUDING TAX WHEN NEW:**
£3,475 (August 1970)

**NUMBER BUILT:**
3,338

# Porsche 914/S
## 1969–73

(This was the UK name for the original 914)

As 914/6 except:

**ENGINE:**
Four-cylinder horizontally opposed, air-cooled; cast-iron cylinders, alloy heads

| | |
|---|---|
| Bore x stroke | 90.0mm x 66.0mm |
| Capacity | 1,679cc |
| Compression ratio | 8.2:1 |
| Induction | Fuel injection |
| Power | 80bhp at 4,900rpm* |
| Maximum torque | 98.3lb ft at 2,700rpm |

*By 1973, Californian version was down to 69bhp

**BRAKES:**
*Front:* Disc (11.0in)
*Rear:* Disc (11.1in)

**WHEELS/TYRES:**
Steel wheels 4.5J x 15in
Tyres Pirelli Cinturato 155 SR x 15in

**WEIGHT:**
18.5cwt (942kg)

**PERFORMANCE:**
(Source: *Motor*)
Car tested: Crayford rhd conversion
| | |
|---|---|
| Max speed | 106.5mph |
| 0–60mph | 12.3sec |
| Standing quarter-mile | 18.7sec |

**PRICE IN UK INCLUDING TAX WHEN NEW:**
£2,261 (July 1971) plus £630 for rhd. Total £2,891

**NUMBER BUILT:**
65,351

# Porsche 914/4
## 1973–75

As 914/S except:

**ENGINE:**
| | |
|---|---|
| Bore x stroke | 93.0mm x 66.0mm |
| Capacity | 1,795cc |
| Compression ratio | 7.3:1 |
| Induction | Fuel injection |
| Power | 73bhp (SAE) at 4,800rpm* |
| Maximum torque | 89lb ft (SAE) at 4,000rpm* |

*US specification (85bhp/102lb ft in German market)

**WHEELS/TYRES:**
Tyres 165 SR x 15

**DIMENSIONS:**
| | |
|---|---|
| Length | 13ft 5.2in |

**WEIGHT:**
19.3cwt (980kg)

**PERFORMANCE:**
(Source: Porsche)
| | |
|---|---|
| Top speed | 110mph |
| 0–62mph | 12.0sec |

(German-market model)

**PRICE IN UK INCLUDING TAX WHEN NEW:**
Not sold in UK

**NUMBER BUILT:**
17,773

# Porsche 914 2.0-litre (inc SC)
## 1973–76

As 914/S except:

**ENGINE:**
| | |
|---|---|
| Bore x stroke | 94.0mm x 71.0mm |
| Capacity | 1,971cc |
| Compression ratio | 7.6:1 |
| Induction | Fuel injection |
| Power | 100bhp (DIN) at 5,000rpm/91bhp (SAE) at 4,900rpm*/84bhp (SAE) at 4,900rpm** |
| Maximum torque | 116lb ft (SAE) at 3,500rpm/109lb ft (SAE) at 3,000rpm*/108lb ft(SAE) at 3,500rpm** |

*US specification
**US specification from 1974

**SUSPENSION:**
Anti-roll bars front and rear

**WHEELS/TYRES:**
Alloy wheels, 5.5J x 15in
Tyres 165 HR x 15in

**DIMENSIONS:**
| | |
|---|---|
| Length | 13ft 3.4in |

**WEIGHT:**
19.2cwt (975kg)

**PERFORMANCE:**
(Source: *Motor*)
| | |
|---|---|
| Max speed | 115.5mph |
| 0–60mph | 9.1sec |
| Standing quarter-mile | 17.1sec |

**PRICE IN UK INCLUDING TAX WHEN NEW:**
914 2-litre: £2,527 (November 1972)
914SC 2-litre: £2,799 (idem)
By October 1973 only SC available in UK, price £3,689

**NUMBER BUILT:**
32,522

Total all 914 four-cylinder models: 115,646

We got a mean 106.5mph top speed round the banked track at MIRA with that Crayford car, 0–60mph in 12.3 seconds with a fifth wheel, and overall fuel consumption of 22.8mpg. Just for the record, because it still seems relevant, our figures for the MGB at that time were 105.0mph, 11.0 seconds and 23.7mpg. If you're a 914 fan, well, I'm sorry but you can't ignore such facts.

In the North American market the 914 was seen as a direct competitor to the Triumph TR6, the Olde English TR being a rather faster car at about the same price. The 914 was also up against the surprisingly nice Fiat 124 Spider and, rather ominously, the Japanese came up with the very impressive Datsun 240Z that entered the market at well under the 914's list price and gave sports car fans a serious jolt worldwide.

American customers were left a bit confused about what exactly Porsche was offering with this model. What exactly was the advantage to be had by opting for the Porsche 914? It was a

*In its final form for 1972, the 916 looked the part with its extended arches. Only 11 prototypes got built, in varying 2.4-litre specifications, but top speed always approached 150mph. Prohibitively expensive, it did not enter production. (LAT)*

good question. Despite the fact that Porsche and VW had created a modern design with plenty to offer the driving enthusiast, there were all those rivals, in other manufacturers' showrooms, that could beat the 914 in several key areas of deep concern to marketing people and potential buyers alike – the especially controversial subjects being performance, looks and price.

The 914/6, of course, was considerably quicker than the four-cylinder base model: my colleagues at *Motor* had tested one in August 1970, shortly before I joined them and they rated it well except for one major drawback: yes, yet again it was the horrendous price. The brutal fact was that, at £3,475 in the UK, most people looking for a sports car would have found it hard to resist saving £1,114 and going for the much faster 4.2-litre Jaguar E-type instead.

Nevertheless, the 914/6 was one of a very small number of cars in those days that could easily exceed 120mph and the *Motor* testers had achieved 8.8 seconds as a 0–60mph time. One more important advantage was that the thoroughbred six-cylinder engine made it sound like a Porsche should sound.

Although the four-cylinder VW engine given to the 914 was one of Wolfsburg's best, it was always uninspiring in a Porsche. No-one could say that about the 'six', which also

came with ventilated discs, wider wheels and other superior components to help turn the whole package into a car that could be seen as 'a proper Porsche'. It was only its very high price that bumped the 914/6 clean out of the picture. The rising value of the German deutschmark at that very time didn't help this already expensive car in export markets one little bit either.

Part of Porsche's problem was the small print of the agreement with VW. Different accounting methods between the manufacturing giant and the smaller specialist company meant that the bodies coming to Porsche to be finished as 914/6s were unusually expensive and in 1972, with fewer than 3,500 made, the six-cylinder model was dropped. Porsche did experiment with some ultra-quick prototypes before the 914/6 line came to an end, a couple having a race-based eight-cylinder engine and reputedly handling well, but it was quite obvious that such extremely expensive variations would never be viable in the market.

Meanwhile, the four-cylinder 914 plugged on and, thanks to detailed improvements – which included a new gearbox and far better gearchange – plus the option of a 2-litre engine, it was a great improvement over the earlier cars. Appreciated by customers, sales rose, notably in the States. Though still a Volkswagen engine, the 914's 2-litre power unit was at that stage exclusive to Porsche and it produced a reasonably respectable 100bhp in European form. In mildly detuned specification it was able to meet emissions requirements throughout the US and still produce 95bhp. In contrast the 1.7-litre, which was still available, was down to a miserable 69bhp in the Californian market, where the rules were the most strict. The relatively lively 2-litre had thus arrived just in time to save the day – especially in North America, where nearly two thirds of all 914s were sold.

In Britain the 914 was simply out of its depth. 'There's so much going against the VW-Porsche that it's almost impossible to resist the temptation to leap to its defence,' we wrote when we

got to test a 2-litre 914SC at *Motor* early in 1973. It still wasn't fast enough for the money, the lift-off oversteer was excessive, the heating was erratic and it still didn't look any less odd to our eyes. Also, it was still only available from the factory with left-hand drive, despite the substantial price-tag. We were all agreed that it was the same old story: the 1973 UK-market VW-Porsche 914SC was interesting, to be sure, but somewhat flawed and massively overpriced.

Differences in accounting procedures between Porsche and VW had cropped up again. In those days, Porsche spread the cost of right-hand drive conversions across all markets but by 1973 VW was in charge of 914 pricing and the policy there was to make each market pay for its own special alterations. It simply wasn't worthwhile for VW to convert a few cars for UK buyers. UK customers could still get that excellent Crayford conversion if they felt like spending over £600.

For the US market the 1.7-litre engine was enlarged for 1974 to 1,795cc, producing 76bhp while still meeting the stringent Californian regulations. Sales were healthier than expected in the States but by then Porsche and VW had been collaborating on another and very different project that would appear later in the 1970s, the front-engined 924; eventually, in 1976, the 914 was discontinued.

I accept that I have said a lot of negative things about the 914. It did have its flaws but by the end it was a pretty respectable machine. There's a lot more going for it now. As classic cars today they can provide interesting Porsche motoring at a very attractive price. They have not held their value as well as a certain rival; incredibly enough the tables have been turned so much that, in the UK at least, a good 914 today is worth rather less than a contemporary MGB in similar condition. That does seems astonishing. While a good 914/6 will fetch considerably more, the difference is far from what it was when these cars were new.

These days the best 914s are likely to be found in California. Europeans who bring such cars back across the Atlantic to a less kindly climate should, I suggest, pay particular attention to guarding against rust. It's alarming how quickly deterioration can set in once a car is transferred from the US West Coast back to Europe. Thirty years ago and more, protection against corrosion, even at Porsche, was far from the fine art it has become today.

Some people have seen the 914 adventure as one of Porsche's few mistakes. But in fact it sold pretty well – close to 120,000 cars of all derivatives in six years – and thus probably served the company well enough from a financial point of view.

Inspired by experience gained in sports car racing, notably with the ground-breaking 904 of 1964, Porsche had tried to exploit the known advantages of a mid-mounted engine in a road car. Naturally enough there was a desire to capitalise upon the company's new-found expertise, and thus get a return on that heavy investment in racing.

Seen that way, the partnership with mighty VW over the 914 had been logical enough in principle but it fell down to some extent in the detail, especially manufacturing cost and showroom pricing. It was an experiment that nearly came off but when 914 production came to a natural end, Porsche was already deeply committed to the new front-engined cars, the 924 and 928. So there was no reason to create a 914 replacement at that time. That 924/928 phase came and went and only then, much later on, did Porsche revert to the mid-engined road-car theme: unlike the 914, which met with that mixed reaction in the 1970s, the modern Boxster hit precisely the right note, brilliantly, in the mid-1990s and Porsche has never looked back.

# Buying hints

**1.** Join the Porsche Club Great Britain (PCGB). These people will rapidly become your best friends. Contact the PCGB's 914 register secretary and you'll discover that there are very few cars in existence in the UK, and they're owned by a tiny band of very keen people who all know each other and support each other. If you do find a car, and you buy it, they'll be delighted to welcome you into their clan.

**2.** Existing owners will probably tell you, in considerable detail, exactly why you should not have bought your chosen car, so the message, as ever with cars of this age, is to get to know these people before you even look at a car. They will know the best independent specialist to go for if you have a gearbox problem, need an engine rebuild or if the body requires fixing in any way. These experts, dotted around the country, are sometimes one-man bands.

**3.** If you're really determined to get a 914 or one of its derivatives, the best way might be to buy from the USA. That's where most of them went and the PCGB will know the latest state of the market. Although all the 914-type Porsches imported into the UK were left-hand drive, some of the US models were rather different in engine specification from the UK cars. Be aware of that and look out for any unwanted later modifications.

**4.** I have never seen a 914 with air conditioning but some US cars were so equipped from new. The installation was done by the dealers and it involved, I am told, considerable cutting about of the bodyshell, which you might not like.

**5.** Obviously, every now and then, one of those keen PCGB members sells a car. He'll want a good home for it. Join the club. That's the message.

# The 'big-bumper' 911

*Nowhere near losing it! The traditional 911SC, seen here on test with Autocar in about 1979, could be pressed to extremes with absolute confidence, on a test track at least. The driver is admittedly racing ace John Miles, but he's relaxed at the wheel and in full control. The trace of steam from the inside left rear wheel shows he has his foot down hard on a damp track, too. John did mention to me recently that lifting off in such conditions would have been more tricky. (Autocar/LAT)*

Going back 30 years, to when the 1974 911 model range got into production, I have to admit that this was when I entered a spell of life away from regular contact with Porsche. I had left journalism to resume full-time racing, paid and under contract to British Leyland via Broadspeed.

Nevertheless, I noted what was going on at Porsche. My impression was that,

while the fabulous 2.7 engine was still going strong, things had been rationalised. The Carrera RS, that incredibly successful homologation special of 1973, was slightly softened for mainstream production and the RS name was dropped except for a small number of race-based exceptions.

For 1974, the top of the range 2.7 911 road car was therefore called the Carrera, pure and simple. It retained a

210bhp version of the engine, however, giving a top speed of 150mph. The duck-tail rear spoiler became optional on these Carreras, except in the UK where it was standard. That funny-looking spoiler was effective but short-lived. At the end of 1974 it would be replaced by the less bizarre-looking whale-tail type that gave even better aerodynamic performance.

The more modest 'T' and 'E' versions were dropped in 1974, too, and all new 911s then showed signs of the changing times with the introduction of impact-absorbing bumpers. Much bigger than earlier 911 bumpers, they didn't appeal at first to 911 fans but, with some regret, we all accepted that there was no way out of that one. The challenge of the new US legislation had to be faced. Built-in headrests also appeared in 911s at that time, for the same reason, but they were not so controversial. We were beginning to sense that the grand old 911 was in a battle against time, which it must lose sooner rather than later. Some top people at Porsche clearly shared those

gloomy thoughts, but how wrong we all were.

Although the 911S name continued, I personally found its use a bit confusing as this particular 'S' had the 2.7 engine in considerably detuned form. At 175bhp it was well down on the 190bhp of the old 2.4 but maximum torque was up a bit, thanks to the increased engine size, and it occurred at 4,000rpm instead of the 5,200rpm of the old 2.4S. Overall, therefore, the performance of the 2.7S was very similar to that of the 2.4S but the big difference was in the fuel consumption. The old model would do little more than 13mpg in hard use but the 1974 2.7S was likely to better 20mpg when driven the same way. It really was an astonishing improvement.

Back in 1974, the 911 range also included a more modest, basic 911 2.7, giving 150bhp and a top speed of about 130mph, and the Targa body became available for all three main road-going models at this time, too.

At that time, what was actually going on dawned on me rather slowly. Fuel

*In 1974 Autocar discovered that the 142mph 911S 2.7 produced a spectacular improvement in fuel economy, thanks to its larger engine. The testers here are Michael Scarlett and Andrew Shanks. (Autocar/LAT)*

consumption was becoming an increasingly important issue and, looking back, Porsche was giving that aspect of the car's performance the urgent consideration it deserved. More than ever, for several years from then on, it became a regular thing for the Porsche range to get a little faster each year while also achieving very significant improvements in mpg.

For 1976, the 2.7-litre base-model 911 continued but the new 200bhp Carrera 3 was announced, having a 3-litre engine based on the die-cast alloy blocks of the Turbo. With electronic fuel injection and that increased capacity, the 145mph Carrera 3 was more flexible than the old mechanically-injected model. Less extreme than the 2.7RS, it was very nearly as quick and customers soon

# Porsche 911/911N/911S
## 1973–75/ 1975–77/1973–77

*(These were British names for selected models on sale in these periods)*

**ENGINE:**
Six-cylinder horizontally opposed, air-cooled; light alloy crankcase and cylinder heads with cast-iron cylinder liners; rear-mounted

| | |
|---|---|
| Bore x stroke | 90.0 x 70.4mm |
| Capacity | 2,687cc |
| Valve actuation | sohc per bank |
| Compression ratio | 8.0:1/8.5:1/8.5:1 |
| Induction | Bosch K-Jetronic fuel injection |
| Power | 150bhp at 5,700rpm |
| | 165bhp at 5,800rpm |
| | 175bhp at 5,800rpm |
| Maximum torque | 174lb ft at 3,800rpm |
| | 195lb ft at 4,000rpm |
| | 174lb ft at 4,000rpm |

**TRANSMISSION:**
Rear-wheel drive; five-speed manual gearbox

**SUSPENSION:**
*Front:* Independent by MacPherson struts, lower wishbones and longitudinal torsion bars; anti-roll bar
*Rear:* Independent by semi-trailing arms and transverse torsion bars; telescopic dampers

**STEERING:**
Rack-and-pinion

**BRAKES:**
*Front:* Disc, ventilated (11.1in)
*Rear:* Disc, ventilated (11.4in)

**WHEELS/TYRES:**
Alloy wheels, 6J x 15
Tyres Dunlop SP Sport Super 185/70 VR15

**BODYWORK:**
Steel monocoque
Coupé or Targa 2+2

**DIMENSIONS:**

| | |
|---|---|
| Length | 14ft 1in |
| Wheelbase | 7ft 5.5in |
| Track, front | 4ft 6in |
| Track, rear | 4ft 5.25in |
| Width | 5ft 3.5in |
| Height | 4ft 4in |

**WEIGHT:**
21.2cwt (1,075kg)/21.2cwt (1,075kg)/21.7cwt (1,105kg)

**PERFORMANCE:**
(Source: *Autocar*)
Models quoted: 911 Coupé and 911S Coupé

| | |
|---|---|
| Max speed | 130mph*/142mph |
| 0–60mph | 7.8sec/6.1sec |
| Standing quarter-mile | 15.8sec/15.0sec |

* Porsche figure

**PRICE IN UK INCLUDING TAX WHEN NEW:**
911 Coupé: £6,249 (January 1974)
911 Targa: £6,650 (January 1974)
911N Coupé: £7,799 (October 1975)
911S Coupé: £6,993 (January 1974)
911S Targa: £7,393 (January 1974)

**NUMBER BUILT:**
911 Coupé: 5,232
911 Targa: 4,088
911N Coupé: 9,904*
911N Targa: 8,182*
911S Coupé: 4,927
911S Targa: 3,051

* Includes 911 Lux

# Porsche Carrera 2.7/Carrera 3
## 1973–75/1975–77

As 1973 Carrera 2.7RS except:

**ENGINE:**
Carrera 2.7 as 1973 Carrera 2.7RS
Carrera 3 as follows:

Die-cast aluminium crankcase derived from 930 turbo model

| | |
|---|---|
| Bore x stroke | 95.0 x 70.4mm |
| Capacity | 2,994cc |
| Compression ratio | 8.5:1 |
| Induction | Bosch K-Jetronic fuel injection |
| Power | 200bhp at 6,000rpm |
| Maximum torque | 188lb ft at 4,200rpm |

**BODYWORK:**
Normal luxury fittings added; rear spoiler optional (except UK) and changed from 'duck-tail' to 'whale-tail'. Impact-absorbing bumpers added 5in to length. Rear spoiler became optional on UK-spec Carrera 3; when fitted, model known as Carrera 3 Sport

**DIMENSIONS:**

| | |
|---|---|
| Length | 14ft 1in |

**WEIGHT:**
Carrera 2.7 Coupé: 22.4cwt (1,135kg)
Carrera 3 Coupé: 21.2cwt (1,075kg)
Carrera 3 Coupé Sport-o-matic: 22.1cwt (1,123kg)

**PERFORMANCE:**
(Source: *Motor/Autocar*)

| | |
|---|---|
| Max speed | 150mph*/141mph |
| 0–60mph | 5.5sec/7.3sec |
| Standing quarter-mile | 14.5sec/15.9sec |

* Porsche figure
Carrera 3 is with Sport-o-matic transmission

**PRICE IN UK INCLUDING TAX WHEN NEW:**
2.7 Coupé: £8,580 (January 1974)
2.7 Targa: £8,980 (January 1974)
Carrera 3 Coupé: £10,997 (October 1975)

*Left: A standard Carrera 2.7 in 1974, as tested by* Motor. *'Most expensive so-called exotica disappoint; a Porsche rarely does,' the magazine said. How true that has been down the years. (Motor/LAT)*

*Opposite: Side view of the 150mph 1974 911 Carrera shows the new 5mph impact bumpers and the more effective new rear spoiler. The late Tony Scott of* Motor *is at the wheel. (Motor/LAT)*

**NUMBER BUILT:**
2.7 Coupé: 1,534
2.7 Targa: 610
Carrera 3 Coupé: 2,546
Carrera 3 Targa: 1,105

Additionally, in 1974 Porsche built 109 Carrera RS 3.0-litres, 49 as evolutionary race cars, the rest as ultimate road cars of their day, complete with luxury trim and 230bhp engine

# Porsche 911SC
### 1977–83

As 2.7-litre 911S except:

**ENGINE:**
Crankcase aluminium-alloy instead of magnesium-alloy

Bore x stroke          95.0 x 70.4mm
Capacity                2,994cc
Power                   180bhp at 5,500rpm*
Maximum torque          188lb ft at 4,200rpm

*Power raised to 188bhp in 1979 and 204bhp in 1981

**BRAKES:**
*Front:* Disc, ventilated (11.3in)
*Rear:* Disc, ventilated (11.6in)
Servo assistance

**WHEELS/TYRES:**
Forged alloy wheels, 6J front and 7J rear
Tyres 205/55 VR 16 front and 225/50 VR 16 rear

**BODYWORK:**
Cabriolet additionally available from 1983

**DIMENSIONS:**
Track, front            4ft 6.25in
Track, rear             4ft 4.75in
Width                   5ft 5in

**WEIGHT:**
Coupé: 24.3cwt (1,233kg)

**PERFORMANCE:**
(Source: *Autocar*)
Max speed               141mph est/146mph
0–60mph                 6.5sec/5.8sec
Standing quarter-mile   15.1sec/14.2sec

(Coupé, 1977/1981)

**PRICE IN UK INCLUDING TAX WHEN NEW:**
Coupé/Targa: £12,600 (December 1977)
Sport models: £14,100 (December 1977)

**NUMBER BUILT:**
Coupé (180bhp): 10,382
Targa (180bhp): 8,108
Coupé (188bhp): 5,010
Targa (188bhp): 3,603
Coupé (204bhp): 16,099
Targa (204bhp): 9,837
Cabriolet (204bhp): 4,096

# Porsche 911 Carrera
### 1983–89

As 911SC except:

**ENGINE:**
Bore x stroke           95.0 x 74.4mm
Capacity                3,164cc
Compression ratio       10.3:1
Induction               Bosch DME injection
Power                   231bhp at 5,900rpm*
Maximum torque          209lb ft at 4,800rpm

*Power reduced to 217bhp if fitted with catalytic converter (from late 1986)

**SUSPENSION:**
*Rear:* Anti-roll bar standard

**DIMENSIONS:**
Track, front            4ft 5.9in
Track, rear             4ft 6.3in

**WEIGHT:**
22.9cwt–23.8cwt (1,165kg–1,210kg)

**PERFORMANCE:**
(Source: *Motor*)

Max speed               151mph
0–60mph                 5.3sec
Standing quarter-mile   14.0sec

**PRICE IN UK INCLUDING TAX WHEN NEW:**
(October 1983)
Coupé/Targa: £21,464
Coupé/Targa Sport: £23,366
Cabriolet: £22,553
Cabriolet Sport: £24,340

**NUMBER BUILT:**
Coupé: 35,517
Targa: 18,468
Cabriolet: 19,987

# Porsche 911 Carrera Club Sport
### 1987–89

As 911 Carrera 3.2 except:

**BODYWORK:**
Coupé two-seater, white only, usually with prominent 'Carrera CS' side lettering

**WEIGHT:**
22.9cwt (1,165kg)
Note that the standard car, at 25.2cwt (1,281kg), had put on weight by then – both these being official Porsche figures

**PERFORMANCE:**
(Source: *Autocar*)
Max speed               154mph
0–60mph                 5.6sec
Standing quarter-mile   14.2sec

(The significant improvement came at higher speeds: at 20.8sec, the Clubsport was 3.9sec quicker to 120mph than a standard model)

**PRICE IN UK INCLUDING TAX WHEN NEW:**
£34,389 (October 1987)

**NUMBER BUILT:**
Coupé: 189
Targa: 1 (yes, one)

recognised it for the very fine everyday roadgoing sports car it was. World economic conditions were pretty bad then but at least Porsche had a great car in the showrooms.

Sport-o-matic, it should be said, was still offered as an option on the 911 in those days. Introduced back in 1967 for the 1968 model year, Sport-o-matic remained in production for ten years before dwindling sales prompted Porsche to drop it late in 1978. Whilst the diehards reckoned it ruined a great car, there were others to whom the Jekyll and Hyde character – of two-pedal operation in one of the world's great performance cars – had a certain appeal. Only a mean-spirited killjoy would want to destroy their pleasure in the Sport-o-matic, so I had better be the one to say that it was a thoroughly rotten idea from beginning to end, and best forgotten, and never mind the fact

that the great Vic Elford, to whose remarkable credentials we should all honestly defer in this matter, thought Sport-o-matics were great in their day. That's a fair point and we shouldn't forget that the vastly superior Tiptronic transmission was still another whole decade away when the Sport-o-matic was finally abandoned.

From 1976, too, the entire 911 bodyshell was fully galvanised with a zinc coating but the age-old motor-industry practice of correcting minor body faults prior to painting could remove this invisible protection in the small areas concerned. Nobody I have spoken to recently remembers it now but I am sure it was in 1981 that Porsche quietly stopped such 'corrections' on all models. From that point on, the bodyshells were fully galvanised and they stayed that way. In those days, that called for an extraordinary confidence in the quality

of the production process but Porsches really were that well built. The bare, unpainted, open 911 Targa rolling shell which over 30 years ago was famously put on display outside the main administrative building at Weissach was still showing no sign of rust when I saw it during a visit many years later.

That dropping of all body correction procedures I remember clearly because by that time, after several years as a full-time race driver, I had become a weekend racer and a full-time Porsche salesman for Gordon Ramsay, then the official dealer for the North East of England. It gave me an extra pride in the product I was selling, knowing that it would not come back with a mysterious rust patch after a few years, revealing the point at which some perfectionist of a worker in Stuttgart had ground off a bit of zinc coating. Despite all the weighty problems of the world around

that time, my faith in the Porsche product was well-placed and stronger than ever.

The late 1970s and early 1980s were a funny time for the 911. Almost everybody was predicting its end by then. The future for Porsche was said to be with the front-engined models. Lots of us believed it and just shrugged our shoulders with regret. Meanwhile the factory kept on turning out a solid series of decent roadgoing 911s with the customary improvements being built in year on year.

For 1978 the 3-litre became standard across the normally aspirated 911 range. These really were first class road cars. Less exciting perhaps than that all-time classic, the 2.7RS of 1973, the 911SC from 1978 was simply an honest, fuss-free 911 that handled beautifully, sounded right, and did everything that the diehard 911 fan wanted. An improved ignition system

pushed power up to 188bhp for 1979 and gained a ten per cent fuel consumption improvement, a pretty staggering achievement when you think about it but there were more spectacular gains in that department just around the corner. Fortunately, the international economic climate was also improving and Porsche was as usual well-placed to take advantage of that.

Performance crept up steadily and I well remember that power rose to 204bhp for the 1981 SC, giving a top speed of 146mph and 0–60mph in 5.7sec. This time the fuel consumption was improved by over 20 per cent!

As I say, I was selling them at the time and I'm reminded of something that rather irritated me then. We all know the customer is always right and I also knew not to risk losing a sale by contradicting a 'prospect', even when he talked rubbish. There was a sports

option on the 911SC in those days that included wider wheels and the tail spoiler. The combination worked rather well for those who wanted to get the maximum roadholding in the faster corners, and quite a large number of customers went for that.

A few other customers had me wanting to scream 'Idiot' at them when they insisted on ordering a new 911SC 3-litre with wide sports wheels but no rear spoiler. I wanted to say 'I drive these cars all the time and I would understand it better if you wanted to have the standard wheels and the spoiler.' But I kept quiet and got the order signed. Everybody was happy about that.

With the sale safely in the bag, at some later point I would be unable to resist mentioning that those spoilers over the engine lid were not mere decoration. It seemed only fair to mention that they actually did a pretty

*Opposite: This standard 1977 model year 911 Carrera 3-litre was tested long-term by* Motor. *Some rare electrical failures occurred, among them the alternator, wipers and cruise control. The then Road Test Editor, Gordon Bruce, is seen here with the newly launched 924 in the background. (Motor/LAT)*

*Right: Rear view of the 1978 model year 911SC Sport, as tested by* Autocar *in December 1977. Traditional Porsche virtues were retained, they said, and the latest Pirelli P7 tyres gave a new edge to handling and roadholding. Porsche has always been quick to exploit advances in tyre technology. (Autocar/LAT)*

good job and I could still add it to the order if they wished.

But I didn't make a big deal of it: I just wanted to behave in a responsible, professional way. We were beginning to get a new kind of Porsche buyer, someone who bought the car because he thought he would look good in it and not because he wanted the ultimate driving experience, day in and day out. For some reason, that type of buyer seemed to reckon that spoilers were for cissies.

How they came to that conclusion still beats me. It would have been a waste of breath talking about the finer points of high-speed handling with them. Never mind, the cars were good,

they sold very well and we still had the pleasure of selling them to plenty of real enthusiasts who did appreciate them properly.

One Saturday in the early 1980s I proved this point about spoilers to myself. All the local roads were covered in thick snow but the sun was shining. I kicked my heels around the parquet floor of the showroom for hours but nobody came in, nobody rang. I was dreadfully bored.

One of the used 911s on display was an early SC 3-litre that had the multiple misfortunes of being a high-mileage machine, painted a sickly light green metallic, with a garish but worn interior, wide sports wheels, and no rear spoiler.

To cap it all, someone else in our company had been far too generous over it in part-exchange, and the poor thing had sat around unsold for months until it owed us much more money than any sensible customer would pay.

For another 15 minutes I paced up and down the showroom, eyeing it. Obviously, what it really needed was a road test. Perhaps if I took it out and gave it a bit of a blast – you know, just to check it over – maybe then my enthusiasm for it would be revived. Perhaps that enthusiasm would rub off onto a customer who might even buy it. I put the trade plates on, just in case.

Another ten minutes and I was off. It

*Opposite: Claimed in 1984 to be the world's fastest convertible, the 3.2-litre 911 Carrera SE Cabriolet was reckoned to be good for 155mph by* Motor *magazine's testers. At the wheel is a young, serious-looking Richard Bremner, now a leading British motoring journalist. His verdict on the car was 'well up to expectations'. Richard adds today: 'Like so many sceptics, I've come around to the 911 as the best serious all-round driver's car – but I always preferred the closed 911'. Bremner knows his stuff!* (Motor/LAT)

*Right: With the top down on the early 911 Cabriolet, the rear wing was less effective, permitting increased oversteer at speed. Telling the owners that was as good as lecturing labradors on philosophy. It was a pretty car, the Cabriolet, but the Coupé remained firmly in first place as the enthusiast's choice.* (LAT)

*Right: Inside the Cabriolet, the interior retained the pure 911 look. This photograph was taken in July 1983.* (LAT)

performed extremely well. On the way back, out in the country, along an absolutely dead straight and deserted section of the old A1 that had long since been bypassed by the motorway, I was cruising along in the sunshine on three inches of packed snow. It was quite beautiful, I could see for miles and there was not a soul in sight. I held it dead straight, lightly feeling everything through my fingers, and edged it up to 70mph. Ahead of me there was nothing, nothing at all, apart from the mildest of brows that I could easily see over. I held the throttle absolutely steady.

As we crested that mild pimple of a crest in the road, the presence of wide, low-profile tyres and the absence of a rear wing made themselves felt. We simply turned round in a graceful straight line, spinning on the snow for a very long time. Eventually, it all came to rest. The trade plates, on elastic straps, had been neatly removed from each end of the car by contact with the snow banked beside the road, but there was not one mark on the car itself.

I refixed the plates and returned carefully to the showroom where the triumphant old beast dripped melting snow onto the parquet for the rest of the afternoon. As a cure for boredom, I can recommend this procedure: it's one hundred per cent effective. I can

add that a rear spoiler would have kept it in line, even at the low speed of 70mph, but it does mean that I can claim to have spun a 911, just once. I am fond of pointing out that I must have driven over 700 911s, mainly at speed, on circuits, in sunshine and in heavy rain, without spinning any of them. I feel that says something about this very special car, in all its forms over so many years.

Within the company the trend, as we have seen, was towards the front-engined models that were expected to take over in due course. That time seemed to be getting very close at the end of the 1970s but it was Ferry Porsche himself who refused to let the

911 be dropped. If the 911 were to die it would not be without a fight. Development continued on all models including not least the great 911 which was again given those spectacular improvements in mpg and speed for the 1981 model year, and that was all at the direct instigation of the man who all those years earlier had created the 356 and the modern Porsche company itself.

The big excitement in 1983 was the arrival of the 911 Cabriolet, a car that

*If you can find one of these today, it's pure gold. It's the 1984 911 Carrera SC/RS, and one of only 20 made. Naturally aspirated but quicker than a contemporary Turbo, this car was featured in* Motor *of 5 May 1984. If 0–100mph in 12.3sec is what you want...* (Motor/LAT)

appealed to yet another entirely new kind of customer. It was a pretty stylish bit of kit from the start but it was not long before I discovered at Brands Hatch that putting the hood down reduces the effectiveness of the rear spoiler, encouraging more oversteer. I never mentioned that to Cabriolet customers. Somehow there didn't seem much point. Few would have had a clue what I was talking about and they might have been needlessly alarmed about something that wasn't a safety issue, merely a matter of interest.

As for the ordinary 'cooking' 911 of this period, it's still a bit of an unsung hero to my mind. Refined for a great driving experience, Porsche quietly turned out this fine machine in healthy numbers for years on end, steadily working in the usual small

improvements. I always liked the old SCs. Good solid, proper production cars, they were fast, real 911s and those with a good service history have proved an outstanding bargain as used high performance cars over the years.

There was no change to the basic character of the standard 911 when the engines were upgraded to 3.2 litres for 1984. That was good news as the old favourite didn't need fundamental changes at that stage. The new engines did give a marked increase in performance, however.

The 3-litre it replaced had produced 204bhp in the old SC. The new 3.2 (actually 3,164cc) format was achieved mainly by adapting known components to produce a logical step up, but new electronic engine management also replaced traditional technology. The

result was an immensely robust engine that produced 231bhp and pushed the standard 911 range to a top speed of 152mph, with 0–60mph in 5.3 seconds, these figures being achieved independently by *Motor* magazine.

A useful improvement was to the timing-chain set-up, greatly increasing the life of that component. To cope with the extra performance, there were bigger brakes and the top two gear ratios were slightly raised.

For this revised 911, Porsche brought the Carrera name back into use for the basic car, which was available in Coupé, Targa and Cabriolet forms. A rather silly option was a Turbo-style body for cars with the standard engine. As that only made it heavier and more of a drag through the air, it was slower than the standard model. Only posers who had some bizarre need to pretend they had a 911 Turbo bothered to fork out the extra cash.

The Sport pack came with low profile tyres, stiffer damping and spoilers at both ends but it also brought the penalty of increased road noise and bump-thump. To my mind, at least, the understated standard Carrera was the thing to get for normal use, possibly with just the spoilers added. The 3.2 Carrera of that era was not remotely flashy but it really should be recognised as one of the great 911s of all time.

My favourite driving experience in a Carrera 3.2 Coupé came in 1987, and it's a story that I fear is likely to make any reader green with envy. During the launch of the 959 at the Nürburgring that year, I had my drive round the new GP circuit in the sensational long-awaited new supercar, and then found that there was a lot of hanging around to do while everybody else had their go. Standing in the hospitality unit above the pits, drinking coffee, had become rather boring. But then I spotted famous Porsche engineer Roland Kussmaul, and we started talking.

Inevitably, the conversation got on to the subject of the old circuit, the famous Nordschleife, towards which I had been casting some wistful glances. The weather was good and I could see that although the GP circuit was closed

*The calm before the storm: these essential workers are seen taking a break in the Porsche factory in 1987. (LAT)*

for our private function, the old track was open to the public that day. Roland, who knew my Porsche racing record well, just smiled and handed me some keys on a Porsche key-ring: 'Take my car. It's the white 911, just outside. I must stay here.'

No second invitation was needed. With brief but profuse thanks, I was off. The fact is that I know the old Nürburgring better than I know Brands Hatch. I've been driving round it since 1965, and racing there since 1981. Being let loose at the place for some fun in a 911 is pretty much my idea of heaven.

What I wasn't prepared for was Roland's car, the then current bog-standard base 911: as soon as I got going, it seemed just too good to be true. The handling was extraordinarily good, naturally slightly 'tail-out' in the proper 911 style, and the engine seemed better than expected. The feeling of precise control provided by the combination of suspension, steering and engine response was delightful. The gearchange, newly improved for the 911 that year, was a further revelation, being far more positive in its action than any previous 911 I had known.

I think I did three laps, which is getting on for 40 miles round that

place, thoroughly enjoying every second of it. It was a quiet day, with little traffic on the Nordschleife, but Roland's 911 flew past every other car I saw there: effortless opposite-lock slides, inch-perfect lines achieved with almost casual precision, all the right noises and that satisfying surge of acceleration followed through corner after corner.

This was the exact opposite of the white-knuckle ride you get with some cars there, nor was there any sense of the thing wilting. It was fast – very, very fast – and it was easy. That had nothing to do with me: it was all because the car was utterly fit for the purpose. As motoring experiences go, a good 911 on the Nordschleife is hard to beat. They are happily at home on that most daunting of circuits.

At the end of a deeply satisfying session, the car felt as fresh as ever – that's a 911 for you – but I decided I had better not abuse Roland's kind offer by going on and on all afternoon, tempting as it was.

When I got back, he laughed as I handed back the keys. Maybe I had a silly grin on my face. 'You must tell me what you have done to it,' I said. 'Nothing,' he replied firmly. 'Surely you've modified something? It feels incredibly good,' I persisted. 'No,' said Roland, looking me straight in the eyes, with a slight smile. 'It's a completely standard, basic 911.'

His relaxed and honest expression made it clear that he was simply telling the truth, as you would expect from a dead-straight, top-class German engineer. I could only conclude that a man like that, who lives with these cars all day and every day, knows how to maintain his 911 better than anyone else in the world – and does so. It was a day to remember.

Slowly, around that time, it began to dawn on some of us that the 911 might not be on the way out after all; maybe it was not inevitable that it would be replaced by front-engined machines. After everything we had heard and feared for years, the fabulous 911 was proving just too good to fade away.

The appearance of the 3.2 Clubsport in that same year helped foster such feelings. Despite reasonable efforts to create another lightweight model, the Clubsport was only marginally lighter than the standard car but it was without question a successful sports version of the 3.2, excellent to drive and absolutely in keeping with the spirit of 911 tradition. In fact, by removing electric windows, back seats, hi-fi, soundproofing and the other such luxury items, they got the weight down by 100kg (roughly 2cwt) and that did make a difference to the feel of the car. The 0–60mph time was unaltered but the Clubsport was 1.8 seconds quicker than a standard car to 100mph and close on four seconds quicker to 120mph. Lower weight also spelt marginally better fuel consumption. It became a minor cult car, reminding real enthusiasts that Porsche was still very much with them in spirit even if the company was courting new business at the same time.

Towards the end of the 3.2 line, Porsche resurrected the Speedster theme for the 911 in 1988 and this model was continued as part of the subsequent and very different Carrera 2 range. I'm afraid that such novelty cars as that Speedster leave me cold because I find it hard to see the point of corrupting the pure 911 theme. If some people find such cars exciting and Porsche gains a few more sales, that's a fine thing. To me, however, the 911 Speedster has all the style of a racing tortoise, if admittedly one which would put the wind up the fastest hare. Give me the magnificent, thoroughbred Coupé every time, please.

The 911 had been around for nearly a quarter of a century even then, in one form or another, and it was still the business. It really was, as I was able to remind myself on that day in Germany in 1987, thanks to Roland Kussmaul's generosity.

# Buying hints

**1.** This era of 'big-bumpered' 911 will provide the pure, classic 911 driving experience at a bargain price.

**2.** The time-honoured advice is to go for a car from the 1984 model year or later because the 3.2-litre engine had the improved, longer-lasting hydraulic timing chain arrangement as well as more power and a reliable electronic engine management system. Advances in manufacturing techniques also meant that the new Porsches of the mid-to-late 1980s were far better protected against rust but many are rotten now.

**3.** That traditional advice, however, hardly gives the full picture today. These cars are now around 20 or 30 years old and how they've been treated over that time matters more than anything else. A well-cared for early model will probably have had

the timing chain set-up modified to the later, more durable specification at some point, so check on that. By all means choose your model carefully but don't jump in and buy a bad car. Check the history thoroughly. Has it had an accident? If so, was it badly repaired? Has it lost its rust protection?

**4.** With cars of such an age, it always comes back to this golden rule – join the club. Take advantage of the vast depth of knowledge that Porsche Club Great Britain officials and fellow members can pass on. Get a car inspected by a recommended specialist if you can.

**5.** Recorded mileage is irrelevant. A well-maintained Porsche engine will run happily for astonishing mileages but one that has been neglected and abused will probably need a proper

rebuild by a recognised expert. Get an idea of much that will cost by seeing an existing owner's recent engine rebuild bills.

**6.** Likewise, does the car need new brakes, a new clutch, a suspension rebuild or a gearbox overhaul? A new set of tyres will almost certainly be needed and the experts' choice of rubber varies from year to year, according to what is available. Gather all the information you can, research the likely expense of getting the necessary work done and then get out your calculator and add up the sums.

**7.** Take all these precautions and you won't waste a fortune. In fact, for a reasonable sum of money you'll end up with one of the most pleasing 911s ever made. And how many other true classic cars can top 150mph, day after day?

*Right:* 'Unworthy of praise' said Motor of the 911 Speedster unveiled at the 1987 Frankfurt show. Discerning critics have not changed their minds. Production total was 171 cars for the 1989 model year. The contemporary Turbolook Speedster shown here sold better, with 2,103 built, despite its serious lack of appeal to diehard 911 fans. (Motor/LAT)

*Below:* In 1987, the new Carrera Clubsport was claimed to be the fastest normally aspirated 911 to date, but had the rare 1984 Carrera SC/RS been overlooked? Stripped of unnecessary luxury, 100kg was saved in the Club Sport and that was felt in the performance of this car, here being tested in Germany when new by Autocar's Graham Jones. It remains one of the most desirable of classic 911s. (Autocar/LAT)

# The 911 turbo

*Introduced in 1975, the 911 turbo Coupé was known as the 930 inside the factory. The fastest German production car of its time, the 3-litre engine produced 260bhp and top speed was over 155mph. Five inches wider than a contemporary Carrera, and with special front spoiler and rear wing, turbos were easily spotted on the road. (Porsche)*

Tricky one, the early 911 turbo. Tricky in all sorts of ways, and I can't say I was a great fan at first. They were certainly quick in their day, they looked great with their widened wheelarches, and they were exciting to drive, I'll say that. Shown at the Paris motor show late in 1974, and in full production for the 1976 model year, the 2,994cc single-turbo engines produced 260bhp, top speed was about 155mph and 0–60mph was achievable in 6.0 seconds.

Strictly speaking, these were Porsche 930s but for obvious marketing reasons they were always sold as '911

turbos' in Europe and Britain, and as turbo Carreras in the US. The most amazing thing about the early 911 turbo is that it was never actually intended for mass-production. Porsche's plan was to make 500, just enough to homologate it for racing. For some reason, those 500 were luxuriously equipped, even having electric windows, and that proved to be some marketing man's touch of genius. Demand unexpectedly took off in a really big way.

I got to drive a fair number of turbos over the years at official Porsche circuit-driving days. One keen

customer, I remember, brought his nearly new car to Donington. It was a 3-litre turbo, some time in the early 1980s, and he asked me to show him what it could do on the circuit. He squeezed into the back, leaving the passenger seat to his girlfriend, and away we went.

Driving someone else's car under these circumstances calls for fine judgement. Just how hard do you try? Big points are lost if you insult owners by going slower than they want. I usually set off at a reasonably brisk rate and, after a couple of corners, ask the owner if the pace is OK. Usually, they say, 'That's fine, thanks' so I don't push things to the very limit.

This chap, a cheerful and likeable Geordie who was making it big in the rag trade, had no doubts: he was up for the full works, he said, and he meant it. On the second lap, through the fast downhill Craner Curves, I fed in the power as the car was teetering on opposite lock. He started laughing. 'Good God, man, it's fantastic,' he said, 'I never knew my car could do this.'

Deep in concentration in the middle of a corner, I think I just smiled. What I was really thinking was, 'Hold on, my

friend. We haven't established that it will yet.' But I kept quiet. The car was behaving well enough, cornering smoothly with just a trace of oversteer, and it was going very fast, but it felt extremely edgy and nervous – as if it were looking for the slightest error on my part as an excuse to fly off the track in one of several possible directions. Frankly, it demanded too much skill even from an experienced driver, and that made serious driving hard work instead of fun.

Those early turbo road cars were not confidence-inspiring and I was far from convinced that selling them to the public was a good idea. I had grown accustomed to driving the fastest normally aspirated 911s and I loved their poise in corners. Approaching a corner at speed on a circuit, I would gently release the brakes and turn in. A typical non-turbo 911 would slide its tail slightly wide, almost imperceptibly – I'm not talking about going wildly sideways – and the driver could then open the throttle progressively and rocket out of the corner on a trace of opposite lock.

The best way to make my point about the early turbo goes like this: suppose the optimum turn-in speed

for a given corner is 60mph. The comforting thing about a good, normal 911 is that if you turn in at anywhere between 45mph and 60mph, it will adopt that same comfortable attitude. You don't have to drive it on the limit to get the full fun of driving it properly. If you turn in a couple of miles an hour too fast, it will go a bit more sideways than is ideal but it still behaves itself reassuringly and the power can be applied as usual. It's not that hard to keep it in that 'window' of handling in which it maintains the classic neutral to oversteering stance.

Those early Turbos were not like that at all. That handling window was still there, of course, but it was incredibly narrow, making it quite hard to hit the spot even on an easy modern racing circuit. On that same corner, an early

## Porsche 911 Turbo (930) 3-litre/ 3.3-litre
### 1974–77/1977–90

ENGINE:
Six-cylinder horizontally opposed, air-cooled, turbocharged, aluminium alloy crankcase and Nikasil-coated bores; rear-mounted

| | |
|---|---|
| Bore x stroke | 95.0mm x 70.4mm |
| | 97.0mm x 74.4mm |
| Capacity | 2,994cc/3,299cc |
| Valve actuation | sohc per bank |
| Compression ratio | 6.5:1/7.0:1 |
| Induction | Bosch K-Jetronic injection; KKK turbocharger; intercooler (3.3) |
| Power | 260bhp at 5,500rpm |
| | 300bhp at 5,500rpm |
| Maximum torque | 253lb ft at 4,000rpm |
| | 303lb ft at 4,000rpm |
| | (318lb ft from 1983) |

TRANSMISSION:
Rear-wheel drive; four-speed manual gearbox until 1988/five-speed manual from 1989 model year

SUSPENSION:
*Front:* Independent by MacPherson struts, lower wishbones and longitudinal torsion bars; anti-roll bar

*Rear:* Independent by semi-trailing arms and transverse torsion bars; anti-roll bar

STEERING:
Rack-and-pinion; unassisted

BRAKES:
*Front:* Disc, ventilated (11.1in/12in)
*Rear:* Disc, ventilated (11.4in/12in)
No assistance (3-litre)
Cross-drilled discs, four-pot callipers and servo-assistance (3.3-litre)

WHEELS/TYRES:
Forged alloy wheels, 7in front and 8in rear
Tyres Pirelli P7 205/50 VR 15 front and 225/50 VR 15 rear

BODYWORK:
Steel monocoque
Coupé 2+2 (3-litre and 3.3-litre)
Slant-nose SE Coupé from 1985; Targa and convertible versions from 1987 (3.3-litre)

DIMENSIONS:
| | |
|---|---|
| Length | 14ft 1in |
| Wheelbase | 7ft 5.4in |
| Track, front | 4ft 8.6in/4ft 8.4in |
| Track, rear | 4ft 11.5in/4ft 11.1in |
| Width | 5ft 9.9in |
| Height | 4ft 4.0in/4ft 3.6in |

WEIGHT:
3-litre: 24.1cwt (1,140kg)
3.3-litre (1979): 25.8cwt (1,308kg)
3.3-litre (1983): 26.5cwt (1,348kg)

PERFORMANCE:
(Source: *Motor/Autocar & Motor*)

| | |
|---|---|
| Max speed | 155mph (min)/ 156mph* |
| 0–60mph | 6.0sec/4.9sec* |
| Standing quarter-mile | 14.1sec/13.1sec* |

*1989 3.3 five-speed, capable of 160mph; 156mph was recorded on Millbrook bowl

PRICE IN UK INCLUDING TAX WHEN NEW:
£14,749 (November 1975)
£26,249 (May 1979)
£31,591 (April 1983)
£57,852 (March 1989)

NUMBER BUILT:
3-litre Coupé: 2,850
3.3-litre Coupé: 14,476
3.3-litre Coupé, slant-nose: 948
3.3-litre Targa: 193
3.3-litre Cabriolet: 918

## Porsche 911 Turbo (964) 3.3-litre/ 3.6-litre
### 1991–92/1992–93

As 930-series 3.3-litre except for power and capacity increases indicated:

ENGINE:
| | |
|---|---|
| Bore x stroke | 100.0mm x 76.4mm (3.6-litre) |

911 turbo would adopt strong understeer if turned in at 55–56mph. At, say, 57–60mph it would start to move its tail, and power could be applied in the normal manner. Take it a fraction over 60mph, however, and the tail would slide too much, forcing the driver to catch it rapidly with an armful of opposite lock, just to stop it spinning.

That sort of extreme sideways driving is exciting but very slow.

*Left: Interior improvements for the 1977 model year 911 included better ventilation and climate control; and the turbo's boost gauge was set into the tachometer dial, as seen here. (Porsche)*

*Opposite: For 1978, the turbo was powered by a new 3.3-litre engine, producing 300bhp and pushing top speed to just over 160mph. The 'tea-tray' rear spoiler came in with it. New cross-drilled brake discs were based on those of the 917 racing car. (Porsche)*

| | |
|---|---|
| Capacity | 3,600cc (3.6-litre) |
| Compression ratio | 7.5:1 (3.6-litre) |
| Power | 320bhp at 5,750rpm* |
| | 360bhp at 5,500rpm |
| Maximum torque | 332lb ft at 4,500rpm |
| | 383lb ft at 4,200rpm |

*355bhp was available with the 3.3-litre Cabriolet with performance kit for the 1992 model year

## SUSPENSION:
*Front:* Independent by MacPherson struts with lower wishbones, coil springs; double-acting gas dampers; anti-roll bar
*Rear:* Independent by MacPherson struts, coil springs; double-acting gas dampers; anti-roll bar

## BRAKES:
*Front:* Disc, ventilated and cross-drilled (12.7in)
*Rear:* Disc, ventilated and cross-drilled (11.8in), with ABS

## WHEELS/TYRES:
Forged alloy wheels, 7in front and 9in rear (3.3) or 8in front and 10in rear (3.6)
Tyres 205/50 ZR 17 front and 255/40 ZR 17 rear (3.3) or 225/40 ZR 18 front and 265/35 ZR 18 rear (3.6)

## DIMENSIONS:
| | |
|---|---|
| Length | 13ft 11.3in |
| Wheelbase | 7ft 5.4in |
| Track, front | 4ft 8.5in |
| Track, rear | 4ft 10.8in |

## WEIGHT:
3.3-litre: 28.9cwt (1,470kg)
3.6-litre: 29.5cwt (1,499kg)

## PERFORMANCE:
(Source: Porsche/*Autocar & Motor*)
| | |
|---|---|
| Max speed | 167mph/174mph |
| 0–62mph/0–60mph | 5.0sec/4.6sec |

## PRICE IN UK INCLUDING TAX WHEN NEW:
3.3-litre: £72,993 (January 1991)
3.6-litre: £80,499 (July 1993)

## NUMBER BUILT:
3.3-litre Coupé: 3,660
3.3-litre Cabriolet: 6
3.6-litre Coupé: 1,437

*Notes:*

(1) Six 3.3-litre Cabriolets also built, with 'performance kit' 355bhp engines – claimed 174mph and 0–62mph in 4.7sec

(2) 86 Turbo S Coupé lightweight 3.3-litres (25.4cwt/1,190kg) also built, with 381bhp engines – claimed 180mph and 0–62mph in 4.6sec. Whether any came to UK is doubtful

(3) Special 3.6-litre models include 76 high-performance slant-nose Coupés made in 1993–94, developing 385bhp – claimed capable of over 174mph and 0–62mph under 4.8sec

# Porsche 911 Turbo (993) 3.6 4wd
## 1995–1998

## ENGINE:
Six-cylinder horizontally opposed, air-cooled, turbocharged, aluminium alloy heads, cylinders and crankcase; rear-mounted

| | |
|---|---|
| Bore x stroke | 100.0mm x 76.4mm |
| Capacity | 3,600cc |
| Valve actuation | sohc per bank |
| Compression ratio | 8.0:1 |
| Induction | Bosch Motronic M5.2; twin KKK K-16 turbochargers; intercoolers |
| Power | 408bhp at 5,750rpm |
| Maximum torque | 398lb ft at 4,500rpm |

## TRANSMISSION:
Four-wheel drive; six-speed manual gearbox

## SUSPENSION:
*Front:* Independent by MacPherson struts with light alloy lower wishbones, coil springs; double-acting gas dampers; anti-roll bar
*Rear:* Independent by light-alloy multi-link system and coil springs; double-acting gas dampers; anti-roll bar

## STEERING:
Rack-and-pinion; power-assisted

▶

**BRAKES:**
*Front:* Disc, ventilated (12.7in)
*Rear:* Disc, ventilated (12.7in)
Four-pot callipers; ABS; servo assistance

**WHEELS/TYRES:**
Forged alloy wheels, 8in front and 10in rear
Tyres 225/40 ZR 18 front and 285/30 ZR 18 rear

**BODYWORK:**
Steel monocoque
Coupé 2+2

**DIMENSIONS:**

| | |
|---|---|
| Length | 13ft 11in |
| Wheelbase | 7ft 5.4in |
| Track, front | 4ft 7.6in |
| Track, rear | 4ft 11.2in |
| Width | 5ft 10.7in |
| Height | 4ft 2.6in |

**WEIGHT:**
28.8cwt (1,507kg)

**PERFORMANCE:**
(Source: *Autocar*)

| | |
|---|---|
| Max speed | 180mph (min) |
| 0–60mph | 3.7sec |

**PRICE IN UK INCLUDING TAX WHEN NEW:**
£91,950 (May 1995)

**NUMBER BUILT:**
Coupé: 5,978

Special models were made in small numbers, including:
(1) 14 Cabriolet turbos with 360bhp engines for 1995
(2) 345 450bhp S Coupés in the 1998 model year – claimed 186mph and 0–62mph in 4.1sec approx

# Porsche 911 Turbo (996) 3.6 4wd
## 2000–05

**ENGINE:**
Six-cylinder, horizontally opposed, water-cooled, aluminium alloy heads/blocks/crankcase; rear-mounted

| | |
|---|---|
| Bore x stroke | 100.0mm x 76.4mm |
| Capacity | 3,600cc |
| Valve actuation | dohc per bank, 4 valves per cylinder (VarioCam Plus timing) |
| Compression ratio | 9.4:1 |
| Induction | Bosch Motronic ME7.8; twin KKK K64 turbochargers; intercoolers |
| Power | 414bhp at 6,000rpm* |
| Maximum torque | 398lb ft at 4,500rpm* |

*Later: 420bhp at 6,000rpm and 413lb ft at 2,700rpm–4,600rpm

**TRANSMISSION:**
Four-wheel drive; six-speed manual gearbox (optional five-speed Tiptronic)

**SUSPENSION:**
*Front:* Independent by MacPherson struts, 'disconnected' light-alloy locating links using elastic rubber bushes, and coil springs; double-acting gas dampers; anti-roll bar
*Rear:* Independent by light-alloy multi-link system and coil springs; single-tube gas dampers; anti-roll bar

**STEERING:**
Rack-and-pinion; power assisted

**BRAKES:**
*Front:* Disc, ventilated (13in)
*Rear:* Disc, ventilated (13in)
ABS; servo assistance
Porsche ceramic ventilated and drilled discs with six-pot/four-pot callipers optional, with 13.8in discs all round

**WHEELS/TYRES:**
Cast alloy wheels, 8in front and 11in rear
Tyres 225/40 ZR 18 front and 295/30 ZR 18 rear

**BODYWORK:**
Steel monocoque
Coupé 2+2; Cabriolet

**DIMENSIONS:**

| | |
|---|---|
| Length | 14ft 6.6in |
| Wheelbase | 7ft 8.5in |
| Track, front | 4ft 9.7in |
| Track, rear | 5ft 11.9in |
| Width | 6ft 4in |
| Height | 4ft 3in |

**WEIGHT:**
30.5cwt (1,549kg)

**PERFORMANCE:**
(Source: *Autocar*)

| | |
|---|---|
| Max speed | 189mph |
| 0–60mph | 3.9sec |
| Standing quarter-mile | 12.3sec |

**PRICE IN UK INCLUDING TAX WHEN NEW:**
£86,000 (July 2000)

**NUMBER BUILT:**
Approximately 22,062

---

Another customer with one of these cars had adopted his own special technique. Any fast corner he took very cautiously and slowly, keeping well out of trouble, but when it came to a slow corner he let the car almost stop, sideways on, as he turned in. As his passenger I got pretty tired of this nonsense. Calmly and politely, I explained that he was wearing out his car and his tyres in a total waste of time and effort.

He said nothing. I waited. Still he said nothing. 'So why do you do it?' I asked politely. I was genuinely puzzled. 'I like it,' was his honest reply. That's fair enough, I thought, but it was perfectly ridiculous. He would have been much quicker by not sliding it at all but he wasn't interested in learning about that. The trouble with monster cars like the early 930s is that they encourage

owners to adopt such laughable tricks in their efforts to tame them.

Infuriating as it was, he had actually been rather clever. What he had done was to evoke part of the old Porsche 356 driving technique of deliberately unsticking the back of the car to get a particular effect. On the earliest Porsches a good driver could hang the tail out a long way and hold the slide in a balanced state, or he could choose to over-correct that slide on purpose and by a precise amount, making the tail swing like a pendulum and thus achieve a rapid and accurate change of direction.

Porsche, however, had long since moved to a higher plane in which the huge slides, such ponderous actions, were ancient history. It had worked all right with skinny wheels but, with the wider rubber in use by then, it simply

slowed us down very rapidly. The fact that this 911 turbo owner had found it at all excited my curiosity but I was offended by his refusal to accept that a more subtle and less leery use of such tricks might prove more effective. In short, his personal combination of intuition and blindness to the next step was frustrating and I was even more frustrated by my own conspicuous failure to enlighten him.

So far I have been talking only of the 3-litre turbos. My memory suggests that they were very much better if the optional limited-slip differential was fitted. These things can be a menace in road cars, making them a shade faster but far less forgiving. With those early 911 turbos, however, the lsd seemed to make them much more manageable. To a considerable degree, having that option somehow widened the speed

*Right: Nearly ready for installation, this 3-litre 911 turbo engine of about 1978 was destined for the USA. (Porsche)*

*Below: A 3.3-litre turbo with slant nose, a special conversion offered by the factory for turbo bodyshells from late 1982. With flatter front wings and pop-up headlights taken from the 944, the slant nose did make the car faster but some were uncomfortable about the style. (Porsche)*

'window' in which the desirable neutral to oversteering corner entry could be achieved, and kept them more stable under power. But, as road cars, they were still a bit wobbly, to put it mildly. Given a twisty bit of road, quite modest machinery could run rings round any of them.

Properly prepared for racing, they were a very different proposition. Many years later, I had a one-off race at Donington in Josh Sadler's 930 and my luck was right in, thanks to some unusual weather. Despite a very fine drizzle, slick tyres were still the right choice: Josh's car, with a standard engine, felt beautifully balanced and it won outright quite comfortably despite being in the third class in that event, and expected to run well down the field.

The weather, as I say, was very much on my side: a couple of 935s were in that race and, as expected, both suffered from severe understeer on slicks in the drizzle that day, so they couldn't use their immense power. Given a dry track, they would have disappeared into the distance. As I say, I was just indecently lucky that day. Josh, of course, is the founder of Porsche specialist Autofarm: his car was perfectly prepared and unusually smooth to drive.

The demands of road and race-circuit driving are linked but obviously far from identical. Roadgoing 911 turbos were always relatively heavy cars and, at 1,300kg, or 25.6cwt, the 3.3-litre turbo, revealed in 1977, was the heaviest 911 road car to that date by far – although still a lot lighter than its contemporary Porsche newcomer, the 928. With the 300bhp engine and 162mph top speed, the enlarged 911 turbo was also the most powerful and the fastest. The 0–60mph time of 5.3 seconds was pretty impressive, but don't forget that the normally

*Above: Very apparent in this side view, the steeply sloping front wings of the 1983 model year 3.3-litre turbo slant-nose. A performance kit with four exhaust tailpipes raised power to 330bhp. (LAT)*

*Left: David Vivian, Road Test Features Editor of Motor in 1987, giving the then-new 911 turbo SE slant-nose the proper treatment. 'I remember that corner,' David told me recently, 'and the fun we had. Perhaps the SE's 935 wannabe nose treatment was embarrassing but it was great to drive: just like the regular turbo but with an extra 30bhp.' (Motor/LAT)*

aspirated and far lighter 1973 Carrera 2.7 could manage the dash to 60mph in 5.5 seconds.

The 3.3 turbo did benefit considerably from chassis development that helped to tame it to a large extent, but the bigger engine (with a new clutch design) meant that there was a 30mm greater overhang at the rear than before. Despite that extra inch plus a bit, Porsche managed to get the best from the latest low-profile tyres – 16in Pirelli P7s, 7in wide front and 8in rear in those days – and the basic grip of the 3.3 Turbo on dry or wet roads amazed all the road-test writers in 1979. Once again, the press sang the praises of the 911 turbo, and quite right, too: it was an incredible car that had just been made yet more unbelievable.

As well as being quicker and better in many other ways, the 3.3 also had better handling than the original 3-litre; but in my view it was still

something of a monster when driven really fast. That said, in normal conditions on the road it was very civilised and devilishly quick for overtaking: a massive maximum torque figure of 304lb ft at 4,000rpm saw to that. If you put your foot down when cruising at 120mph, it gave you a good push in the back. The big brakes were well up to the job, and the 3.3 turbo also had that typically Porsche feeling of having an unburstable engine, yet still being very easy and free of fuss when driven slowly around city streets.

Maybe it was still a bit of a big bruiser with slightly primitive ventilation and only a four-speed gearbox, but it could be hard to resist its raw appeal at times. And it certainly had other major plus points, including a 12,000-mile service interval that was unique for such a fast car at the time. Porsche claimed that the 3.3 turbo offered racing performance with saloon-car comfort: it was a pretty fair claim.

*Above: Typical 911 turbo interior, with suitable script neatly cut into the rear seat backs. This is a 1983 model. (LAT)*

*Below: Rear view of the 3.3-litre 911 turbo. This famous number plate has been used on numerous cars loaned to the press by Porsche Cars Great Britain Ltd. At the time of writing, 911 HUL is a 3.6-litre model first registered in August 2007! (LAT)*

Above: Targa and Cabriolet versions of the 3.3-litre turbo went on sale in the spring of 1987. This contemporary publicity shot gives a good comparison of the new styles available for the turbo. (Porsche)

Left: Autocar & Motor tested this 3.3 turbo, with the then-new five-speed gearbox, in March 1989. Road tester Andrew Frankel drove the maximum speed test, 156mph round Millbrook, and remembers it fondly, but adds that it could be 'a tricky bugger if ever there was one'. He was right there! (Autocar & Motor/LAT)

Opposite: The good-looking 964-bodied version of the 911 turbo did not arrive until the 1991 model year, using a cleaner and more powerful (320bhp) edition of the familiar 3.3-litre engine. This looks like a good sideways shot until you look very closely – either the driver was parked in that attitude or the photographer used an extremely fast shutter speed! (LAT)

Buyers in the US missed out on the turbo for a few years around that time because of their country's emissions regulations, and when the model eventually went on sale there it was considerably less powerful than its European counterpart. Porsche, as ever, addressed the problem and eventually restored proper power to US turbo buyers.

Detailed improvements were made for 1983 and a radically different look was offered in 1985 as an optional package but, thanks to a hefty price, it remained relatively rare. Known in Britain as the SE (Special Equipment) this 911 turbo had a slanted nose with pop-up headlights, even wider rear arches and wheels, and engine power raised to 330bhp. The result was a road car that bore a strong resemblance to a racing 935, and its better shape raised the top speed to 171mph.

Two years later, this special look was offered in Targa or Cabriolet form in addition to the classic Coupé. Other non-turbo models had been offered with the turbo-style wide body but the genuine turbo always retained the large rear wing. It had to, because that wing also contained the large intercooler that had been made standard with the 3.3-litre turbo.

Once praised to the skies, the old monster was however finally beginning to show its age. People began to see it as mighty and wicked, but flawed. It wasn't, however, quite finished yet. For 1989, the turbo got a five-speed gearbox at last (whether it needed it or not), plus firmer torsion bars and stiffer anti-roll bars. This, the last of the line of 911 turbos with the traditional torsion bar suspension, could manage 0–60mph in 4.9 seconds but it felt a bit fussy in the lower gears when used hard. It had a short production life, being discontinued at the end of the 1989 model year, and was replaced, after a brief hiatus, by a revised turbo using the all-new 964 chassis with its coil-spring suspension.

The last of the rear-wheel-drive 911 turbos, announced for 1991, were thus a development of the Carrera 2, initially with the 3.3-litre engine. They were impressive machines, even more so after the 3.6-litre version had appeared at the Paris show late in 1992. In this form, with 360bhp, the 911 turbo was capable of 0–100kph (62mph) in 4.8 seconds and could reach 174mph. With ABS brakes and the more modern chassis, turbos based on the coil-sprung 964 body were much more drivable than the early turbos had ever been, and also benefited from a bodyshell that was twenty per cent stiffer than that of the previous turbo.

But these interesting models were not that heavily promoted – probably for the good reason that the true future of this flagship performer in Porsche's range lay with four-wheel drive. Tiny numbers of very special turbos were

# The racing 934

It's worth taking a look here at one extraordinary competition version of the 911 turbo. Apart from anything else, it reveals an interesting anecdote on Porsche rear wing performance – so this is an excusable little digression, I hope. When Porsche fit these things they are not decorative items, they perform a function.

Earlier I mentioned that driving many 911 cabriolets with rear spoilers on track days in the 1980s, whether turbos or not, I noticed that when the hoods were lowered the effect of the rear wings was greatly reduced. They tended to oversteer more easily in the faster corners. They were all safe with the hoods up or down but there definitely was a very noticeable difference.

When you get up to extremely high speeds, any small differences can become far more noticeable. An early competition version of the 930 was the 934, one of which I raced in 1980–82, sharing the drives with owner Richard Cleare. It proved the point, to me anyway.

Porsche built 30 examples of the 934 in 1976. Based closely on the production 911 turbo road car, they were mainly for private entrants in serious competition. At first, the 3-litre engine produced 485bhp, giving a top speed of 186mph in a car that weighed 1,122kg, or roughly 22cwt.

When we were driving Richard's car, the 934 was getting a bit long in the tooth but the performance was still unbelievable. What's more, as each month went by it seemed, further 934 improvements filtered through from the factory's excellent customer racing department, under Herr Schmidt. Before long we had 625bhp and virtually no turbo-lag, meaning we could drive the 934 on the throttle in corners, just like a normal car. It really was quite some machine.

With what was by then a magnificent battle-wagon we won our class all over the place, including Le Mans in 1982, where it did a timed 205mph on the Mulsanne Straight. The 934's behaviour on the classic French circuit fascinated me at the time. Richard had a 3.3-litre engine for qualifying and, with fewer fuel stops in mind, a 3-litre engine for the race.

In qualifying, we ran with the 3.3-litre 'tea-tray' rear spoiler and we were joined for that long race by Richard Jones, who proved an excellent, quick driver and fitted in with the team, and all went to plan in practice.

Then the fun began. The scrutineers told Richard Cleare that, as he had specified a 3-litre engine for the race, we would have to run with the much less impressive-looking 3-litre rear spoiler. It was simply a flip-up tail, lacking the raised edges around the sides. There was much talk, and Richard became very unhappy.

Secretly, I thought the scrutineers were right, and I still do. However, worried that this might all end in tears, even that we might be chucked out, I said he should face the inevitable, give in to the scrutineers' demands and instruct chief mechanic Don Holland to fit the older spoiler. 'I don't suppose it will make any difference anyway,' I said.

Well, I was dead wrong about that. After much grumbling, Richard did give in and, when it came to the race, we found our car was immediately, on lap one, a massive four seconds a lap faster than it had been with the bigger engine and the tea-tray spoiler. The extra speed was an unexpected bonus that amused and delighted me even if it was a bit embarrassing to have got our set-up so fundamentally wrong in qualifying.

This huge difference in lap times was entirely a result of the reduced drag of the smaller spoiler. We were getting up to the same speed, 205mph on the long and then still chicane-free Mulsanne Straight, but so much earlier and the car felt quite different. Whereas in practice it had been rock steady, in the race I could feel the air passing over the back and spilling first to one side of the spoiler and then to the other, in a curiously regular motion.

At the same time the rear of the car was 'hanging down' towards the gutter – before the chicanes appeared, the genuine old *Route Nationale* public highway sloped down from the crown of the road towards each side – so a trace of opposite lock was needed on the straight for us, and changing lanes required some care.

The lesson is that even between small spoilers like that, there can be a surprisingly big difference in effect. The faster you go, the more such differences will be noticed. But, I mean, four seconds a lap! Over 24 hours at Le Mans, it must have been worth at least twenty extra laps. Those awkward scrutineers had actually done us a big favour and we finished thirteenth overall as well as first in class. The whole thing made me laugh.

*Richard Cleare's 934, with the author on the limit in the Esses during the 1982 Le Mans 24Hrs, en route to a class win and 13th overall. The 934 was a production-based 911 turbo Group 4 race car, built in 1976. With factory help, power was steadily increased to 625bhp by 1982 and the car was clocked at 205mph on the Mulsanne Straight. Differences between 'tea-tray' and 'whale-tail' rear spoiler performance were very obvious at that speed. Richard Jones shared this drive with us. (Jeff Bloxham)*

occasionally made in the early 1990s, such as six high-performance Cabriolets, but they are almost too rare to be worth mentioning. The factory records do show 76 slant-nosed Coupés with 385bhp engines made in the 1994 model year, with 'more than 174mph' claimed, and a devoted collector would probably reckon one of those to be well worth tracking down.

On paper the 964-based turbo – called by some the 965 – was a mighty impressive machine which handled well and could outperform any rival on power to weight, acceleration and top speed. But people reckoned it lacked passion: it felt more like a GT than a sports car, the steering lacked that characteristic sense of engagement and, although it was fast, the engine lacked that 911 howl.

Going against the trend to GT comfort, however, the suspension tended to thump even on quite smooth roads, while there was too much noise from the huge, low-profile tyres. Looking back, the snag must have been getting that much engine performance to act on the rear wheels in a safe and civilised fashion. In their quest Porsche's engineers undoubtedly

succeeded but the last of the rear-wheel-drive 911 turbos, despite its unforgettably mighty performance, did not sell in huge numbers in its four-year production run. I suspect the general public hardly noticed it was there. There was, however, something rather special just around the corner.

The next new 911 turbo arrived for 1995, based on the 993 series of 911s.

*Above: Still very much a classic Porsche interior for the 1991 model year 911 turbo, despite the all-new 964 body. (Porsche)*

*Below: The 360bhp 3.6-litre engine became available in the 964-bodied turbo for the 1993 model year. Distinguished by 'turbo 3.6' badging on the engine lid, performance remained much as with the 3.3-litre – still stunning, with a top speed of 174mph.*

It came with four-wheel drive, and almost immediately it was obvious that this was the real thing. None of us, not even rabid 911 fanatics such as myself, had any idea of just how impressive this new turbo would be. In fact, when I heard that the 911 turbo had been revived in that form, I confess I had some doubts. I approached my first drive in the then-new 1995 turbo with a certain scepticism, namely a fear that it might combine the worst features of previous turbos with the ghastly feel of the early Carrera 4.

As soon as I saw the new 408bhp Porsche 911 turbo, a sense of reassurance began to build in me. For a start, the stylists had updated the look so perfectly that even the beautifully curved, fixed rear wing appeared to be a proper part of the machine and not some afterthought. First impressions were good, and just a few miles down the road from Stuttgart, I was more than reassured. I was astonished.

By a long, long way, this was the finest Porsche turbo yet: streets ahead of its ancestors, it was an absolute revelation. A year before the car came out, the Carrera 4 had been given that viscous coupling to replace the mechanical central differential of the early models. That change had made

all the difference, transforming the normally aspirated four-wheel-drive 911 into a car that handled as well as a good rear-wheel-drive model.

An even more advanced version of that all-wheel-drive transmission went into the new turbo, helping it become a truly formidable road-eating device. While the first generation of 911 turbos might have been a novelty, something to make your friends gawp in amazement simply because of the stunning straight-line performance, those early turbos could be decidedly tricky and had always been somewhat unwieldy. Even in skilled hands they were never easy machines to handle.

Not so the 1995 four-wheel-drive version. That 911 turbo was a serious motor car. At its heart was the traditional air-cooled 'boxer', flat-six engine in the latest 3.6-litre form. With twin turbos and a massive intercooler under the rear wing, plus twin three-way catalysts, power was up to 408bhp and the old bogey of turbo-lag was rendered a thing of the distant past. The 1995 turbo pulled like hell, instantly, from almost any revs, and it was fast: 0–100kph in 4.5 seconds and a top speed of 180mph were modestly claimed. When *Autocar* tested an early example they got from rest to 60mph in just 3.7 seconds and were well past

a genuine 100mph when ten seconds had elapsed.

Inevitably, this car drew comparison with the twin-turbo, four-wheel-drive 959 supercar of a decade before. One major difference in the engine this time was that the 959's two turbos blew in series, but this car had a separate turbo on each side. Electronic engine management had advanced in bounds, too. Torque, even at medium revs, was very impressive and the new engine was unexpectedly smooth for a car of such very high performance. For outright speed, the 959 remained king, being good for nearly 200mph, but this was really a much more advanced motor car. It made the 959 a museum piece: fascinating, yes, but still a museum piece.

The manual gearbox had the most positive feel to its lever that I had ever experienced in a 911, and now with six well-chosen speeds there was always the right gear available to give your passengers the feeling of being thrust forward with great force, yet uncanny smoothness.

That smoothness of the entire machine did surprise me. After all, this car had an immensely strong steel monocoque (zinc-coated on both sides of each panel by that time, too) and mated to it was this ingenious

*Left: Rear view of the 3.3-litre 911 turbo created from the 964 body for the 1991 model year. (Porsche)*

*Opposite, top: The wider, flatter look of the 993 body was extended further for the 911 turbo from the 1995 model year. Four-wheel drive, the twin-turbo engine and the advanced limited-slip transmission made it a revelation to drive. This example is from the 1997 model year. (Porsche)*

*Opposite, bottom left: From all angles, the 1997 911 turbo 3.6 Coupé was a beautiful car. The effective rear spoiler looked far more 'part of the car' than such important additions had in earlier days. (Porsche)*

*Opposite, bottom right: Interior of the 1997 911 turbo and, yes, it remains firmly in the Porsche mould. There are differences but it's hard to tell it apart from the previous 964. (Porsche)*

transmission with four double-jointed driveshafts and a tough suspension system, all of which had to be quite heavy to cope with all the massive forces that engine could bring to bear. Somehow the engineers had put it all together to produce a car that had not the slightest hint of the crude, agricultural character that had been associated with four-wheel-drive vehicles only a few years before. It was so smooth. How did they do it?

Well, I don't really know, but the answer can only lie in innumerable minor technical details. All I can say is that they achieved it, and very cleverly too. Under normal conditions, nearly all of the torque was sent to the rear wheels, but the variable distribution allowed up to 40 per cent to be diverted seamlessly to the front wheels when appropriate, so maintaining traction and balanced handling.

Suspension, front and rear, was by double wishbones, coil springs, advanced gas dampers and anti-roll bars. All these things meant that the new turbo, like the then current Carrera 4, handled like a good rear-

wheel-drive car when driven hard. It understeered at first, shifting to stable oversteer as cornering force approached the limit. It did not wobble, nor did it teeter uncertainly on opposite lock like some of the old turbos had. Few drivers ever try to take such a car to the limits of its cornering ability but the vital point is that, with the four-wheel-drive turbo, they were not in for a nasty shock if they really did find themselves on the ragged edge one day. It was not a car to lead the ignorant into any traps yet at the same time it was one to satisfy the experts, particularly those with 911s in their blood.

On the straight, if the road was not absolutely smooth, one could even feel the steering writhing in the hands slightly, despite the power assistance. That to me was in the best 911 tradition. Some might call it a fault, but I could not disagree more: vital messages come back through such a steering system and, if you go with it, interpreting the sensations that reach your hands, it's not tiring and it's not irritating; it is, quite simply, part of

*Opposite: After a break in turbo production, the 911 turbo Coupé returned in January 2000 as part of the 996 range, with water-cooled engines. This time, we see the familiar 911 HUL registration on a turbo during an Autocar road test in 2000. The front grille arrangement, with three inlets, distinguished it from other models. Some felt that the turbo's styling had become almost too understated but the testers' overall verdict of the 414bhp, 189mph machine was a clear: 'Even better than we'd hoped'. (Autocar/LAT)*

*Above: With 473bhp, the 911 turbo could manage 0–60mph in 3.6 seconds, as measured by Autocar magazine in 2006. The rear wing is seen at rest here, the upper part only rising when 75mph is reached ('Yes, Officer'); it moves back down at 37mph. (Porsche)*

the reassuring pleasure of driving a true 911, and that's exactly what that turbo was.

The brake callipers were painted red, a bit of marketing-department fun, no doubt. More to the point, all four discs were drilled and ventilated and the brake circuits were split front and rear.

*Extremely stylish, as well as potent: the 996-based 911 turbo Cabriolet. (Porsche)*

*The mighty flat-six, twin-turbo engine, as fitted to 996 models of the 911 turbo, produced 473bhp and up to 502lb ft of torque from 3,600cc. Turbo lag was effectively eliminated from Porsche engines many years ago and in this form the performance became more stunning than ever. (Porsche)*

Non-asbestos pads were already in use. Not only that, but by 1995 advances in anti-lock braking software were able to provide another major feature which put that turbo way ahead of the old 959: truly reassuring feel at the brake pedal.

Despite the low-profile tyres, the ride was more than acceptable for a sports car and, like the 959, the special wheels had hollow spokes to save weight and effectively to raise the quantity of air within the tyres, thus improving ride: it appeared to work.

While the 959 had been a low-volume production experimental supercar, a further decade of development had enabled Porsche to produce this car, the 959's true roadgoing descendant, in far greater numbers and for half the price that the 959 had cost all those years before. What's more, the thousands of small improvements added up to a car that was immensely more sophisticated. There was no occasional dead, clicking sensation at the brake pedal, no crudely shifting torque split under pressure. Quicker responses than had been possible with the 959, in all vital areas, made this a more appealing car for the serious driver.

Thus, the return of the Porsche 911 turbo had been achieved triumphantly. As a traditionally minded 911 enthusiast, I loved it, I was surprised by it, and my faith was fully restored.

On a trip to Germany the following year, I had the chance to drive the latest 1996 911 turbo and to compare it directly with four other new 911 models – the standard Carrera, the 4S, the RS and the GT 2 – which are all covered elsewhere in this book.

In that illustrious contemporary repertoire of Porsche models, the place of Porsche's all-wheel-drive 911 turbo was clear. In terms of price it fell neatly between the overtly sporting RS and GT 2 models. But to say simply that it was a well-sorted all-rounder would have undersold the mighty turbo. I wouldn't argue with those who insisted that, for ultimate sports car driving satisfaction back in 1995, one of the contemporary rear-wheel-drive 911s would still have been the thing to get. They made a fair point. For those who could afford it, however – apart from the price, fuel consumption could drop to around 15mpg when used very hard – by 1996 the turbo had become an immensely powerful supercar that was ideal for everyday use as well.

Also, it was hard to believe the new turbo was in any way related to its wild and worrying, lag-prone 1970s ancestor. Just a few years before, virtually every mile in the old 911 turbos had been white-knuckled. How

different it had become: more speed, more response, more thrills of the right kind, more of everything – except turbo lag and prematurely white hair.

It was undeniably pleasing to be seen in such a superior piece of kit but, at last, the real pleasure of Porsche's 911 turbo undoubtedly lay in driving it. The *raison d'être* of most four-wheel-drive cars has always been to improve traction on slippery surfaces but, with the turbo, there was so much torque that four-wheel drive had become a dry-road boon as well, helping to maintain a natural balance during hard cornering.

Under such conditions, no excessive physical effort was required at the wheel: the turbo's steering felt only slightly heavier than that of the rear-drive models. And you could do just about anything you liked with that car because it was so easy to anticipate its responses to driving input.

'Fabulous brakes,' I jotted in my notes, as a first snap judgement. It was astonishing how that car could wipe away speed at more than 1g without

the slightest loss of stability. I became convinced that if you needed to stop in a hurry you were better off in a current 911 than in any other car on the road.

Porsche's implementation of the latest ABS technology had become second to none but the telling difference between the turbo and its contemporary 'super 911s' was that the driver could relax in comfort when required. It was indeed a brilliant all-rounder, and stunningly fast. The combination of huge performance and driver-friendly manageability was unique in my experience.

From that point on, the 911 turbo just got better and the four-wheel-drive turbo layout was well-suited to the all-new, larger, water-cooled Type 996 range that came in from 1997 onwards. There was a short gap in turbo production before it got the 996 treatment but by the turn of the century the 911 turbo had become a truly outstanding car. Even the most hardened traditionally minded 911 enthusiasts began to admit that it might just be the pick of the 911 bunch for road use.

# Buying hints

**1.** If you've never owned a very high-performance car, the 911 turbo probably isn't the best place to start. Of all the Porsche road cars available, the 911 turbos can be the most expensive to maintain.

**2.** The early models were certainly the trickiest to drive. They felt ferociously quick in a straight line, especially the 3.3-litre versions, a sensation enhanced by turbo lag and the subsequent mighty kick in the back. The early 911 turbo was an homologation special which gave the factory an opening to race and rally 911s with many hundreds of horses. For road use, I have always felt that matters got slightly out of hand with this model. In fact, you always needed a lot of clean shirts handy if you were going to drive hard in any rear-wheel-drive 911 turbo.

**3.** Don't forget that several later 911s of the normally aspirated variety have been more powerful and faster as well as being a whole lot more user-friendly. And given a meandering country road, even a standard Carrera is a lot more fun to drive and often considerably quicker because the power is so much more usable.

**4.** Later four-wheel-drive 911 turbos were beautifully drivable and controllable, putting them in a completely different league. But I wouldn't care to be the recipient of a bill for the restoration of such a complex car, superb though it is.

**5.** So, my buying hint is simple: don't do it unless you have a very good reason for taking that path. Wealthy owners might want one or two turbos

to complete their Porsche collections, and such experts need no advice whatsoever from me.

**6.** That said, if you really do feel a deep personal need to go for an early 911 turbo, take all the usual steps. Join the Porsche Club Great Britain, meet existing owners, take your time and find a car that has never been wrapped round a tree and has a decent, checkable history. It's that 'never been wrapped round a tree' bit that needs special attention – and might be tricky.

**7.** To conclude on a positive note, a recent four-wheel-drive 911 turbo, one that has always been looked after by the original official Porsche Centre and still has an attractively low mileage, would make a very fine purchase for road use.

# *The* 959

*Porsche's dramatic unveiling at the 1983 Frankfurt show seemed like something out of science fiction. With 400bhp, four-wheel drive, six-speed gearbox, advanced electronics and a rumour of 200mph, the mysterious 'Porsche 911 Group B' caused a sensation. Neither the name '959' nor the price was mentioned, but the required 200 deposits for competition homologation were taken immediately. Production would begin early in 1984, Porsche said. (LAT)*

Helmuth Bott, one of Porsche's greatest engineers and the big chief behind the 959 project, said in 1986 that it was 'a car which demonstrates the abilities of the Weissach development team in every aspect of automobile design'.

That summed it up with neat precision. The essence of the extraordinary 959 was exactly that: under Manfred Bantle, the 'Father' of the 959 development team in Porsche factory language, every conceivable example of the latest technology was applied to it. The result was that, for some time, the Porsche 959 was undeniably the world's undisputed top supercar. The 959 was much faster than any other road car you could buy; but its superiority over other cars was more than a mere matter of speed.

The all-wheel-drive 200mph 911-based concept was first revealed at the Frankfurt show as a Group B competition prototype in 1983, and 200 deposits were soon accepted. Production would start early in 1984, we were told, but it wasn't that easy for

Porsche to deliver the goods: delays, as much the result of Porsche's shifting internal politics at that time as of the many problems of an engineering nature, meant it was at least three long years before road cars began to be delivered to the amazingly patient customers.

When that day came, in 1986, they were not disappointed. The 959 looked fabulous, it was outrageously quick, and it did everything that had been claimed for it. In the UK, we were told that the 959 would cost £155,266, that just 12 British owners had been accepted and that deliveries would be from March 1987.

Part of the challenge for those owners was learning how to get the best from their new cars: the 959 drove like no previous rear-engined car, nor any previous road car for that matter. It was already a proven winner, too, in that a simplified version had won the daunting Paris–Dakar rally first time out in 1984; in complete contrast, even though it was not really considered a race car, it was also adapted, with even more power, to be surprisingly successful at Le Mans.

As one of the fortunate few journalists invited to the 959 press launch at the new Nürburgring in 1986, I was fascinated by its many new features. First of all, however, the performance must not be forgotten. Even by today's standards, close on 200mph is indecently fast but it's easy to forget that this was more than 20 years ago. Even in modern company, the 959 remains a true supercar in that respect.

Engine response, with twin sequential turbos going a good way towards eliminating the dreaded lag, was superb, giving a smooth but mighty push in the back, especially from 4,000rpm up to the 7,500rpm rev limit. Speeds available in intermediate gears were 37mph, 64mph, 93mph, 127mph and 161mph, and a 959 could get very close to that 200mph mark on a level, straight road. In terms of acceleration, the 959 Sport could manage 0–60mph in 3.6 seconds and 0–100mph in 8.2 seconds.

Such figures make it sound like a

ferocious beast but in reality it was always controllable, luxuriously comfortable and, when driven slowly, docile and easy to handle around a crowded city. Such was its potential that most drivers, coming to it for the first time, simply could not get their head round its capabilities. When they found that its limits were way above anything they could understand, or even approach, they were awestruck.

In keeping with Porsche tradition, the 959 engine was a horizontally opposed six-cylinder. Based on Porsche's racing technology, it displaced 2,847cc and had four valves per cylinder, four camshafts, the twin turbochargers with two intercoolers, air-cooled cylinders and water-cooled heads, Bosch Motronic ignition and injection, and the customary dry-sump lubrication. It produced a massive 450bhp at 6,500rpm, with maximum torque of 370lb ft at 5,000rpm.

Driving a car with a six-speed gearbox, variable four-wheel drive, electronically-controlled differentials and programmable traction control was a completely new experience for most of us back in 1986. On the modern Nürburgring circuit I recall clearly the unaccustomed sense of the mighty 959 thinking for me at speed in

*Finally launched in 1986, the production 959 was faithful to the sensational design unveiled at the Frankfurt show in 1983, with the addition of air inlets around the nose and high in the rear arches. Easily the world's top supercar at the time, it was a technological landmark. (LAT)*

a slippery corner. It worked like magic, the controlled traction and massive torque making it incredibly quick out of corners, and it was extraordinarily safe.

Even so, it seemed a ponderous thinker to me at the time. You could actually feel it making all the right decisions as you planted your foot with the car loaded up in a corner. That was a new sensation at the time, but time has moved on. It's hardly surprising that better software has long since made such systems much sharper.

It was a similar story with the brakes. Thanks to four-pot callipers on big ventilated discs, they were incredibly powerful, stopping the car safely in astonishingly short distances, but the system could do strange things. The pedal felt dead and inconsistent when used hard: it also required a progressive technique. If you hit it fast yet with what seemed no more than usual effort, pedal travel could

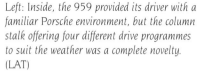

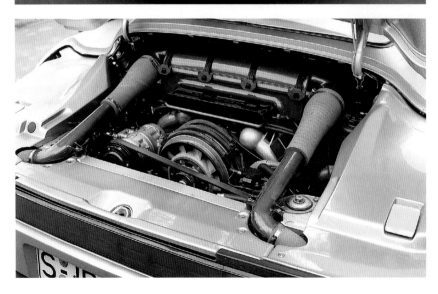

Left: Inside, the 959 provided its driver with a familiar Porsche environment, but the column stalk offering four different drive programmes to suit the weather was a complete novelty. (LAT)

Centre: The sleek body had a very low drag coefficient and lift at speed was eliminated. Once in a corner, the traction control was effective if somewhat ponderous by Porsche standards today. A technological tour de force in every way, the 959 made its drivers think afresh about long-established advanced driving techniques. It was a new world. (Motor/LAT)

Bottom: Concealed in its bay, the 959's 2.85-litre, 450bhp flat-six was based on race technology, but adjusted to run smoothly on 95-octane fuel. Sequential turbocharging gave a quick response from low revs and water-cooled heads meant that the cabin heating system was the best to date in a Porsche! (LAT)

occasionally be longer than expected, accompanied by a weird pumping action caused by an anti-lock system that seems primitive now. It still worked when that happened, even so, but it was rather alarming. The wise driver did not push his luck with ultra-late braking. In fact, our normal understanding of brake 'feel' is exactly what it lacked. Anti-lock brake systems have come on a lot since those early days, as have many other aspects of car technology.

Another surprise was to find that the 959 had no anti-roll bars in its suspension design, that task being performed by the damper software, we were told. There were double wishbones, coil springs and adjustable, speed-sensitive Bilstein dampers all round. It ran on the latest 17in hollow-spoke magnesium centre-lock wheels with tyre-pressure sensing built in. Rim size was 8in front, 9in or 10in rear and the tyres were Bridgestone RE71s. Steering was by rack-and-pinion with power assistance: stability was exemplary at all times.

With everything that had been packed into it, the fact that Porsche

# Porsche 959
## 1987–88

**ENGINE:**
Six-cylinder horizontally opposed, water-cooled heads, aluminium/magnesium alloy heads/blocks/crankcase; titanium rods and crankshaft; rear-mounted

| | |
|---|---|
| Bore x stroke | 95.0mm x 67.0mm |
| Capacity | 2,849cc |
| Valve actuation | dohc per bank, four valves per cylinder |
| Compression ratio | 8.3:1 |
| Induction | Bosch Motronic management; twin water-cooled, sequential KKK turbochargers; twin air-to-air intercoolers |
| Power | 450bhp at 6,500rpm |
| Maximum torque | 370lb ft at 5,500rpm |

**TRANSMISSION:**
Variable, programmable four-wheel-drive; six-speed manual gearbox

**SUSPENSION:**
*Front and rear:* Independent by double wishbones, coil springs (double at front), dual Bilstein electronically-adjustable dampers. Fichtel & Sachs hydropneumatic ride-height adjustment, speed-sensitive with override switch.
No anti-roll bars at first, this function being performed by automatic damper adjustments However, anti-roll bars were fitted, front and rear, to production models.

**STEERING:**
Rack-and-pinion, power-assisted

**BRAKES:**
*Front/rear:* Racing 956-type ventilated and cross-drilled discs (12.7in /12.0in)
Assistance by high-pressure hydraulics; four-channel Wabco-Westinghouse anti-lock system

**WHEELS/TYRES:**
Cast-alloy hollow-spoked wheels, 8in front and 9in or optional 10in rear; Denloc bead-retention and pressure-monitoring sender units
Tyres Bridgestone RE71: 235/45 VR 17 front and 255/45 VR 17 rear or optional 275/35 VR 17 rear (Later cars: ZR rating)

**BODYWORK:**
Steel monocoque coupé with aluminium doors and front bonnet and other panels in polyurethane, Kevlar, Aramid, glassfibre (RRIM or autoclave)
Left-hand drive only

**DIMENSIONS:**

| | |
|---|---|
| Length | 13ft 11.7in |
| Wheelbase | 7ft 5.4in |
| Track, front | 4ft 11.2in |
| Track, rear | 5ft 1in |
| Width | 6ft 0.4in |
| Height | 3ft 11.2in |

**WEIGHT:**
Comfort model: 28.5cwt (1,450kg)
Lightweight Sport model* 26.6cwt (1,350kg)

* Minus air con, ride height control, rear seats, most sound deadening and passenger door mirror

**PERFORMANCE:**
Lightweight Sport model
(Source: *Motor*)

| | |
|---|---|
| Max speed | 197mph |
| 0–60mph | 3.6sec |
| Standing quarter mile 11.9sec | |

**PRICE IN UK INCLUDING TAX WHEN NEW:**
Approximately £167,000 (personal import)

**NUMBER BUILT:**
292

kept the weight down to 1,450kg (28.5cwt) was impressive. In this version of the classic 911 coupé shape, the steel bodyshell had Aramid and Kevlar parts, aluminium doors and lids and a polyurethane front skirt.

Back in the mid-1980s, the 959 gave a clear look into the automotive technology of the future. There simply wasn't anything else like it. Advantages of the design included superior safety in accidents, an ability to turn into corners much more sharply than any front-engined car could, amazing traction, and the fact that the car remained so very stable in the corners. Despite all that power, it did not want to spin out.

A steering column stalk enabled drivers to select one of four transmission modes of traction control: Dry, Wet, Snow or Traction. Basically, 80 per cent of the drive went to the back wheels in normal dry conditions. Working through these modes, a greater percentage of the drive was sent to the front until you got to 'Traction', in which everything was locked 50:50 front/rear, to let the car crawl out of a slippery spot.

Transmission electronic controls were designed to ensure a smooth shift from one mode to another on the move and many foolproof systems were built into the 959 to stop drivers damaging the machine by their mistakes. To ensure a positive turn into corners, drive to the front was always reduced under braking.

An automatic/manual ride height control was fitted to the Comfort model but not to the Sport, which sat permanently on the low setting. Further, to make it as light as possible, the Sport model did not include air conditioning, electric window lifters or electric seat adjustment. It also had less soundproofing material. Accounts vary, but all these deletions from the specification produced a weight saving in the Sport model that was probably very close to 100kg, or roughly 2cwt.

Porsche's 959 remains an incredible machine to drive but it's important to remember that it's now a classic car from a couple of decades back. You only have to drive any 911 Turbo of recent years to realise that such later machinery, developed from all that groundbreaking 959 technology, actually does the job a whole lot better. The truth is that the 959 is relatively crude these days but, with every imaginable gizmo packed in, it was nothing short of mind-blowing in 1986.

Any 959 today should be preserved as a star exhibit in the motor house of the wealthy Porsche collector. As a technical tour de force, the 959 was way ahead of the game and that guarantees its status as one of the truly great classic cars of all time. It commands lasting, genuine respect. In the end, 283 were said to have been made but this figure was later revised to 292. Perhaps they should have charged a lot more for it but despite the unexpectedly long and costly development, the factory stuck to its word and did not raise the price. Porsche did not make money out of the 959 – it cost the factory a fortune, in fact – but it did make a lot of friends, quite apart from throwing the opposition into confusion.

# The 959 in competition

Intended for Group B rallying, the 959 seemed set to take the world by storm when the 1983 motor show concept car was first seen. Then three basic prototypes were entered in the 1984 Paris–Dakar, running with much-simplified four-wheel-drive systems and different 225bhp engines, to cope – it was said – with poor fuel in desert conditions.

Star driver Jacky Ickx, the inspiration behind the whole Porsche effort in that event, finished sixth after many minor problems but he played a good team game to the end,

*Paris-Dakar rallies, won by Porsche 959s in 1984 and 1986, proved invaluable for development. Jacky Ickx/Claude Brasseur, seen here, finished second in 1986 behind team-mates René Metge/Dominique Lemoine. Porsche engineer Roland Kussmaul, navigated by Hendrick Unger, was sixth in the third works entry. (LAT)*

supporting experienced Frenchman René Metge, who sailed through to win easily with the second car. The third entry, driven by Porsche engineers Roland Kussmaul and Eric Lerner, was there to back up the others. Despite that, and despite stopping several times to send Ickx back on his way, they finished 26th. It was a good start.

A year's development saw a team of much more advanced works 959s entered in the 1985 Paris–Dakar but all three retired, damaged, so the factory decided to use the Egyptian Pharaohs Rally to develop the cars further. By then the competition 959s had proper 400bhp engines and more advanced four-wheel-drive systems. This time, Ickx's car was destroyed early on when the turbos ignited the wiring and that in turn set the fuel ablaze.

The 959 that won by a large margin was driven by local rally champion Saeed al-Hajri, but it had been prepared by David Richards, the top outfit in that

line of work in England. His people had altered the wiring so that the heat from turbos couldn't harm it.

The many lessons learned meant that when Porsche returned to the Paris–Dakar in 1986 the latest 959, driven by René Metge again, won by two hours. Jacky Ickx, delayed again, finished second and Kussmaul, this time partnered by another colleague, Hendrick Unger, came sweeping in behind in sixth place. That was an emphatic achievement but there was to be no more rallying for the 959. The powerful, lightweight Group B rally cars had turned out to be much too dangerous to their crews and after other works teams suffered a number of grim accidents on special-stage events the entire category was abandoned by the FIA in favour of the simpler and safer Group A.

As far as rallying was concerned, therefore, those unexpected events meant the 959 was sidelined before it

could tackle the main events for which it had been designed. As 959 production had not even begun before Group B was banned from rallies, the required 200 cars had not been built and it was therefore not eligible to run as a Group B racer either. It was, however, adaptable to the Le Mans 24-hours, where it was able to run in the IMSA GTX class. Known as the Porsche 961, the 1986 Le Mans racing version of the 959 developed 640bhp at 7,800rpm and 465lb ft of torque at 5,000rpm.

Whereas the desert rally cars had been geared for a maximum of 145mph, the endurance-racing 961 had a theoretical top speed of 213mph. Other sources have suggested much higher potential speeds for the 961 but that's the factory's own figure. The problem was that aerodynamics held it down to 193mph in the first racing trim tried. Roland Kussmaul and his team adjusted the bodywork apertures so that that when it came to the race the

961 driven by René Metge and Claude Ballot-Lena proved good for 198mph on the straight. Despite an unscheduled pit stop after a tyre failure, which caused further damage, they finished as high as seventh overall and won the class.

Under those IMSA GTX rules, relatively narrow rims were required, and the 961 was restricted to 11in-wide rear wheels – hence that failure at Le Mans. Even so, an attempt was made in October in the final round of the 1986 Camel IMSA GT Championship, the Daytona 3-hours race. There the steep banking on the famous US track caused even more tyre trouble and a humiliating need to slow down for the sake of survival. Finishing in 24th place overall, it would have been better not to have gone there at all. It was not a great day for Porsche, all in all, for although 962s finished second, third, fourth, fifth and sixth, the outright winners were Bob Tullius and Chip Robinson in a Jaguar XJR-7. You can't win 'em all.

*Developed from the 959, the racing 961 proved surprisingly successful at Le Mans. Car 180, the works entry of René Metge and Claude Ballot-Léna, is seen here at the start of the 1986 24-hours. Having qualified 26th on the grid, they won the GTX class and finished a remarkable seventh overall. (Porsche)*

The final attempt at Le Mans for the 961 came in 1987 but ended in retirement when the transmission started playing up and the car spun off the track. Nobody really noticed, because Porsche won the race outright in fabulous style with a 962C Group C car.

For a rally car, the 959 had proved better than expected when adapted to endurance racing. But we should remember it not for that but for its outstanding victories in the desert and its invaluable contribution to safety in road cars. In the long run, that last point is perhaps the most important of all.

# The 924

*The first right-hand-drive 924s arrived in the UK early in 1977, this one being featured on the front cover of* Motor *in February. Its aerodynamically efficient design made the most of the 2-litre Audi engine's 125bhp. Fuel consumption was good and the car exceeded 120mph quite comfortably. It was expensive to buy but relatively cheap to run. (Motor/LAT)*

As an exercise in automotive engineering design, Porsche got it just right with the 924 and it has to be said that it did sell well from the start. Although VW and Audi parts were adapted for use in the 924, the design was Porsche's own. Some of the things they got wrong, however, had nothing to do with engineering, and those mistakes did this efficient little sports coupé no good at all.

It's a big stretch of the imagination, but just suppose British Leyland had designed the 924 as a replacement for the MGB GT in the early 1970s. The whole world would have heaped praise on it for the very good reason that it was fundamentally a fine car. But it was Porsche who launched the 924, rather than the ill-fated British combine, and – with the conspicuous exception of the UK – the company did not do the best possible public-relations job.

The negotiations with original partner Volkswagen dated back to the early 1970s and the initial intention had been for VW to sell the car as a VW

or perhaps as an Audi. Porsche's subsequent decision to go it alone was bold and it was not Porsche's fault that it took too long to get the 924 into production. Launched in Germany in November 1975, in a sense it paved the way for the bigger new front-engined Porsche, the V8-powered 928, a project that in fact had been started before the 924. The first right-hand-drive 924s began arriving in Britain in 1977.

At the root of the 924's trouble was the feeling that this relatively modest car was 'not a real Porsche', and too many people at the factory made little or no effort to overcome that. In some ways, it was indeed a fair point, for the original 924 had a four-speed gearbox, poor-quality rear dampers that soon went soft, and rear drum brakes that had a tendency to lock the left wheel. Steel wheels were standard, alloys being an optional extra.

Despite all that, there was nothing wrong with the car – except that greater things were expected of the Porsche name. Having committed themselves to the venture, however, that prejudice should have been overcome, probably by raising the specification of the car. Perhaps even that move would not have stopped the negative feeling about the 924 that came from certain factions within the factory itself. That was inexcusable, yet undeniable. Somehow, Porsche allowed the world to sneer at the 924 because the engine was said to come from a Volkswagen commercial vehicle. True, it wasn't that exciting an engine, especially in the higher part of the rev band, but it was tough, reliable and well up to the job.

On top of all that, Mazda priced its RX-7 very keenly for the American market, and the interesting rotary-powered rival damaged 924 sales there. A curious pricing anomaly then existed: in Britain, an important market for such cars, the 924 and the RX-7 were about the same price in 1978, at around £7,000. In the US, however, both cars were effectively cheaper but the incredible fact was that the RX-7 was half the price of the 924 on the other side of the Atlantic. The 924 was

Above: Despite a number of recognisable VW components, it looked reasonably like a Porsche inside the 924 and there was plenty of room in the front, thanks to the rear-mounted transaxle. The four-speed gearbox, as here, was standard but there was a five-speed option. A criticism was that the steering wheel was a little low and too far away. For racing, I had a six-inch column extension made. (LAT)

Below: The 924 was surprisingly quick across country but critics commented on the lack of sporting feel from its reliable 2-litre, overhead-cam engine – and sneered rather unfairly at the engine's roots. It came from an Audi saloon unit that in turn was derived from the VW LT light van engine, but don't knock that – it was tough and efficient! (LAT)

# Porsche 924/924 turbo/924 Carrera GT

## 1976–85/ 1978–82/1980–81

**ENGINE:**
Four cylinders in line, cast-iron block, light alloy head

| | |
|---|---|
| Bore x stroke | 86.5mm x 84.4mm |
| Capacity | 1,984cc |
| Valve actuation | sohc, two valves per cylinder |
| Compression ratio | 9.3:1/7.5:1/8.5:1 |
| Induction | Bosch K-Jetronic injection/idem plus KKK turbocharger, intercooled on Carrera GT |
| Power | 125bhp at 5,800rpm |
| | 170bhp at 5,500rpm* |
| | 210bhp at 6,000rpm |
| Maximum torque | 121.5lb ft at 3,500rpm |
| | 181lb ft at 3,500rpm* |
| | 203lb ft at 3,500rpm |

*Series 2 turbo engine, for 1981 model year, uprated to 177bhp (and 184lb ft at 3,500rpm) thanks to digital ignition and 8.5:1 compression ratio. Performance little changed but fuel economy improved by claimed 13 per cent

*Note: 1981 Evolution Carrera GT variants, the 245bhp GTS and 375bhp GTR, were intended for competition*

**TRANSMISSION:**
Rear-wheel drive; torque tube to rear-mounted Audi four-speed manual gearbox (optional VW three-speed automatic)
Porsche five-speed manual gearbox optional from 1978 and standard on turbo/Carrera; Audi five-speed standard on regular 924 from 1980

**SUSPENSION:**
*Front:* Independent by MacPherson struts; optional anti-roll bar (standard on 924 from 1981 model year and standard on turbo/Carrera).
*Rear:* Independent by semi-trailing arms and transverse torsion bars; telescopic dampers; anti-roll bar on turbo/Carrera.
924 turbo: stiffer dampers, stiffer rear torsion bars, stronger rear trailing arms, anti-roll bars standard front and rear, 911-type five-stud hubs

924 Carrera GT: lowered, stiffened and strengthened; altered steering geometry

**STEERING:**
Rack-and-pinion; unassisted

**BRAKES:**
*Front:* Disc (9.4in) on 924; ventilated disc (11.5in) on turbo/Carrera
*Rear:* Drum (7in) on 924; disc (7in) on turbo/Carrera
Servo assistance

**WHEELS/TYRES:**
Steel wheels, 5.5 x 14in or (optional) cast alloy 6 x 14in; later option of 15in wheels (924)
Alloy wheels, 6 x 15in or optional 16in (turbo)
Forged alloy wheels, 7J x 16in front and 8J x 16in rear (Carrera)
Tyres Dunlop SP 185/70 HR 14 (924); 185/70 VR 15 or optional 16in (turbo); Pirelli P7 205/55 VR 16 front and 225/50 VR 16 rear (Carrera)

**BODYWORK:**
Galvanised steel monocoque
Coupé 2+2
924 Carrera GT: special wide polyurethane front

wings and rear wheelarch extensions, prominent bonnet air-scoop, flush-fitting screen and special aerodynamic frontal treatment

**DIMENSIONS:**

| | |
|---|---|
| Length | 13ft 10in/14ft 2in (Carrera) |
| Wheelbase | 7ft 10.5in |
| Track, front | 4ft 7.8in |
| Track, rear | 4ft 6in |
| Width | 5ft 6.3in (excluding mirrors)/5ft 8in (Carrera) |
| Height | 4ft 2in |

**WEIGHT:**
924: 20.2cwt (1,026kg)
turbo: 23.7cwt (1,204kg)
Carrera: 19.7cwt (1,180kg)

**PERFORMANCE:**
(Source: *Motor*)

| | |
|---|---|
| Max speed | 121.3mph/140mph est/150mph est |
| 0–60mph | 8.2sec/7.0sec/6.5sec |
| Standing quarter-mile | 17.0sec/15.4sec/not quoted |

(924 figures for 4-speed manual car)

**PRICE IN UK INCLUDING TAX WHEN NEW:**
924 Coupé: £6,999 (February 1977)
turbo: £13,629 (January 1980)
Carrera: £19,211 (February 1981)

**NUMBER BUILT:**

| | |
|---|---|
| Coupé: | 121,510 |
| turbo: | 12,427 |
| Carrera GT: | 406 (plus 59 GTS and 19 GTR competition 'Evolution' models) |

# Porsche 924S
## 1985–88

As 924 except:

**ENGINE:**
Four cylinders in line, alloy block and head

| | |
|---|---|
| Bore x stroke | 100.0mm x 78.9mm |
| Capacity | 2,479cc |
| Compression ratio | 9.7:1/10.2:1 |
| Power | 150bhp at 5,800rpm 160bhp at 5,900rpm (1988 model year) |
| Maximum torque | 144lb ft at 3,000rpm 155lb ft at 4,500rpm (1988 model year) |

**STEERING:**
Power assistance optional

**BRAKES:**
*Front:* Disc, ventilated (11.1in)
*Rear:* Disc, ventilated (11.4in)

**WHEELS/TYRES:**
Alloy wheels, 6 x 15in; 16in wheels optional
Tyres 195/65 VR 15

**WEIGHT:**
23.1cwt (1,172kg)
22.9cwt (1,164kg) for 1988 model year

**PERFORMANCE:**
(Source: *Motor*)

| | |
|---|---|
| Max speed | 135.1mph 137.1mph (1988) |
| 0–60mph | 7.8sec/7.4sec (1988) |
| Standing quarter-mile | 16.1sec/15.7sec (1988) |

**PRICE IN UK INCLUDING TAX WHEN NEW:**
£16,040 (December 1985)
£21,031 (November 1987)
£23,649 (1988 model year 924S Le Mans)

**NUMBER BUILT:**
1985–87: 12,195
1988 model year: 4,079

---

in many ways a better car than its Japanese competitor, but not that much better.

The British concessionaires, led by John Aldington, realised that they had a task on their hands with the launch of the 924. The British boss himself had become an instant 924 fan when the first car arrived in Britain: he drove it home that night and found not only that it took no longer than the same journey in his 911, but that he had actually really enjoyed the drive.

The message about the new car had to be got across to the dealers as well as to the public. Aldington's PR chief, Mike Cotton, came up with the idea of a one-make championship for standard 924s, which would run for just one year. Each of the main dealers would run a car, paying recognised professional or semi-professional

*Opposite: The 924 Lux in late 1981. This car was tested over 12,000 miles by* Motor's *Jeremy Sinek, who pointed out the excellent way it had kept its value; although it had cost £10,020 with extras when new, it was still worth over £9,000 after a year. All 924s had been five-speed since late 1979. (Motor/LAT)*

drivers to take part. It worked: many of the top touring car drivers were signed up and the nine-race series produced close racing of high quality with relatively few of the body-smashing incidents so often associated with one-make races. It was also better-policed than many such race series as far as engine legality went, and that was extremely welcome. A couple of infringements in that line did occur and they were dealt with quickly – if rather too discreetly for some of us.

Before that championship was announced I became personally involved with the 924. At the time, very early in 1978, I was under contract to British Leyland, driving Broadspeed-prepared Dolomite Sprints in the British Saloon Car Championship. That contract did not exclude non-conflicting drives for others, so when Porsche Cars Great Britain Ltd approached me and asked me to try out a 924 on a circuit, I accepted readily. The object of the test was to run the car on a Dunlop intermediate race tyre, see how it stood up, and give an opinion on whether the cars were suitable for the proposed series.

The answer was positive – with

reservations about the brakes, which tended to get rather hot in racing conditions. That was my first experience of 924 driving and the car didn't feel that fast. I was surprised, however, at how incredibly quick the lap times were, given the modest output of the 2-litre engine. Clearly, this was a high-quality product at heart, being aerodynamically efficient and having fairly even front/rear weight distribution.

By that stage, Porsche's own five-speed gearbox, with first on a 'dog-leg', was a 924 option. It was a fine gearbox but the linkage was weak in this application and it didn't take long before the gearlever was leaning over at a strange angle, with gear selection impossible: we soon learnt that the only answer was long hours spent by the mechanics, grinding and polishing the linkage so that it became super-smooth. With that done, it did not snag and fail.

With a front-mounted engine and rear-mounted gearbox, and little weight in between, the 924 handled safely but rather like a weight-lifter's dumb-bell. It would understeer gently as it approached its surprisingly high roadholding limit and it needed a very

*Celebrating a double World Championship success in racing, the 'Martini' was a good-looking special edition of the 924 produced in January 1977. The suspension was uprated with anti-roll bars front and rear, and it had 6J x 14 alloy wheels. Inside it was finished off with attractive red and blue material worked into the seats and carpeting. (Porsche)*

sensitive touch to maintain it in that attitude.

Ultimately the tail would come out but that was quite harmless because there was no risk of losing control. It simply allowed the car to flop sideways briefly, which was annoying because vital forward motion was lost. Allowing that to happen, in a corner on a race circuit, produced a harmless twitch that was not alarming in any way; it just lost a great deal of time. It was extremely safe, therefore, but quite difficult to get the very best lap times from it.

Those of us used to putting a 911 very slightly sideways on entering a corner, and then applying throttle to drive through and away on a touch of opposite lock, found the 924 less satisfying to drive but it was certainly astonishingly quick for what it was. The

handling, for racing purposes, was a bit frustrating. During one test day I spotted some bags of cement behind the pits at Donington, so I 'borrowed' about 2cwt of the stuff, slid the passenger's seat forward and stuck the heavy bags inside for a couple of laps. This made the car more satisfying to drive because it took away that violent lurch from understeer to oversteer as the cornering limit was reached. Approaching the limit, the car became neutral: what it lacked then was sufficient power to take advantage of the stability provided by the more even weight distribution created by that cement.

No doubt acceleration suffered slightly with an extra 2cwt on board but the lap times were absolutely the same with or without it. I put the cement bags back where they came from and accepted that I would have to 'drive round' that little problem, as we say. I then convinced myself that, in this case for once, being tall was an advantage as it put my own weight lower and further back within the car. In fact, I have no doubt whatsoever that this gave me an edge, improving the balance of that 924 and of other

production cars that I have raced.

As a road car, the 924 was remarkably effective and efficient. On a fast, twisty road it was indecently quick for what it was on paper, regardless of the weather, and easily able to embarrass drivers of more powerful machinery. On a motorway, the quality of the body design and build meant there was very little wind noise at high speed. The overall gearing was also pleasantly just on the long side.

With its slippery shape and rugged if low-powered engine, this was a car that could exceed 125mph. Normal driving gave fuel consumption of about 30mpg, there were long service intervals, and the car was amazingly cheap to service, even at official Porsche dealers' workshops. Reliability was excellent, the only problems being those cheap rear dampers, which lasted only a few hundred miles at full efficiency, to be honest, and the fact that the spotlights tended to collect dirt and lose their earth.

The 0–60mph time of under 10 seconds was just respectable enough. For a sports car, the 924 had a huge luggage compartment under the glass rear window, and that space became truly vast if the backs of the occasional rear seats were folded down. Those rear seats were ideal and safe for children up to the age of about 10–12 years. Driving comfort was good except for the fact that with the seat slid back for tall drivers the steering wheel was too far away.

When Gordon Ramsay, then the official Porsche dealer in the North East, rang up and asked me to drive for his racing team in the 1978 Porsche 924 Championship, I accepted immediately. The first thing I did when we took delivery of the race-prepared car from Broadspeed was to have a 6in steering-column extension built by Gordon Ramsay Racing Team mechanic Tom Ferguson, so that I could drive it comfortably. It made a big difference.

My car had been prepared at Broadspeed, alongside Chris Craft's Lancaster Garages entry, by the same team of mechanics. To show how close the series was, we won six of the nine races but we only took pole position once and that was for the very last race, long after the championship outcome had been decided.

For the road, I have always felt that the 924 was basically a superb little car that was almost ruined by the PR disasters mentioned above. Despite steady improvements, the mud stuck to its name. The dampers were uprated in 1978 – although I still maintain that even then they were not that good. Then Audi's five-speed gearbox, reliable and easy to use, and with fifth in the conventional place, became standard in 1980, while there were countless other improvements to specification and quality over the years.

Some really great cars would eventually emerge from this line of development, but Porsche's front-engined four-cylinder cars never seemed to recover completely from the marketing setbacks of the early days of the 924. Although many of them did sell well enough in their day, perhaps the sales story would have been even better if, from the start, the 924 had been equipped with discs all round, a five-speed gearbox, better-quality dampers, alloy wheels – all as standard – plus a little more top-end power. That might have answered the critics who branded it, only slightly unfairly, as not being the real thing.

Be that as it may, the 924 remained in production until mid-1985, when it was replaced by the 924S, which was powered by Porsche's own

*The 1978 924 one-make championship was part of Porsche Cars Great Britain's successful British launch of the new car. The dealers all entered cars and attracted known saloon and sports car drivers to race them – and the author managed to win the championship. This is on the way to victory for the Gordon Ramsay team in a hectic race at Thruxton.*
(Author's collection)

counterbalanced 2.5-litre four-cylinder engine from the 944 (which is covered in another chapter). Announced back in 1981, the 944 was proving a success, and thus for the 924S the engine had to be detuned to 150bhp to save 944 owners from being humiliated.

The point was that the 924S had the 944's brakes and suspension but it retained the narrow body, without wheelarch extensions, and that meant that in a straight line it had the aerodynamic potential to be a faster car. In its final year the 924S was at last uprated to 160bhp, and by the time production ended in August 1988 the 924 was a very fine, fast, comfortable and economical little sports car.

Before we leave the 924 to rest in peace, I cannot resist telling the story of one unhappy customer. Hundreds of

*A smiling Rex Greenslade and Mike McCarthy (with stopwatch board) testing the new 140mph 924 turbo for* Motor *in January 1980. The exhilarating performance, they said, was at least the equal of many so-called supercars, proving that 'Germany sets the standard for sports cars in the 1980s'. (Motor/LAT)*

owners have allowed me to drive them round circuits in their own cars. I have only ever had one complaint and that was over 20 years ago. It came from a lady of about 60 who became speechless with rage after I had taken her round the old Nürburgring in her husband's 924.

We were at the classic German GP circuit, that spectacular spot in the Eifel mountains, as part of a trip organised for his customers by Gordon Ramsay, then still the Porsche dealer in Newcastle-upon-Tyne. I had been engaged for the day to 'chauffeur' the customers around the circuit, which I already knew extremely well from racing there.

After our lap, she complained to Gordon, accusing me of treating her with contempt by driving obviously slowly, 'because she was a grandmother,' even though she had specifically asked to be taken 'flat-out, as fast as possible'.

For once, I was speechless. Not far into our 12-mile lap, I had noticed that she seemed bored and irritable. As for me, I could feel my shirt getting wet: slightly irritated by her boredom, I had started to try really hard and was soon going absolutely as fast as that car could go.

She did not believe it. In fact, she was mightily displeased, to put it mildly. Afterwards I protested that I could not have gone any faster, not even to save my life. She thought I was some sort of wimp. I said that the 924 was like that, a very smooth car, and the fact was that I had not made a single mistake. I was tempted to add that a standard 924 couldn't pull the skin off a rice pudding, but I refrained from insulting her husband's car. Anyway, I had retained a sneaking respect for the 924 and was not about to start running it down.

I agreed to take her round again. As before, she seemed unimpressed at first. In fact, it was exactly the same all the way until we got to the flat-out top-gear Pflanzgarten roller-coaster section, at which point a German *hausfrau* in a lime-green Opel saloon – I can still see it now, very clearly – pulled across my path just as I was going to pass her. She was doing about 40mph. My speedo was showing over 115mph, so braking was out: I swerved by, over the blind crest and half on the grass, missing her by inches.

The ensuing fishtailing slide certainly engaged my attention but, as I collected it all together, I simply said, 'I hope you feel you've had your money's worth now'.

Would you believe it? That wicked old granny was still sitting there impassively. She spoke calmly. 'That was more like what I was expecting,' she replied. Good grief. Maybe she'd seen some rally driving on the telly.

Even as the standard 924 was going into production, Porsche was already planning a genuine high-performance version. Here would be the reassurance to satisfy most Porsche enthusiasts, even if some remained permanently unimpressed by all 924s: the 924 turbo was stylish, very quick, properly equipped with high-quality parts and very attractively priced. Announced early in 1978, production began for the 1979 model year and it reached British buyers about a year later.

Those who failed to appreciate its finer points, perhaps by its association with the efficient but less exciting standard 924, were missing out on a

Right: Based on the standard 924 engine, the 924 turbo produced 170bhp at 5,500rpm. The robust components handled that easily provided owners remembered not to switch off when the engine was very hot – a couple of minutes, ticking over, was all that was needed. I had two of these cars from new, covering over 20,000 miles. They felt like supercars, the throttle lag was easy to overcome, and they gave no trouble at all. (LAT)

Below: A new 924 turbo, probably seen in late 1979, when it first went on sale in the UK in right-hand-drive form at £13,629; it had been available in Germany for a year. This was not simply a 924 with a turbocharger – it was a fully re-engineered and very fine car in every respect. Note the five-stud wheels. (LAT)

very fine road car. It was distinguished in appearance from the standard car by four air-intake slots in the nose, a NACA duct in the bonnet for the turbocharger, high-quality five-stud 6J alloy wheels and a neat spoiler mounted at the back of the rear window. With that fitted, Porsche claimed the lowest drag coefficient of any production car at the time (0.35). It was easy to spot the differences, too. Such things matter in the market place.

Under the skin, the turbo was a very different machine from the normally aspirated 924. It had ventilated disc brakes all-round and a suspension package that was up to the job. Although the engine was at heart a modified 924 unit, only the block, crankshaft and conrods were retained.

In effect, this was a new engine, boosted by a KKK turbo mounted very close to the exhaust manifold on the underside of the heavily-canted block and head. It produced 170bhp at

5,500rpm and 181lb ft of torque at 3,500rpm, and there was no question about it: this gave the performance required. The 924 turbo was far from out of its depth in company with more expensive machinery such as Ferrari's 308 GT4, Maserati's Merak SS and Jaguar's XJ-S.

Once you got the turbo spinning, which was easy for any reasonably competent driver, the performance was superb: top speed 140mph, 0–60mph in 7.0 seconds and truly remarkable

*The few '924 Le Mans' special models of the 1981 model year that came to the UK were all snapped up instantly. Unlike many limited-edition cars, this model was genuinely attractive with its drag-reducing turbo spoiler, attractive alloy wheels, low-profile tyres, firmer suspension and special interior. All were finished in Alpine White. (Porsche)*

acceleration when using the right revs through the gears for overtaking at speed.

Fuel consumption was becoming ever more important, even at this end of the market, and the 924 turbo was outstandingly good, never dropping below 21mpg and in normal fast driving doing far better than that. Its 14-gallon fuel tank gave a range of 340–400 miles between stops.

I ran two of them in succession as regular road cars in 1981–82, thanks to the fact that I was then selling Porsches for Gordon Ramsay, for whom I had raced in 1978. The personal use of those 924 turbos was quite a perk. Technically they were demonstrators, of course, but I really enjoyed my road driving at that time, clocking up well over 10,000 miles in each of them.

Quiet and comfortable at speed, the 924 turbo had exceptional roadholding plus well-balanced handling. These qualities made long journeys over fast, twisty main roads something to relish. The turbo rode bumps well and gave a sense of effortless speed, partly thanks to its long gearing in all but first gear.

Speeds in gears were 35mph, 62mph, 91mph and 119mph. There was a mild engine boom at about 4,000rpm, corresponding to almost 100mph in fifth, but it was not unpleasant. To withstand the torque, the 924 turbo retained Porsche's own five-speed gearbox, with first on a dog-leg.

The car was no city-street hot-rod, however. In confined spaces the steering was a bit low-geared and the occasional need for first gear, the turbo lag and the firm low-speed ride were irritating in such conditions. The secret was to drive with cool dignity around town before enjoying the full potential on the open road. One soon got the hang of using the turbo boost to best advantage, which usually meant changing up at about 5,800rpm instead of hanging on to the red line at 6,500rpm.

My two 924 turbos were totally reliable, as were those of most of our customers, all of whom were very pleased with their cars. A few ran into trouble with premature turbo failure. But that was clearly the result of abuse, such as driving too hard on a cold engine or, even worse, getting it hot and then stopping and switching off immediately. It was also possible to damage the discs by failing to cool them off before stopping.

Respected journalists at the time started to suggest that the 924 turbo was giving us a glimpse of the supercar of the future. Back in the early 1980s, it seemed to prove that the days of the 911 were well and truly numbered. That was plain wrong, as things turned out, but the 924 turbo was a fine

machine which led to some even greater cars before Porsche finally dropped this line of development many years later. Although 924 turbo production ceased as long ago as mid-1982, that was far from the end of the story: nearly three years later, the 944 turbo arrived.

Today, these early 924 turbos don't rate highly as classics, being worth considerably less than, say, a late MGB, complete with those ugly rubber bumpers. Much as I understand the appeal of the old 'B', I know which I would rather be driving. Other factors holding 924 turbo values down today must be the potentially high cost of maintaining an old one and the fact that a later 944 is easier to find and likely to be a much better bet.

Special editions of the normally aspirated 924 appeared around then. Hugely better than earlier 924s, most were too sparingly available as well as being a bit late in the day. Some special-edition 924s were certainly attractive cars, notably the 'Martini' series in 1977 which commemorated Porsche's double World Championships in sports-car racing in Group 5 and Group 6. They were painted in the Martini colours over white, with luxury trim added.

Even better was the rare 'Le Mans special model' of the 1981 model year, which is probably forgotten now. This version celebrated the three works 924 GT prototypes which ran in the Le Mans 24-hours in 1980, and one of which I shared with Andy Rouse. The special road car was a long way off the specification of the works racers but it was still well worth having. Finished in Alpine White with a discreet all-round stripe in German colours and a luxury interior with a special steering wheel, it differed from the standard car in having sports dampers, anti-roll bars front and rear, special turbo-like 6J x 15 alloy wheels (albeit still with four studs), and a turbo rear spoiler. This came very close to the specification I thought the standard 924 should have had from the start. We were allowed three to sell from the dealership: all were sold with two hours of the announcement, long before the actual cars arrived.

In summer 1985 the original 2-litre standard 924 was dropped after 137,500 had been made. It was replaced in September of that year by the 924S, with the 944's 2,479cc engine, in 150bhp form, and 944-style high-quality suspension parts. Well-balanced, superbly built, economical and pretty quick (top speed 137mph, 0–60mph in 7.4 seconds), here truly was the kind of 924 that diehard Porsche enthusiasts had expected the company to produce a decade earlier. A Le Mans special edition based on the 924S should not be confused with 1980's 924 Le Mans model mentioned above. The 924S was a very attractive 'entry-level' Porsche in every way except, unfortunately, its price. It cost about £15,000 in the UK, which was

well over the price of its one-time rival, Mazda's RX-7, which by that stage cost about £11,500. With improvements two years later, including the 160bhp engine, the 924S became an even better car, but its UK prices started at about £22,000 (and no less than £23,649 for that 924S Le Mans special edition) when the model was discontinued in August 1988. Expensive? Outrageously so, even if it was a very good car.

But if the 924S was the most rounded of the range, it seems appropriate to end this chapter with a look at a special variant that was effectively a minor-league supercar. In 1979 Porsche had indeed decided to give the 924 the full treatment – and when the incredible 924 Carrera GT appeared at the Frankfurt show, in

'THE 924S', *reads the registration plate, and it was exactly that in this remarkable* Motor *road test photograph of November 1987. Late in the 924's life, the engine was uprated to 160bhp, pushing top speed close to 140mph. With its narrower body, it confused people by being faster than a 944. Better than ever? Sure. Testers' verdict? 'For what it offers, this car is too much money.' The very last 924S models, after this, had the 944-style rear diffuser.* (Motor/LAT)

*New engine, new gearbox, new suspension: some felt the new 924S, seen as tested by* Autocar *in February 1986, at last had the specification that the 924 should have received from the start in order to merit its Porsche badge. The five-stud wheels, similar to the 928's, indicate a most superior 924, powered by Porsche's own 2,479cc engine tuned down to 150bhp.* (Autocar/LAT)

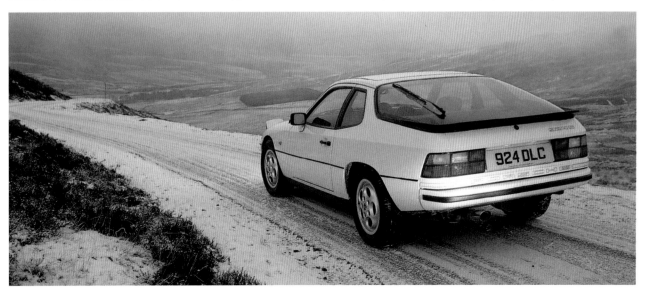

Opposite: The 924 Carrera GT, produced for 1981 and seen here with earlier Carreras, was an astonishing performer, well worthy of the name with its 210bhp engine, butch looks, nimble handling and 150mph performance. Little wonder that my sponsor, Geoff Fox, had his brand new road car nicked from outside our hotel when we went to Monza for me to race Richard Lloyd's 924 Carrera GTR. Geoff's fabulous car, of which only 406 were made, was never seen again. (LAT)

Above: Porsche publicity photograph from 1980 shows the special wheelarches and bonnet scoop of the new 924 Carrera GT. Wide wheels were used, 7J x 15 being standard, but options included 16in wheels with 7J rims front and 8J rear. (Porsche)

Right: So this was an LT light van engine? Don't make me laugh. Yes, the 924 Carrera GT engine was based on the same major components as the modest 924 but it was one tough engine, well up to producing a reliable 210bhp for road use like this. Racing versions produced around 350bhp, it was said, and that certainly felt an honest claim on the track. (Porsche)

September of that year, 924 critics were knocked sideways.

This was no cynical special edition with a pretty paint job. It was the real thing, as if some hard nut at the factory had said 'OK, if we really have to do the 924, let's show 'em.' The 924 Carrera GT had all the style of an aggressive street-fighter and it offered genuine supercar performance. Available in black or Guards Red, with 'Carrera' embossed on the front right wing, only 406 were to be made, 75 of those in right-hand drive and available in the UK for £19,210 on the road.

A few months later, two even hotter versions were offered, both intended for serious competition drivers and

Le Mans pit-stop, 1980, with the works 924 Carrera GT Prototype: I am handing over to co-driver Andy Rouse. We finished 12th overall despite valve trouble for the last 10 hours. This car differed considerably from production GTR racers and, beware, there is a fake out there somewhere; the genuine car remains concealed in the factory's museum! (Jeff Bloxham)

# Buying hints

**1.** This may be the 'cheap' Porsche but it's still a Porsche and some parts will be expensive. There are 924s on eBay for a few hundred pounds these days and most of them must be MoT failures. If you buy one of these, don't worry if the engine is wrecked as you can get the VW-based straight four rebuilt relatively cheaply. It's the condition of everything else that matters, especially the body.

**2.** All the obvious things apply. Has it been repaired after a crash and is it rusty? What's the trim like inside and how much will it cost to put that right? As ever, join the Porsche Club of Great Britain and have a chat with the 924 Register Secretary. He'll know whether there any 924 specialists near you and they can tell you the likely cost of any work.

**3.** Bear in mind that you may well decide that a slightly younger 944 is a better car for not that much more money. A pure 924 does have its own charm, however, and if you're really set on getting one it's best to take your time and search for one of those rare cars that has been perfectly maintained and kept in the right conditions. Find that car, look after it

and you'll be surprised at how enjoyable it is to drive and how little it costs to maintain compared with other classic sports cars.

**4.** However good a nice original 924 is, you'll still have some work to do. Most 924s, especially the early ones, had pretty poor dampers as original equipment. They were just not good enough, so you'll need to choose a set that works better and lasts longer.

**5.** A 924 turbo was a far faster car with superior suspension, braking and transmission. Even if the bodyshell is totally sound, one of these could cost a fortune to put in proper working order if everything else is ruined. They were great cars to drive but you really must just walk away from the wrong one now.

**6.** Not all 924s were inexpensive and a few are very valuable now. A Spanish enthusiast contacted me recently to say that he'd been offered the 1980 924 Carrera GT Prototype that I drove at Le Mans. Somebody wanted a lot of money. We established that the real car still belongs to the factory and remains hidden away. Take care!

definitely not meant for road use. The GTS, only in red, cost about £27,500 from the factory (ie before tax, import duty and so on). It had more air intakes, glass-covered lights instead of pop-ups, plus side and rear windows in lightweight plastic. A mere 59 were made. The even more extreme GTR cost a basic £34,600 from the factory (almost £40,000 tax-paid in the UK), and just 19 were produced. Remember that the original Porsche 924 of 1976/77 produced 125bhp and had a top speed of 126mph, with 0–60mph in 9.7 seconds. Porsche then produced the civilised and impressive 924 turbo in 1978 and the 924 Carrera GT was based on that. For the GT, the compression ratio was raised from 7.5:1 to 8.5:1, the turbo boost went from 0.65bar to 0.75bar, and a large intercooler was fitted.

This engine did not give much below 4,000rpm but after that there was tremendous performance available, with 210bhp at 6,000rpm and a rev limit of 6,600rpm. In this form the 924 looked, felt, sounded and went like a serious sports car. The Carrera GT sold out in no time, the entire UK allocation being spoken for long before the first one arrived in the country. Top speed was 150mph, with 0–60mph in 6.5 seconds. The competition versions, the GTS and GTR, developed 245bhp and up to 375bhp respectively, offering top speeds of over 155mph and up to 175mph for private teams wishing to compete in races or rallies at various levels.

It's still a shockingly brutal car to look at, the 924 Carrera GT, but the styling is hard to fault. It's one of those cars that looks exciting when it's parked, thanks to those broad front wings, special aerodynamic nose, large bonnet scoop and wide rear wheelarch extensions. At the same time, being built around the very practical 924 theme, the Carrera GT is a sensible car for daily use or long journeys. As with all 924s, there is that huge luggage area, for a sports car at least, which becomes amazingly capacious if the occasional rear seats are folded flat. The 924 Carrera GT looks low, squat and purposeful and it feels it on the road. It offers that hard-to-define quality of excellent driver involvement, and there's a kind of raw appeal without harshness in both the looks and the driving experience. Since those days, cars have been developed to take advantage of more modern tyres, sophisticated suspension geometry, better brakes and dampers, plus all manner of electronic stuff, but this 1980 machine with a 1,984cc four-cylinder engine is still marvellously quick.

The standard seats are set low in the cabin and the driving position is very good except that, for taller drivers, as in all early 924s, the steering wheel is too far away and there's no fore-and-aft adjustment. That can be overcome: that special steering column extension I had built for my successful 924 racer in 1978 wasn't hard to do.

Driving the standard 924 Carrera GT, first gear is on that 'dogleg' but the lever is easily shifted and, on the move, the top four gears are a pleasure to

use. First is quite low, giving just 39mph, but 70mph is available in second, 102mph in third, 133mph in fourth and a genuine 150mph in fifth. Despite such high performance, typical fuel consumption is 22–25mpg. It's true of all 924s that the performance figures don't tell the full story. All of them are much faster cars across country than their figures suggest and that holds true for the Carrera GT, which is powerful enough for throttle control to become a factor in the handling.

Predictable and responsive when driven hard, the GT has no nasty vices if you have to lift off. Dry-weather grip was amazing in its day, though some complained of too much understeer in the wet. But this was always a stable car, and the brakes are also extremely good for a car of those days. The ride is sportingly firm, and there's some engine and road noise inside but again, like all 924s, wind noise is very low even at the highest speeds. This car is a high-quality product, no doubt about that.

Probably the best-handling car I have ever raced was the works 924 Carrera GT prototype that I shared at Le Mans with Andy Rouse in 1980. It was a three-car team and it's often said that those cars were GTRs. That is not strictly correct for they had one-piece front

bodywork and a different and immensely stiff chassis construction. Later I shared Richard Lloyd's superbly prepared racing GTR in major international events with much pleasure and some good results. It was quick but it never had quite the same feel as that 1980 factory-entered prototype.

For road use, then or now, the standard 924 Carrera GT really did come close in spirit and feel to those much faster racers. Without doubt, it has always been one of the most attractive sports coupés around. In some ways it was too attractive. The principal sponsor of the Gordon Ramsay Racing Team at that time was customer and friend Geoff Fox. He and I went to Monza, where I was to drive Richard Lloyd's car in the 1,000Km race, and Geoff's lovely new 924 Carrera GT was pinched from the hotel during the night. Those Carrera GTs were always at high risk from the sort of low-lifers who steal cars. We never saw it again.

*The author at the old Nürburgring with Richard Lloyd's Canon-sponsored 924 Carrera GTR in the 1982 1,000Km. Lloyd and the author, with Hans Volker, finished fifth overall and first in the IMSA GTO category. (LAT/Jeff Bloxham)*

# The 928

The number plate was misleading! A dozen years after its introduction, the 928 became a serious car for the enthusiast. The 171mph 928 GT, introduced in the summer of 1989, is seen here on test with Autocar & Motor. The magazine's short verdict: 'Sacrifices refinement for excitement'. (Autocar & Motor/LAT)

The 928? What are we to make now of the dear old 928? It appeared in a glorious blaze of publicity in 1977, winning the international title of *Car of the Year* 1978. That particular title was all the more valuable because it almost invariably went to some worthy, affordable family saloon.

The writing really seemed to be on the wall for the 911 when the 928 came along. This svelte newcomer from Stuttgart – and it did seem that way then – had a big 4.5-litre V8

engine, producing 240bhp at first. Obviously, it would be well able to develop the power required and meet emissions legislation for years to come. And, we all thought, with its front-mounted engine it would always pass the crash tests that we feared the 911 might shortly be failing.

The 928? It was a Porsche, folks, but not as we had known them and learnt to love them. The world was changing, we had to keep up, and that meant getting used to the idea of no more new 911s. We had all been

*Right: The original 928's water-cooled, 4,474cc, 90-degree V8 engine had belt-driven camshafts, hydraulic tappets, two valves per cylinder and a compression ratio of 8.5:1. Running on regular fuel and producing 240bhp, the engine was reliable and there was plenty of scope for further development. Top speed was 143mph. (LAT)*

*Below: An early left-hand-drive 928 in 1977. With a V8 engine in the front, this was an entirely new kind of Porsche. Its design, modern construction and advanced features, including the 'Weissach' axle system, won it the 'Car of the Year' title for 1978. (LAT)*

brainwashed to think that way and we were, of course, completely wrong.

The 928 was perceived as an example of very modern engineering and styling in the 1970s, and the patented 'Weissach axle' rear suspension attracted particularly favourable publicity. After years of fighting accusations of sudden oversteer in their rear-engined cars, Porsche was determined that no such problem would afflict its first big front-engined model. The 928's rear suspension design incorporated anti-toe-out geometry that successfully reduced abrupt oversteer on lift-off during cornering.

Other notable details of the design were the transaxle rear-wheel drive, the integrated plastic-clad impact-absorbing bumpers, the strong steel bodyshell that was hot-dip galvanised on all surfaces and the use of aluminium for the doors, bonnet and front wings.

Despite the 928's glittering start, Porsche rapidly got into a muddle over the 928 project, it seems to me; before very long, it became a confused mission. Conceived as a flagship model, and probably the 911's replacement given time, early 928s were sold to many customers who had

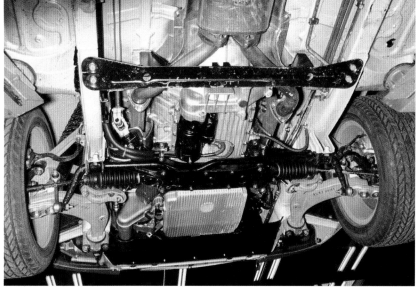

Above: Most 928s were automatics, many customers feeling that this better suited the high-performance mile-eater. The so-called 'op-art' seat panels seem a curious item of fashion history now, and not unattractive, but they were controversial at the time and the US importers got them dropped from the American market as soon as possible. (LAT)

Left: Looking under the front of an early 928 shows how neat this design was from the start, with all vulnerable items kept well out of harm's way. The gearbox, not seen here, was a transaxle between the rear wheels – five-speed manual or three-speed automatic. (LAT)

# Porsche 928
### 1977–82

**ENGINE:**
V8, aluminium block and heads, water-cooled; front-mounted

| | |
|---|---|
| Bore x stroke | 95.0mm x 78.9mm |
| Capacity | 4,474cc |
| Valve actuation | sohc per bank, two valves per cylinder |
| Compression ratio | 8.5:1 |
| Induction | Bosch K-Jetronic injection |
| Power | 240bhp (DIN) at 5,000rpm (from late 1981 5,250rpm) |
| Maximum torque | 257lb ft (DIN) at 3,600rpm (from late 1981 280lb ft) |

**TRANSMISSION:**
Rear-wheel drive; torque tube to rear-mounted five-speed manual gearbox; optional three-speed Mercedes-Benz automatic

**SUSPENSION:**
*Front:* Independent by double wishbones and coil-sprung MacPherson struts; anti-roll bar
*Rear:* Independent by lower wishbones, upper transverse links with patented Porsche-Weissach axle geometry, and coil-spring struts with double-acting dampers; anti-roll bar

**STEERING:**
Rack-and-pinion, power-assisted

**BRAKES:**
*Front:* Discs, ventilated (11.1in)
*Rear:* Discs, ventilated (11.4in)
Servo assistance

**WHEELS/TYRES:**
Alloy wheels, 7J x 16in
Tyres Pirelli P7 225/50 VR 16 or optional 215/60 VR 15 (standard from late 1981)

**BODYWORK:**
Galvanised steel monocoque with alloy doors, bonnet, front wings
GT 2+2-seater

**DIMENSIONS:**
| | |
|---|---|
| Length | 14ft 7in |
| Wheelbase | 8ft 2.5in |
| Track, front | 5ft 1in |
| Track, rear | 5ft 0.3in |
| Width | 6ft 0.3in (excluding mirrors) |
| Height | 4ft 3.8in |

**WEIGHT:**
28.9cwt (1,468kg)

**PERFORMANCE:**
(Source: *Motor*)
| | |
|---|---|
| Max speed | 140mph |
| 0–60mph | 7.0sec |
| Standing quarter-mile | 15.2sec |

(manual car)

**PRICE IN UK INCLUDING TAX WHEN NEW:**
£19,499 (October 1978)

**NUMBER BUILT:**
17,669

# Porsche 928S/ 928 S2
### 1979–1983/1983–86

As 928 except:

**ENGINE:**
| | |
|---|---|
| Bore x stroke | 97.0mm x 78.9mm |
| Capacity | 4,664cc |
| Compression ratio | 10.1:1/10.4:1 |
| Power | 300bhp (DIN) at 5,500rpm 310bhp at 5,900rpm |
| Maximum torque | 283.5lb ft (DIN) at 4,500rpm 295lb ft at 4,500rpm |

**WEIGHT:**
928S: 32.3cwt (1,640kg)*
928 S2 30.3cwt (1,537kg)

* *Motor* figure, with fuel for 50 miles. Porsche quotes kerb weight as 1,450kg

**PERFORMANCE:**
(Source: *Motor/Autocar*)
| | |
|---|---|
| Max speed | 155mph/158mph |
| 0–60mph | 6.2sec/6.2sec |
| Standing quarter-mile | 14.2sec/14.5sec (manual car) |

**PRICE IN UK INCLUDING TAX WHEN NEW:**
928S: £25,251 (April 1980)
928 S2: £30,679 (May 1984)

**NUMBER BUILT:**
928S: 8,315
928 S2 and S3: 14,347

# Porsche 928S4/GT
### 1986–91/1989–91

As 928 except:

**ENGINE:**
| | |
|---|---|
| Bore x stroke | 100.0mm x 78.9mm |
| Capacity | 4,957cc |
| Valve actuation | dohc per bank, four valves per cylinder |
| Compression ratio | 10.0:1 |
| Power | 320bhp (DIN) at 6,000rpm 330bhp at 6,200rpm |
| Maximum torque | 317lb ft (DIN) at 3,000rpm 317lb ft at 4,100rpm |

**BRAKES:**
*Rear:* Discs, ventilated (11.8in)
ABS standard

**WHEELS/TYRES:**
Alloy wheels, 7J x 16in front and 8J x 16in rear; 7.5J/8J x 16in front and 9J x 16in rear (GT)
Tyres 225/50 VR 16 front and 245/45 VR 16 rear; Dunlop D40 225/50 ZR 16 front and 245/45 ZR 16 rear (GT)

**BODYWORK**
Detailed changes all round included a larger rear wing, the whole effect reducing the Cd from 0.39 to 0.34 or 0.352, depending on the positioning of the automatically controlled engine-cooling duct

**WEIGHT:**
S4: 30.9cwt (1,571kg)
S4 Clubsport: 28.5cwt (1,450kg)
GT: 30.8cwt (1,564kg)

**PERFORMANCE:**
(Source: *Motor/Autocar*)
| | |
|---|---|
| Max speed | 164mph (S4 auto)* 168mph (S4 manual)* 165mph (GT) |
| 0–60mph | 6.4sec (S4 auto) 5.6sec (GT) |
| Standing quarter-mile | 14.9sec (S4 auto) 13.8sec (GT) |

*Porsche figures

**PRICE IN UK INCLUDING TAX WHEN NEW:**
S4: £48,935 (December 1986)
GT: £64,496 (January 1991)

**NUMBER BUILT:**
17,894 (including Clubsport models)

# Porsche 928 GTS
### 1992–95

As 928GT except:

**ENGINE:**
| | |
|---|---|
| Bore x stroke | 100.0mm x 85.9mm |
| Capacity | 5,397cc |
| Compression ratio | 10.4:1 |
| Power | 350bhp at 5,700rpm |
| Maximum torque | 362lb ft at 4,250rpm |

**BRAKES:**
*Front:* Disc, ventilated (12.7in)

**WHEELS/TYRES:**
Alloy wheels, 7.5 x 17in front and 9 x 17in rear
Tyres 225/45 ZR 16 front and 255/40 ZR 16 rear

**WEIGHT:**
30.9cwt (1,600kg)

**PERFORMANCE:**
(Source: *Autocar*)
| | |
|---|---|
| Max speed | 168mph |
| 0–60mph | 5.4sec |
| Standing quarter-mile | 14.1sec |

**PRICE IN UK INCLUDING TAX WHEN NEW:**
£64,998 (September 1992)

**NUMBER BUILT:**
2,831

previously owned Porsche's great rear-engined cars. Looking back on it in 2003, John Aldington, the former MD of Porsche Cars Great Britain, recalled how he had taken a different tack. 'We never promoted the 928 as a sports car,' he told me. 'After all, the 911 was still being made and that was the sports car. The 928 was a GT.'

Fair enough, but can we be sure that Aldington's view was shared wholeheartedly in the boardroom at Stuttgart? Years before, it must have taken a great deal of nerve from the board members when they committed the company to this massive project at the height of an international crisis but once the car had been in production for a couple of years that resolve did not seem to be quite so firm.

John Aldington was a wise and intelligent man and it saddens me that he died before this book came out. A small point recalled by him the last time we spoke was a dispute with the factory regarding sunroofs for 928s. The main problem, as the British concessionaires saw it, was that the company was dominated by engineers who always insisted they were right and expected customers to toe their line of logic. This was true even of small details: in the case of the 928, the engineers had dictated a low roofline for aerodynamic reasons. Most British GT customers expected a sunroof but that low roof rather restricted the headroom. The

engineers' answer was that a sunroof was not necessary because the car had air conditioning. This was not a German attempt at humour: they meant it.

British Porsche sales teams had a slightly harder time because of that but, even so, the new car did sell reasonably well. Some customers liked them very much but, for sure, some did not. There was a fair bit of that misjudged salesmanship in the showrooms, with 928s being sold inappropriately to loyal Porsche customers who were really diehard 911 enthusiasts.

A serious step in the right direction did come with the updated 928 S, introduced for the 1980 model year as an addition to the range. With the engine enlarged to 4.7 litres, and power raised to 300bhp, the 928 was given the true high performance expected of a model that purported to be some sort of flagship for the marque. Not only could the much more sporting 928 S manage about 155mph, the acceleration (especially in rare manual models) at last felt stunningly quick and, to top it all in best Porsche tradition, there was a marked improvement in fuel consumption, as much as about seven per cent in typical use. The standard 4.5-litre 928 was not dropped until late 1982. A year later, in 1983, the 928 S2 was announced, the differences being a small increase in power to 310bhp and

the fitting of ABS anti-lock brakes, normally then an expensive extra, as standard on all 928s.

When the 911 did not die away it seems that Porsche had the good idea of selling 928s to a new kind of Porsche buyer. For some years, accordingly, it was developed into an ever softer grand touring machine. The years ticked by and the 928 was steadily modernised, but meanwhile the core of its basic design steadily slipped out of date.

Much later on Porsche suddenly surprised us all by giving the 928 a complete change of character, when it launched the 928 GT. Out went the old man's comfortable tourer and in its place came a firmly-sprung, aggressively powerful sports model. In that guise the 928 became a mighty road burner, and surprisingly good fun for press-on drivers. Proving the point, the 928 GT was a car chosen by former Grand Prix driver Jonathan Palmer, who definitely never liked wallowing barges for road use.

But let's look at the 928 driving experience in a bit more depth. Throughout the 1980s I raced a couple of standard 928s for AFN and the story of those cars reveals much about the character of this once-mighty GT machine. The idea behind racing the 928 in British Porsche Club events, from AFN's point of view, was probably not so much to win as to demonstrate that their comparatively big, luxury machine could hold its own among the 911s. There was a real danger in those days of it being seen as a bit soft.

The highlight of the 1983 season was the Willhire 24-hours race at Snetterton when I was joined by the strong team of Andy Rouse, Win Percy and Phil Dowsett – a good bunch of real winners. First qualifying was in the dark on Friday night, and there was a rainstorm. The opposition was demoralised when I put the AFN 928 on provisional pole by the huge margin of five seconds. The 928 S2 was genuinely a great car in the wet, but even in the dry, for the final session the next morning, I qualified our car over two seconds clear of the field.

Andy took the start of the race,

Opposite: 'The 928 that goes like a Porsche should,' they wrote. On the high-speed bowl at Millbrook test track, here is a 928 S under test with Motor early in 1980. With the engine enlarged to 4.7 litres, and producing 300bhp, top speed was raised to 156mph with this model. Manual transmission, as fitted to this car, became slightly more popular with buyers of Porsche's smooth and sophisticated supercar. (Motor/LAT)

Upper right: On the 928 production line, a completed bodyshell being lowered for attachment to a fully-assembled drivetrain and suspension. This procedure was impressively quick. (LAT)

Lower right: I took this snap, showing a 928 drivetrain assembly on its trolley, during a factory visit in the mid-1980s. What I like about it now is that it also shows leading journalists of those days, including Denis Jenkinson (left foreground) and LJK Setright (right), both no longer with us. (Author)

Below: Another of my own photos from that mid-1980s factory visit. As the 928s came off the production line they were driven briskly at a steady pace over what looked like a pair of ladders bolted to the concrete. In fact, this rumble strip settled the suspension prior to final adjustments. (Author)

Left: Ferry's Porsche 75th birthday present from the factory was this one-off four-seater 928 S. He is seen receiving the car at his home on 19 September 1984, surrounded by Porsche company top brass. (Porsche)

Below: In 1988 and 1989 I raced this 928 S4 SE manual for AFN in the British Porsche Championship. Once handling guru Rhoddy Harvey-Bailey had sorted the damper and spring rates for racing, it was a pretty handy circuit car. It could take pole occasionally but, with standing starts, there were usually half a dozen of those damned quick 911s ahead of it before the first corner! I do remember that this 928, however, was especially good in the wet. (Chris Harvey)

coming round well in the lead at the end of lap one, steadily pulling away, and that's how it continued. I shall never forget crossing the finishing line a day later, and seeing the crowds waving from both sides of the Norfolk circuit. It wasn't exactly Le Mans but it remains the only 24-hour race that I have won outright, and I treasure it!

Most of our races were effectively sprints, however, and the 928's problem was that it could put up a good time in practice only to be left behind by the rear-engined 911s at the standing starts. It didn't matter how well you got away in the 928, you were likely to find some 911s ahead of you at the first corner. Then the hard work began but we did win some races with the S2.

After that, in the mid-1980s my Porsche racing was mainly in the classic 911 2.7RSL mentioned in an earlier chapter. Meanwhile the 928 S2 continued in production with regular minor improvements. However, I returned to AFN and a 928 in 1988–89, driving the latest S4 SE. Non-Americans, by the way, sometimes wonder what the 928 S3 was because it was not seen outside the US. In the later days of the S2, Porsche put a catalytic converter on the 4.7-litre engine, as required for that market's emission regulations, and restored performance with four valves per cylinder and two camshafts per bank.

That was the S3, and the S4 – launched for the 1987 model year – inherited the quad-cam four-valve arrangement, only with the engine capacity enlarged to 4,957cc, this giving an output of 320bhp and better low-down torque.

Back home in England, the new S4 proved a much trickier beast on a circuit than the S2 had ever been, at first anyway. The problem was twofold: first; the suspension was inclined to develop an up-and-down motion at speed; second, the ABS system was too keen to interrupt braking effort whenever the suspension was on one of its 'up' strokes, so to speak.

Testing the brand-new standard S4 SE at Snetterton I found that this combination of problems meant that, about one in ten times, the car would end up flying into corners 20mph too fast. It was unpredictable and I had to spin it a couple of times during that initial day's testing, just to get out of trouble. After disabling the ABS system, I was able to lap consistently but it still didn't feel right.

The team went away, scratched their heads and fitted much stiffer springs and dampers; but that only made it much worse, as a later test proved. At that point I insisted on calling in handling guru Rhoddy Harvey-Bailey. After analysing it, he went back to the much softer springs and specified revised damper rates. He did his best to explain that the problem was caused by an incompatibility between the spring rates and damper rates, exacerbated by a further incompatibility with the software in the ABS braking system.

While he spoke of compatible frequencies I tried to look intelligent; as soon as I drove the car, I realised that he had solved the problem completely. Our AFN S4 SE was transformed, but although we took pole several times, the 911s were stronger than ever in British Porsche Club racing by then and we never got a single win with that 928. Our one big chance came at Phoenix Park in Dublin where we looked set to win in the wet but the sun came out, the circuit dried, and I was picked off one by one by a string of 911 men.

About that time, I remember that one of AFN's customers complained about his new S4 SE. Although he was unaware of our secret tweaks, he could have been describing the race car before we installed Rhoddy's special dampers. Our 928 racers were all manual cars, I should add, but most customers bought automatics for the road and that, I felt, would make the problem feel even worse.

Even so, the sales people at AFN asked me whether I would have a word with their customer and put him right on his driving technique. I replied that there was nothing to suggest any fault with the man's driving; he had been remarkably clever to identify the real problem accurately. The best thing, I said, would be to offer him a new set of our special dampers.

That, I recall, is what they did but it did take a bit of persuasion to get people at AFN to believe that there could ever be anything wrong with the basic product. The idea that Porsche never made mistakes was deeply ingrained in their thinking, and for good reason: it had been perfectly true for decades. I must not, however, mislead anybody with this single anecdote. It was always a great pleasure to work with the AFN people and drive for them. Something of the old days, almost the atmosphere of a rather good club, lingered within the firm: it was business-like and efficient, yes, but there was a fundamental decency in the way the AFN team went about its daily business. That, together with their intelligent, typically dry wit made them all very good company.

All the AFN mechanics were great people but one deserves a special mention: Peter Caulfield, for whom nothing was too much trouble, especially when we were racing the unlikely 928s. Peter, who died tragically young in 2003, was a 16-year-old AFN apprentice when he first began to prepare cars for me but already he was able and confident, yet modest. Peter symbolised the AFN attitude: he was one of the best.

Over in Stuttgart in the late 1980s, however, Porsche really did seem to be losing the plot even more with the 928.

Contrary to expectations, the 911 most definitely had not faded away and nobody seemed quite sure of exactly what future purpose the 928 was meant to serve in the light of that. The 928 S4, as it was by late 1986, was a potent 5-litre car with four camshafts, 32 valves and a peaky 320bhp at 6,000rpm that gave it 160mph-plus performance – but even the professional road testers were becoming puzzled by it.

In that year alone the UK price of a new 928 had risen from £35,524 for an S2 to £48,935 for the S4 and that was almost all because of currency fluctuations rather than any change in specification. But no-one was asking whether the latest 928 was worth the money. What we all wanted to know was this: what was it for? Nine out of ten sold were autos and we couldn't work out whether it was an unusually relaxed supercar or an overpowered luxury cruiser which made too much road noise from its back wheels and which had bizarre suspension settings that made it unexpectedly sharp to drive. Impressive as it was in many ways, the whole 928 mission seemed to have drifted into confused old age.

That's when Porsche decided to take a bit of bold action. They changed the 928 completely, turning it into an uncompromising sports GT quite unlike the wallowing luxury barge it had been becoming in S4 form. The 928 GT didn't look very different from previous 928s but it was set up to satisfy those who like to drive hard, yet still not scare the pants off them if they started playing seriously; it was also sold only with manual transmission.

By 1992, when the subsequent 928 GTS appeared, a four-speed automatic gearbox was again an option in some markets but not, I think, in the UK, where informed journalists were openly predicting that, whatever transmission it had, we were looking at the last form of the 928. Its 1970s design really had become very obsolete, whatever was done to update it. Yet there was still widespread praise for the GTS because, at long last, the 928 had been made into a true driver's car, and it had bags of character. Whilst the confused S4 had seemed to wear a

# Buying hints

**1.** There was a time when a second-hand 928 was a bargain. You could take your pick from a range of desirable used cars, all with low mileages and perfect service histories. If you bought one then, you did very well, but that was some years ago. Such cars may still be found at attractive prices but good examples aren't so common.

**2.** The 928 has been moving out of the ordinary second-hand market, leaving nearly all the survivors to be regarded as classic cars for use on special occasions. Some remain superb, but not all. Those people who bought the bargains ten years ago, and have neglected them ever since, still expect to sell them for the price of a properly maintained car. Such is life.

**3.** Although the 928 never changed dramatically in appearance, it had several different guises throughout its time in production. You must be clear about whether you want a pleasant GT cruiser, probably with old-fashioned automatic gears, or one of the later GT or GTS versions, which were fabulous things to drive, especially with the manual gearbox.

**4.** By comparison with the early 928s, the high-performance GT or GTS cars were road racers, somewhat raw and uncompromising. Never mind the surprisingly low purchase price – can you really afford to run one of these cars? Check the fuel consumption figures in an original road test. Find out how much a new set of tyres will cost.

**5.** Remember that 928s were powered by a magnificent V8 engine which, when it comes to rebuild time,

can produce a suitably impressive bill. These engines were well made to survive many years but nothing lasts forever without the right attention. Don't just inspect the car itself; go through the paperwork and check the service history with great care before buying. If there's no proper history, or there are big gaps, be very wary indeed.

**6.** Before buying it's essential to join the Porsche Club Great Britain and get the latest advice from the 928 Register's technical adviser. Meet other owners through the club, find the top 928 specialists through them and try to test drive a few cars before you settle on buying one. If you take the precaution of getting one of those specialists to inspect it first, that would be wise. Get all that right and you'll have a fabulous car.

*Opposite: People were confused by the S4 of late 1986. New spoilers set it apart from earlier models, but it felt somewhere between a stunning high-performance supercar and a very fast luxury machine. The 928 was changing and at this stage the compromise was not completely successful – but with 5 litres, four cams, 32 valves and a claimed top speed of 168mph it was most definitely quick. (LAT)*

veneer of effete respectability, all of that was stripped away to create a sophisticated bruiser of a muscle-car. That was the 928 in its final guise – by this stage the GTS being the only 928 model offered.

The 32-valve V8 had steadily increased in size over the years and now it took on another 440cc to become a 5.4-litre that produced 350bhp at 5,700rpm and 362lb ft at 4,250rpm. With a top speed of 170mph and 0–60mph possible in 5.4 seconds, the manual GTS was a fast machine indeed, but such numbers hardly convey the thrust available for overtaking, all to the tune of a distant bellowing and clattering from the great alloy V8.

It's worth mentioning the pleasure of driving the rare manual versions of the 928 in any of its forms from late 1977 onwards. The lever was no neat little twig: you knew you had control of a big gearbox, and there was a correspondingly long throw, but it was not as heavy as some critics have said: when used with precision at speed, it was satisfying to shift, being perfectly in keeping with the generous, big-chested feel of the whole motor car.

It still looked respectable enough, this final 928; it remained docile in traffic and retained the traditional Porsche virtue of long-term reliability even when used enthusiastically. Never mind if the fuel consumption was likely to be between 14mpg and 20mpg, it was a hard man's car at heart and all the better for that. The last batch of them to come to the UK was sold in early 1996, when the list price was £72,950. Finally, contrary to expectations, the 928 had come out as a strong, growling beast; at the end, there really was something rather grand and magnificent about it.

*Above: Purposeful luxury inside the 1989 928 GT, with manual gearbox – the funny 'op-art' look of 928s in the 1970s was long forgotten when this 171mph supercar came along. There was no mistaking what it was – an uncompromising, high-performance driver's car. (LAT)*

*Below: 'An intoxicating cocktail of driver appeal and luxury,' said* Autocar & Motor *of this, the last word in the long line of 928s. The 5.3-litre 928 GTS produced 350bhp and 369lb ft of torque. Manual versions were capable of 0–60mph in 5.4sec, top speed remained a claimed 171mph – and just 2,831 were made from late 1991 to 1995. (Autocar & Motor/LAT)*

# The 944 and 968

The first hint of the 944 came at
Le Mans in 1981, when a
prototype powered by an all-
Porsche 2.5-litre four-cylinder engine
ran to an impressive seventh overall at
Le Mans.

As Jacky Ickx, partnered by Derek
Bell, scored a record fifth Le Mans
victory that year in a Porsche 936/81,
the modest '924 GTP 2.5' driven by
Walter Röhrl, Jürgen Barth and 'Sigi'

Brunn did not hit the headlines. But it
was noticed by those in the know:
sharper journalists immediately
reported that it was the prototype of
an upmarket 924-based road car, to be
called the 944. The main difference,
they said, was that the Le Mans car
was a fully race-prepared turbocharged
machine, whereas the new road car
was to be a more modest normally
aspirated version.

*Right: Similar inside to the 924, the 1982 944 was comfortable, with excellent seats and plenty of legroom in the front, but the steering column was still rather low. On the move, there was little wind noise but road noise was noticeable. Even so, it felt relaxed at speed. (LAT)*

*Below: Testers were genuinely surprised by the easy-revving nature and the lack of vibration and boom periods of the 944's counterbalanced engine, which produced 163bhp at 5,800rpm from 2,479cc. It really did feel unbelievably smooth for a straight four-cylinder. (LAT)*

An official announcement confirmed the story a few days after the race. Based on the 924, the 944 was nevertheless perceived by the outside world as one hundred per cent Porsche from end to end. That should have nailed the marketing problem that had blighted the innocent 924 all along. Fair or unfair, we all know that the 924 had never been fully accepted as a proper Porsche and it was only five years old when the more sophisticated 944 came along. That said, the 924 continued to be available alongside the 944 throughout most of the 1980s.

From the very start the 944 had plenty going for it. The chassis had all the good bits from the 924 turbo, with widened wheelarches that gave it a stylish, muscular look. To power it, Porsche produced a superb four-cylinder engine of 2,479cc with two counterbalancing shafts that made it extraordinarily smooth. The cylinder head design was based on that of the successful 928 V8 and the 944's engine was made largely of aluminium alloy. In truth it could be called a 928 engine that had been split in half. Bosch L-Jetronic fuel injection and a single overhead camshaft with self-adjusting hydraulic tappets were further features of the design.

With 163bhp, and an impressively flat torque curve, the 944 was an immediate success the moment it went on sale, late in 1981 in Germany and from early 1982 elsewhere in the world. Seen as the responsible driver's sports car, it was relatively clean in its emissions, economical, and easy to maintain. Service intervals were at

# Porsche 944
# (944 Lux in UK)
### 1982–89

**ENGINE:**
Four cylinders in line, alloy block and head, counter-balance shafts, water-cooled

| | |
|---|---|
| Bore x stroke | 100.0mm x 78.9mm |
| | 104.0mm x 78.9mm |
| Capacity | 2,479cc/2,681cc |
| Valve actuation | sohc, two valves per cylinder |
| Compression ratio | 10.6:1/10.9:1 |
| Induction | Bosch injection |
| Power | 163bhp at 5,800rpm |
| | 165bhp at 5,800rpm |
| Maximum torque | 151lb ft at 3,500rpm |
| | 166lb ft at 4,200rpm |

**TRANSMISSION:**
Rear-wheel drive; torque tube to rear-mounted five-speed transaxle

**SUSPENSION:**
*Front:* Independent by MacPherson struts with double-acting dampers; anti-roll bar
*Rear:* Independent by semi-trailing arms and transverse torsion bars; double-acting telescopic dampers; anti-roll bar

**STEERING:**
Rack-and-pinion
Power assistance optional for 1984 and standard from 1985 model year

**BRAKES:**
*Front:* Disc, ventilated (11.1in)
*Rear:* Disc, ventilated (11.4in)
Servo assistance
ABS standard on 2.7-litre

**WHEELS/TYRES:**
Alloy wheels, 7J x 15in
Tyres 215/60 VR 15; Continental Super Contact 195/65 VR 15 on 2.7-litre

**BODYWORK:**
Galvanised steel monocoque
Coupé 2+2

**DIMENSIONS:**

| | |
|---|---|
| Length | 13ft 10in |
| Wheelbase | 7ft 10.5in |
| Track, front | 4ft 10.3in |
| Track, rear | 4ft 9.0in |
| Width | 5ft 8.3in |
| | (excluding mirrors) |
| Height | 4ft 2in |

**WEIGHT:**
2.5-litre: 22.5cwt (1,143kg)
2.7-litre: 26.0cwt (1,320kg)

**PERFORMANCE:**
(Source: *Motor/Autocar & Motor*)

| | |
|---|---|
| Max speed | 137mph*/136mph |
| 0–60mph | 7.2sec/7.0sec |
| Standing quarter-mile | 15.1sec/15.7sec |

*Porsche figure

**PRICE IN UK INCLUDING TAX WHEN NEW:**
2.5-litre: £12,999 (May 1982)
2.7-litre: £25,991 (December 1988)

**NUMBER BUILT:**
944 Series I (1982–84): 64,486
944 Series II (1985–87): 41,174
944 (1988): 5,480
944 2.7-litre (1989): 4,426

# Porsche 944 S/S2
### 1986–93

As 944 except:

**ENGINE:**

| | |
|---|---|
| Bore x stroke | 104.0mm x 88.0mm (S2) |
| Capacity | 2,990cc (S2) |
| Valve actuation | dohc, four valves per cylinder |
| Compression ratio | 10.9:1 |
| Power | 190bhp at 6,000rpm |
| | 211bhp at 5,800rpm |
| Maximum torque | 170lb ft at 4,300rpm |
| | 207lb ft at 4,000rpm |

**BRAKES:**
*Front:* Disc, ventilated (12.0in) (S2)
*Rear:* Disc, ventilated (11.8in) (S2)
ABS optional; standard on S2

**WHEELS/TYRES:**
S2: Forged alloy wheels, 7J x 16 front and 8J x 16 rear
Tyres 195/65 VR 15 (944S); Dunlop D40, 205/55 ZR 16 front and 225/50 ZR 16 rear (S2)

**WEIGHT:**
944S: 25.0cwt (1,270kg)
944 S2: 26.6cwt (1,350kg)

**BODYWORK:**
From 1989, S2 Cabriolet also available

**PERFORMANCE:**
(Source: *Motor/Autocar & Motor*)

| | |
|---|---|
| Max speed | 138.1mph/146mph |
| 0–60mph | 7.5sec/6.0sec |
| Standing quarter-mile | 15.7sec/14.4sec |

**PRICE IN UK INCLUDING TAX WHEN NEW:**
944S Coupé: £23,997 (November 1986)
S2 Coupé: £31,304 (March 1989)
S2 Cabriolet £36,713 (March 1989)

**NUMBER BUILT:**
944 S (1987–88): 7,324
S2 Coupé: 9,352
S2 Cabriolet: 6,980

# Porsche 944 turbo
# /turbo SE
### 1985–88

As 944 except:

**ENGINE:**

| | |
|---|---|
| Compression ratio | 8.0:1 |
| Induction | KKK turbocharger, intercooler |

---

12,000 miles and 944s would turn in 25mpg even when driven fairly hard on the road; 30mpg was easily achievable. So, despite a top speed of 137mph and a 0–60mph time of 7.2 seconds – making it a pretty quick car in 1982 – it also beat many much slower family saloons when it came to fuel economy.

On paper, so far so good. Just as important, however, was the rewarding nature of the 944 to drive. I got to know the model well through Porsche's UK Driving Days at circuits such as Brands Hatch, Silverstone, Donington, Thruxton and Snetterton. Fun days, those, when I was paid to meet my

friends, pass on driving skills to the keenest car owners to be found anywhere, and enjoy driving their cars with them. Those Driving Days provided a first class opportunity for us, as temporary employees, to compare the relative merits of the entire range of recent Porsche cars and I have to say that the 944 was immediately impressive on every circuit we went to. It was a good motor car, simple as that.

Not only did it achieve surprisingly good lap times, it was easy and satisfying to balance in the corners, plus it had the feel of a high quality

sports car, that delightful sense of effortless performance about it. Measured against the contemporary 911s, of course, it was a modest machine but even so it sounded right and it felt right. As with the 924 on which it was based, the 944 had plenty of room within a well-designed interior, including that renowned load-carrying ability which was so remarkable in a sports car.

Well-equipped, the standard package included electric windows and mirrors, tinted glass and a good radio/cassette player. Power-assisted steering, an option from 1983, became

| Power | 220bhp at 5,800rpm* |
| | 250bhp at 6,500rpm |
| Maximum Torque | 243lb ft at 3,500rpm |
| | 258lb ft at 4,000rpm |

*There was a special series of 1000 944 turbo S 250bhp models in 1988, based on the Turbo Cup racing specification

**BRAKES:**
Front and rear: Disc, ventilated (11.8in)
ABS standard from 1987
Uprated to four-pot with larger callipers for turbo SE

**WHEELS/TYRES:**
Cast alloy wheels, 7J x 16in front and 8J x 16in rear (turbo)
Forged alloy wheels, 7J x 16in front and 9J x 16in rear (turbo SE)
Tyres 205/55 VR 16 front and 225/50 VR 16in rear (turbo)
Tyres 225/55 VR 16 front and 245/45 VR 16in rear (turbo SE)

**WEIGHT:**
turbo: 24.8cwt (1,258kg)
turbo SE: 26.8cwt (1,361kg)

**BODYWORK:**
Coupé 2+2, Cabriolet (handful only)

**PERFORMANCE:**
(Source: Motor/Porsche)
Max speed 157.9mph/161mph
0–60mph 5.9sec/5.7sec
Standing quarter-mile 14.5sec/13.9sec

**PRICE IN UK INCLUDING TAX WHEN NEW:**
turbo: £25,312 (late 1985)
Later turbo SE: £39,893 (1989)

**NUMBER BUILT:**
| turbo Coupé | 17,627 |
| turbo S Coupé | 1,635 |
| (1989–91) turbo Coupé | 3,738 |
| (1989–91) turbo Cabriolet | 528 |

# Porsche 968/968 Club Sport
## 1991–95

As 944 S2 except:

**ENGINE:**
| Valve actuation | VarioCam variable valve timing |
| Compression ratio | 11.0:1 |
| Induction | Bosch DME injection |
| Power | 240bhp at 6,200rpm |
| Maximum torque | 225lb ft at 4,100rpm |

**TRANSMISSION:**
Six-speed transaxle gearbox; optional four-speed Tiptronic (not CS)

**WHEELS/TYRES:**
Tyres 215/60 VR 15
(In some markets, options include 7.5J x 17in (front) and 9J x 17in (rear) wheels, with 225/45 ZR 17 and 255/40 ZR 17 tyres; this combination standard on Clubsport)

**DIMENSIONS:**
| Length | 14ft 2in |
| Track, front | 4ft 10.1in |
| Track, rear | 4ft 9.1in |
| Height | 4ft 2.2in |

**WEIGHT:**
Coupé 27.0cwt (1,370kg)
Cabriolet 28.4cwt (1,440kg)
Clubsport 26.0cwt (1,320kg))

**PERFORMANCE:**
(Source: *Porsche Cars, otherwise Autocar & Motor)
Max speed 153mph/157mph*
0–60mph 6.1sec/6.1sec

**PRICE IN UK INCLUDING TAX WHEN NEW:**
Coupé: £34,945 (August 1992)
Cabriolet: £38,724 (August 1992)
Clubsport: £28,750 (January 1993)

**NUMBER BUILT:**
Coupé 5,731
Cabriolet 3,959
Clubsport Coupé 1,538

# Porsche 968 Turbo S
## 1993–95

As 968 except:

**ENGINE:**
| Valve actuation | sohc, two valves per cylinder |
| Compression ratio | 8.0:1 |
| Induction | Turbocharged, with intercooler |
| Power | 305bhp at 5,400rpm |
| Maximum torque | 369lb ft at 3,000rpm |

**TRANSMISSION:**
No Tiptronic option

**BRAKES:**
Front: Disc, ventilated (11.7in)

**WHEELS/TYRES:**
Alloy wheels, 8J x 18in front and 10J x 18in rear
Tyres 235/40 ZR 18 front and 265/35 ZR 18 rear

**BODYWORK:**
Coupé 2+2

**DIMENSIONS:**
Height 4ft 1.4in

**WEIGHT:**
25.6cwt (1,300kg)

**PERFORMANCE:**
(Source: Porsche)
Max speed 174mph
0–62mph 5.0sec

**PRICE AT FACTORY**
(without UK tax and duty paid):
DM 175,000 (Late 1992)

**NUMBER BUILT:**
14

Magazine road testers are expected to push cars, especially sports cars, to the limit on a track and report back to the readers. This test of a 944 S in 1986 told of the need for 'a firm hand' but said lift-off oversteer was 'easy to correct'. But the driver lost it this time... (Motor/LAT)

Above: The 944 S, which first arrived in late 1986, was set apart by its very smooth 16-valve cylinder head, with double overhead camshafts. Acceleration in the upper speed ranges was improved but overall the 'S' wasn't that much quicker than a standard 944. The quality was there but all 944s were expensive by then and rivals had caught up on fuel economy. (LAT)

Left: '16 Ventiler' reads the script in black plastic, indicating that the 2,479cc engine of the 1987 model year 944 S had four valves over each of its four cylinders. Power rose from 163bhp to 190bhp, torque was up to 170lb ft at 4,300rpm, and top speed was a claimed 142mph. (LAT)

standard in 1985 and further improvements, such as optional ABS from 1987, were built in annually until the two-valves-per-cylinder 944 was superseded in late 1989. In that, its last year, the basic 944 had a 2.7-litre engine, thanks to a bigger bore, but we'll get to the details of that later.

The 944 was never that cheap to buy but over time it proved a deceptive bargain for owners, always being relatively cheap to run. Strong owner satisfaction and fuss-free performance were very much part of the package. The 944 has proved pretty durable and these days I keep hearing of people buying second-hand examples more than 20 years old for ridiculously small amounts of money, and finding that they still give excellent service.

Late in 1986 the more powerful

944 S was added to the range, featuring the four-valve head on the 2.5-litre engine, and giving 190bhp. At lower revs there was a slight loss of performance but in the higher rev range it was a fair bit quicker on acceleration in the intermediate gears. The power increase did not make much difference to the top speed but it did get there considerably more quickly.

As the early 'S' cost a fair bit more than the standard car, most people in Britain thought it rather an indulgence, especially as it was slightly thirstier. The more powerful engine produced a boom at very low revs but there was no loss of that superb top end smoothness. As for noise at speed, the 944 S was typical of all the four-cylinder Porsches of those days: very low wind noise but some road roar on certain surfaces.

*The diffuser under the rear immediately distinguished the new 3-litre 944 S2, seen here early in 1989. The increased capacity not only made it the world's biggest four-cylinder car engine, but also provided increased punch – which really told on the road. With a lookalike body, it appeared identical to the turbo but for its badge and the wheels. (LAT)*

Around this time the many 944 variants available started to become confusing. Some were more powerful, but also much heavier, so they weren't always that much quicker. What was going on? Essential new technology for the future was piling on the kilos but the poor buyer was hard-pressed to make an intelligent choice. The consolation was that all 944s were consistently good to drive and economical to own, even

Above: The Cabriolet was introduced with the S2 series for 1989. It was a great-looking car, whether with top up or down, but there was a considerable loss of luggage space. The top was electrically operated but there was still plenty of fiddling about with clips and the cover back in those olden days. (LAT)

Below: Strictly for the rich seeking fun in style: the off-white leather treatment inside this 944 S2 Cabriolet cost an extra £2,575 back in 1989, lifting the showroom price to £39,288. The possibly preferable Coupé S2, priced from £32,024, offered better value. (LAT)

if the company's marketing wasn't that brilliant.

Then, seven years down the line from its launch, the standard 944 came under threat from 'lesser' cars bearing badges such as VW and Nissan. Porsche was ready for the 1989 model year with a bored-out engine for the 944, up from 2,479cc to 2,681cc. This 2.7-litre version pushed the power up a little to 165bhp but the key point was a big increase in torque at lower revs, to 166lb ft at 4,200rpm – which was handy, as the 944 was inevitably and steadily putting on that little bit of weight. As smooth as ever, the increased urge of the bigger engine gave a noticeable improvement in acceleration from normal cruising speeds, making overtaking easier. ABS became standard, too. All this kept the very desirable basic 944 well enough up to the mark.

The best was yet to come, however. Enthusiasts with any sense of history know that a well-made three-litre, four-cylinder, rear-wheel drive sports car is something of a classic package. Bentley did it way back in the early 1920s, producing one of the greatest Vintage sports cars of all time. The same concept had produced the early Big Healey of 1952, admittedly a 2.7-litre but still a true classic 'big-pot four'. With 1990s Porsche technology behind it, the pleasure of driving a thumping great four-cylinder sports car was greater than ever.

When Porsche revealed the 944 S2 for 1989, the result was by far the best 944 to date. Knowledgeable owners of earlier models noticed that there was a big, big difference with this latest version. At 2,990cc, it was at the time the largest four-cylinder car engine in the world. The new cylinder block had the same 104mm bore as that of the 2.7 but the stroke was 88mm; the 16-valve format was retained. The result was a truly outstanding, thoroughbred machine with a 211bhp engine, a top speed of 146mph and a 0–60mph time of 6.0 seconds. The new 3-litre S2 overlapped in 1989 with the last of the basic 944 models, which had been uprated to 2.7 litres for its final year in production, as mentioned before.

Despite joining a very high-performance section of the market, the 944 S2's fuel consumption was still extremely competitive: in normal use it easily did better than 25mpg and even when pressed hard on the road it still turned in just over 20mpg.

It really was a great car to drive: the superbly lusty normally aspirated 3-litre engine was perfectly attuned to the well-balanced chassis, enabling confident use of the throttle in corners. Adding to its appeal, the S2 got the turbo-look 944 body and all the important beefed-up parts from the turbo's chassis and drivetrain. The S2 was a deeply satisfying car to drive, with no serious faults.

All right, so there was an occasional lack of smoothness in first-gear traffic-jam motoring caused by the rather abrupt fuel cut-off. This, to me, was so trivial a hardship that I feel tempted not to mention it at all. If the minor controls needed a bit of updating by then, that was even less important. Essentially, the 944 was good to start with but now it had become magnificent.

*Below: The turbo version, first seen in 1985, moved the 944 into a new performance league. Autocar measured a mean 153mph top speed in this car, with a best one-way speed of 158mph. Despite some reservations about road noise, the terrific performance and predictable, sporting handling made the 944 turbo an extremely exciting car. But it also had that Porsche logic and quality about it, making it reliable, accessible and easy to live with. (Autocar/LAT)*

Above: In 1988 the 944 turbo SE was tested by Autocar against the equally new 911 Carrera CS, both topping 150mph and making 0–100mph in around 14sec. 'There's no doubt which stands out as being the most rewarding driving machine,' they wrote, choosing the animal magnetism of the 911 over the sophisticated feel of the 944, adding, 'Across country, the cars are as quick as each other.' Poor old 944! It was brilliant but the 911 still had its own magic. (Autocar/LAT)

Left: The 944 turbo SE engine, seen in a 1988 car, produced 250bhp and 258lb ft of torque. With 0–60mph in 5.7sec and a top speed of 152mph (Autocar), the performance was well up to the required mark. A problem was that this car cost £41,250 and Porsche customers at the time were also offered the new 911 Carrera Clubsport, with equal performance, for £35,850. (Autocar/LAT)

Right: Interior of the original 944 turbo for the 1985 model year included new electric Recaro seats, new steering wheel, redesigned instruments and a new facia and console. Power steering was standard on the turbo, which also had a suitably uprated chassis, including ventilated discs all round and four-pot callipers. (LAT)

Below: Once you'd got out and clipped down the cover for the convertible top, the 944 Cabriolet did look good. This is one of a small number of turbo models made only for the 1991 model year, and 944 production finally ended that May. Admittedly, the mechanism of the convertible top was considerably improved for this model, being easier to latch shut. (LAT)

Autocar & Motor Road Test Editor David Vivian assessing a pre-production 968 in Germany in 1991. 'It's the real thing,' he said, but was still unconvinced despite many new features and its superb cornering balance. The Variocam engine felt less flexible than expected, the early 968 lacked some refinement and the steering wheel was still low, as in the 924 and 944. Great in parts, yes, but this tester had some prescient doubts. (Autocar & Motor/LAT)

Apart from the Coupé there was also by then the 944 Cabriolet, first shown at the Frankfurt show in 1985 but not put into production until 1989, as an open-topped version of the 3-litre S2. Personally, I preferred the looks and feel of the Coupé – and still do – but it must be said that for those who insist on open air motoring, the 944 S2 Cabriolet was hard to beat in terms of performance, dependability and plain fun.

Unlike many convertibles – regardless of price – the open 944 felt

taut in its chassis, was remarkably lacking in scuttle-shake and, as for wind noise, with the soft roof closed it was hard to tell it apart from the Coupé (the reduction in glass area, however, was noticeable). The behaviour on the move reflected the standard of engineering integrity that Porsche enthusiasts had come to expect quietly over the decades, but the Cabriolet's extraordinary superiority, as a proper Porsche, can still come as a surprise to people who have only driven open-topped cars of other makes.

Just a couple of points against the 'Cab': for those used to the push-button ease of today's soft-tops, the electrically-driven roof will appeal but even so there is still a lot of messing around required with handles, clips and the hood bag whenever the top is put up or down. Furthermore, the soft-top's stowing area meant much of the 944's admirable luggage space was lost. With the hood down, however, I

have to admit that this Porsche looked great, and still does.

The 944 S2 range continued to the end of the 1992 model year, when it was replaced by the 968. And a range it had indeed become, not least with the arrival of the sensational 944 turbo back in 1985. So far, only the normally aspirated 944s have been covered because it seemed better to deal separately with the much faster turbos. I well remember travelling alone to the Nürburgring from Calais late one night, driving what was then the latest 944 turbo S, or SE as it would then have been called in UK-market form. It must have been some time in 1988. Before the days of the motorway that now goes south-east off the main drag through Belgium – past Spa and into the land of Bitburger beer – I used to cut across country to get to the 'Ring, partly to save some miles but mainly for the pleasure of driving.

That night, however, I decided to

THE 944 AND 968

stick with the autobahn, driving straight on into Germany, which made it quite a lot further but just as quick thanks to the faster roads. Anyway, with that car I wanted to get on the unrestricted autobahn and try a bit of straightline speed. That 944 turbo S seemed to give almost supercar performance, without fuss, and I wanted to see what it would really do.

Soon after crossing the border near Aachen, I speeded up and at 120mph found myself overtaking a heavily modified 928. It had been dolled up with a wild-looking non-factory body kit – huge arches, deep skirts, big exhaust, a gigantic rear wing, the lot – and it looked very silly indeed. The comedian driving it obviously thought that being overtaken by a 944 on British plates was too much. He probably also thought that I was exactly what he had been waiting for as he trundled along the nearly empty autobahn at 200kph. So he put his foot down.

What happened next made me laugh for the rest of my journey. The two cars continued to accelerate at exactly the same rate, until we reached 150mph. This was no death-defying chicken run: we were on a nice, open straight stretch of road, so it was merely interesting.

It was obvious that he didn't lift off. As we approached 150mph, however, his car began to run out of acceleration. All that cosmetic junk that he had glued onto that innocent 928 was acting like a parachute. He must have been really choked to see 'my' 944 (it was actually a Press car I had on test) sail away into the distance at almost 160mph. He'd wasted his money, probably a great deal of it, on making his car ugly and much slower. I never saw him again but it still makes me smile.

The 944 turbo, launched in 1985, was indeed a very likeable car, and one that appealed strongly to me – and not just because of that bit of fun with an

*Production 968s released to the press in 1992 were much better than the pre-production cars tested a year earlier, but observant writers suggested the car should have been called a 944 S3. They had a point as the 968 was a major facelift rather than a new model, but the handling, fuel economy, performance and six-speed gearbox attracted praise, as did the exemplary build quality and reduced price, cut to £34,945. (LAT)*

'S' on the autobahn. From the start, the 944 turbo combined all the best qualities of the normally aspirated model, plus there was that big boost to performance. With 220bhp from the 2,479cc engine in 1985, it offered 0–100mph in 14.9 seconds, and that put it into a different league altogether. It handled superbly, even sideways on, and it was not upset by bumpy roads.

Three years on, in 1988, a Special Equipment version based on the Turbo Cup racers was offered, producing

Left: Journalist Andrew Frankel chased the 1992 Mille Miglia re-run in this 968 Cabriolet Tiptronic, here seen with its headlights raised. On twisty mountain roads, the high gearing of the Tiptronic's ratios proved a weakness – but he said it was the second-best cabriolet he'd ever tested. Yes, and no prizes for guessing, Frankel's top choice was its 911 stablemate, which then cost £13,500 more than the 968 Cabriolet. (Autocar & Motor/LAT)

Below: It didn't look any different but the 1993 968 had many environmentally friendly changes, including water-based paint with reduced solvent, special high-boiling-point brake fluid and CFC-free air conditioning. Dual airbags became available in the UK market. (LAT)

Right: David Vivian also tested the new
Cabriolet in 1991 when he went to Germany for
a first drive in the pre-production 968 range.
Despite some carefully considered reservations,
he did report that the rear-drive chassis was even
better than that of the hugely rewarding 944 it
replaced. (Autocar & Motor/LAT)

Below: Unmistakeable Porsche style is seen in
this 1992 comparison between the 968
Cabriolet and Coupé. Some critics complained
that the 968 looked too much like a cross
between the 944 and the 928 but the rest of us
couldn't see what was wrong with that! (LAT)

250bhp and delivering a whopping 258lb ft of torque at 4,000rpm. That brought the 0–100mph time down to 13.5 seconds but, at around £41,000, it cost £5,000 more than a 911 Carrera Coupé and that didn't seem so clever. The 250bhp engine became standard the following year in a model called 944 turbo S (or 'SE' for the British market) but even so it was not long before the basic 911 crept back into its proper slot, ahead of all 944s in Porsche's price list.

For a time, we had been given the strong impression that the factory intended the 944 turbo to replace the 911 in due course. That was definitely the plan at one stage, whatever anyone tells you now, and the small front-engined Porsche had become good enough, on paper and on the road, to take on that rôle. Of course, there's more to this game than that and you don't need me to tell you that. Good as the 944 turbo was, we know now that nothing could replace the unique appeal of the 911. Even so, the 944 turbo SE brought the 944 line to a close with a flourish. It was an accomplished design with 160mph-plus performance and it was a fabulous thing to drive.

There was a 944 turbo SE Cabriolet listed towards the end of the model's production run, but they were extremely rare beasts: just 51 came to the UK in 1991, then 44 in 1992 and the last five in 1993. If you can find one of these, you will have secured a rare gem.

Both normally aspirated and turbo 944s gave way in 1992 to one of the most underrated Porsches ever, the 968. A heavily re-engineered 944, this short-lived model represented the final stage of development of the small front-engined Porsche theme and was destined to last no more than three years. In 1995 a new MD, Wendelin Wiedeking, came in and called a halt to the long struggle. Wiedeking had the brains to see that it was a lost cause; he also had the guts and the vision to take effective action. For twenty years, enormous effort had gone into the front-engined sports cars but different times demanded fresh thinking; the time had come for renewed

concentration on 911 development and the creation of an entirely new kind of Porsche 'entry model'.

So the 928 and the 968 both got the chop. Early in December 1995 the 968 disappeared from UK price lists. It had been a fabulous car to drive but for some reason its tremendous virtues went mysteriously unappreciated. Not enough people wanted to buy it. The 928 GTS soon followed, presumably after remaining stocks of the bigger car had been sold off. There was another fabulous car that simply wasn't selling well enough by then.

As a business decision we can look back and say that Wiedeking got it dead right, returning as he did to core values by concentrating on the trusty 911 before branching out into fresh ground. First there was the Boxster and, then the hugely successful Cayenne and, more recently, the delightful Cayman. It takes a bold man to grasp the nettle like that but Wiedeking's commercial thinking was sound and many loyal Porsche 911 fans agreed, purely for sentimental reasons, that the axe did need to fall on the 968.

That said, let's just put it firmly on record that the short-lived 968 CS (Clubsport) was a truly great driver's car, whatever those diehard traditional purists ever thought about it. The hallmark of the 968 was always its wonderfully controllable handling. It struggled a bit in the market place when cheaper rivals appeared, apparently offering better value for money, higher performance and superior roadholding. More grip is all very well, if it can be put to good use. The trump card of the 968 was its surefooted controllability, the feeling of confidence it gave to the driver. When pressed really hard on an unknown road, the 968 was a brilliant machine, a real thoroughbred able to humiliate the upstarts that had seemed better on paper. You had to drive the 968 to appreciate its finer qualities, and then everything became very clear indeed.

It was a combination of chassis development, coupled with perfectly attuned engine characteristics and

good gearing, that did the trick. The 968 felt balanced because it was exactly that, making for one of those rare cars that a good driver feels he can do anything with. It was an outstanding machine in that respect.

The styling was updated neatly, with improved aerodynamics helping the 968 to a top speed of 153mph; it got a six-speed gearbox and the 240bhp straight-four three-litre engine had variable valve timing. An early Tiptronic option was also offered but it was not that desirable in those days: Tiptronic technology was to improve greatly in subsequent years thanks to better-chosen ratios and, above all, to software developments that gave much smoother changes.

Fuel economy and build quality were exceptional for a car in that class. Until that cheaper competition appeared, it seemed competitively priced and there was still a very attractive Cabriolet version. Yet, for some reason that still escapes me, all that was not enough to make for commercial success in the tough world of motor manufacturing.

Is it absurd to suggest there remained some lingering prejudice against the 968 dating from the original 924? Did that ghost blight the 968's chances? Who knows for sure? Either way, it's perfectly ridiculous that such an outstanding machine should have been dismissed so lightly by sports car buyers.

There are also some people who are mistaken enough to look down on four-cylinder engines, however brilliant they are. This is feeble-minded snobbery. Give me a fabulous 'four' over an indifferent engine with more cylinders any day.

Whatever the cause, an image problem probably did persist. It was unfair, it was wrong but it seemed there was apparently nothing that could be done to alter it. Looking back at the 968 Clubsport of 1993, that model looks like a last-ditch defiant gesture, an attempt to say to the world 'Look, this car really is the business. Can't you see that, you fools?'

It was the best of its kind: out came the back seats, much of the sound insulation, the electric window lifters and mirror motors, the central locking,

Above: Framed on the famous Spa GP circuit, a fine image of the 968 Clubsport, which became available in early 1993. The CS model indicated that Porsche was making a healthy return to its roots after some years lost in the wilderness. The UK price was £28,750, nearly £5,000 less than a standard 968. More to the point was a saving of 85kg in UK models. With unnecessary luxury items removed, it was noticeably better to drive. (LAT)

Right: Wind-up windows, manually adjustable mirrors, no back seat, no central locking, no rear wiper, etc, etc, but who cared about all that? With the 968 Clubsport you did get these lightweight racing seats, 17in alloy wheels, a ride height lowered by 20mm plus stiffer suspension. It wasn't the fastest machine for close on £30,000, but it was a truly great driver's car with excellent steering and handling. (LAT)

*Right: With an eight-valve head and KKK turbocharger, the turbo S engine produced 305bhp, making the car good for 174mph, at least, with 0–60mph well under 5.0sec. Before this car appeared, the factory had said it would be too expensive to produce a 968 turbo but they based this one on the old 944 turbo top end and made a handful of 968 3-litre specials to go racing. More race car than road car, it was also more than a bit wild. (LAT)*

*Opposite top: Rare beast – a 968 turbo S Coupé. Although they said up to 100 might be built, a mere 14 of these raw road-racers were made through the 1993–94 model years. Intended to win the German ADAC GT Cup race series, with a turbo RS version, the 968 turbo S did show a revived dynamism in Porsche's intentions. Never officially listed in the UK, it could be ordered specially for about £70,000. (LAT)*

*Opposite bottom: Two small ducts in the bonnet and an adjustable rear wing distinguished the turbo S Coupé from other 968s, as did the three-piece 'Cup' wheels and the suspension, lowered by 20mm. Like the Clubsport, the turbo S was stripped of unnecessary luxuries to reduce weight. It belonged on the track, where its ferocious performance could be fully exploited. (LAT)*

the rear wiper, the alarm, the electric tailgate lock and even the engine-bay light. In went lightweight, genuine racing seats and big alloy wheels from the 911 turbo. The finished car was 85kg – or 1.7cwt – lighter than standard, and nearly £5,000 was lopped *off* the price of a lightweight special this time. It was superb, an unrivalled sports car in the classic mould. Undercutting opposition nonentities on price and far excelling them in road manners, it should have hurt those rivals more than it ever did.

Towards the very end, for 1994 there was a 305bhp 968 turbo S, capable of 174mph. Despite a single overhead cam and an eight-valve head, it was clearly a flying machine. Only 14 of those extreme cars were made but why more people didn't rush out and buy any 968 I shall never know. That remains one of life's mysteries.

# Buying hints

**1.** Unlike most 924s, the 944s and 968s had real Porsche engines and, just take note, one day you might have to face real Porsche engine rebuild prices. Don't be frightened off by that, however; just bide your time and take special care to buy the best. Some oil leaks are normal but look out for any alarmingly big puddles underneath the car's customary parking place.

**2.** These cars were well made in the first place and if they have been properly cared for, as I think quite a few still have, you can find a superb example at a very good price. There are also plenty of grim, abused old 944s around, however, and they do need to be avoided. As the values aren't that high, even for the best examples, some 944s will cost far more than they're worth to get them roadworthy, let alone into a condition in which you'd be proud to show them to your friends.

**3.** Before buying, try to get out there and look at as many cars as you can, and drive them if the owners will let you. You might be surprised at how they vary. Apart from the engine, feel the steering and, on later models with power steering, listen for any inappropriate noises. The steering pumps have a reputation for failing, so find out the going rate for replacements. See whether the car runs straight and stops properly.

**4.** After seeing half a dozen you'll be beginning to think like an expert but don't kid yourself. Still don't buy anything until you have joined the Porsche Club Great Britain and done all your homework. The club has separate registrars for 944s and for 968s and these people will be your best friends at this stage of the game. Genuine experts, they will always point you the right way.

**5.** Some final thoughts on 944s and 968s: ignore anybody who sneers about them not being proper Porsches. An early 944 doesn't seem that quick now, perhaps, but it's quick enough on today's roads and it's a proper rear-wheel-drive sports car. They aren't 911s, obviously, but they were all good cars to drive in their own right and there were some really outstanding special models.

**6.** If you can find a good one, a rare 968 Clubsport is a terrific bargain as a track day car though possibly somewhat extreme for normal road use.

# The 911, Types 964 and 993

*Greeted by most of the press as the best 911 yet, the 3.6-litre Carrera 2, which arrived in late 1989, shared the 964 body of the Carrera 4 launched a year earlier. Experienced 911 enthusiasts were pleasantly surprised by an incredible improvement in the gearchange. However, almost idiot-proof handling made these cars safe but, for some of us, unsatisfying when driven hard. (LAT)*

Constant development and occasional total re-engineering have kept the 911 with us for well over 40 years. However good a new car may be, it cannot remain in production unaltered forever. Hence the 911s for the 1990s, the Carrera 4 launched late in 1988 and the Carrera 2 that appeared a year later, were really totally new cars.

They were greeted with universally ecstatic praise by the motoring press.

Despite being known within the factory as the 964, the good old 911 name was retained for sound marketing reasons. Call them what you will, I'm sorry to say those 964s just weren't my sort of motor cars at all, not at first anyway.

How can I say that? I'd be the first to admit that the new models, so different under the skin from previous 911s, really did seem to answer all the old criticisms that outsiders had levelled against rear-engined Porsches for decades. It was as if the Old Guard among senior Porsche engineers had finally defeated every enemy the 911 ever had.

On paper it was quite a car. Coil springs replaced the traditional torsion bars, suspension geometry was revised, and all this was installed in a completely new and very strong bodyshell. An intriguing detail was that both the Carrera 2 and the Carrera 4 had a discreet rear spoiler that rose at 50mph and dropped flat when the car's speed fell below 6mph, the primary function of this clever feature being to pass air through the engine's oil cooler. There was no doubting the quality of both execution and design of these new 911s, while in terms of styling Porsche had taken great trouble to retain the traditional 911 look in a beautiful, modern form. No, I had no objection to the way they looked.

How could anyone not like these cars? Well, let's consider the early Carrera 4 for starters. When that car first appeared, I was racing a 928 in British Porsche events for Porsche Cars Great Britain Ltd, under AFN's colours. So I was close to the clan, if you like, and bumped into plenty of friends at the British launch of the new Carrera 4.

One sales manager I knew well was bubbling over with enthusiasm for the new model, having just driven it himself around a circuit. My turn came and I found that the Carrera 4 was indeed one of the safest road cars I had ever driven. The stability under braking, and the stopping power, were both incredibly good. And, despite the four-wheel drive, the car turned into corners accurately, reasonably sharply and took up a nicely balanced stance. So far so good.

Then I put on the power, and the new Porsche accelerated hard through the corner with ever-increasing understeer. The more the power was applied, the more it understeered: quite simply, it just wanted to go straight on, quite harmlessly, and one

was forced to back right off. There was no way round that. When I did lift off, even abruptly, there was no hint of oversteer; all that happened was a marked reduction in the understeer.

Perhaps rather kindly, I decided that this four-wheel-drive car was most probably intended for the mountains in winter, where it might prove very effective; but I could not judge that aspect of its performance on a bone-dry racing circuit in summer. The trouble was that in those normal conditions it just didn't give the driving experience expected from a 911. The expression, 'utterly idiot-proof' came to mind. I could accept that anybody who had felt a little challenged by 911s in the past might find this new device just the job, so I smiled politely and avoided comment. I was glad I did not have to write a road test on it as I feared my words might have lost me a few friends.

The Carrera 2, which appeared in

1989, was effectively a rear-wheel-drive version of the Carrera 4, and it was a greatly superior machine to drive anywhere except possibly, I am prepared to concede, where ice and snow were to be found. But even the 964 Carrera 2 still wasn't to my liking, which seems ungrateful when I confess that I was then paid to race one for AFN for a couple of years. As soon as the new rear-wheel drive 911 came out, AFN's racing 928 S4 was pensioned off and we went on to win a lot of races outright in that Carrera 2.

So what was the problem? Let me answer that with a story. Before we had

*Another appropriate number plate, fitted to a series of Porsche GB test cars. The 911 Carrera 4 was launched for 1989 with a new 3.6-litre engine and, of course, four-wheel drive. These '964' Carrera 4s felt supremely safe but understeered on an open throttle. (LAT)*

Above: The blue Carrera 4 and the red Carrera 2 looked identical in late 1989. Both were heavy but the red car was 100kg lighter, faster on 0–60mph acceleration, 2mph faster on top speed, more agile and quicker on twisty, dry roads. In Britain, the 2's list price was £41,504, the 4's £47,699. The 4 was meant for snowy winters but some buyers chose it because it cost more, assuming it had to be better. (LAT)

Left: Developed for the 964 series, the new 3.6-litre, flat-six, double-overhead-cam engine was superb, developing 250bhp at 6,100rpm and giving the Carrera 2 (seen here) a claimed top speed of 161mph. The same engine was fitted to the Carrera 4. (LAT)

Left: The discreet rear spoiler of the Carrera 4 (as with the 2) rose automatically at 50mph and returned to rest as the speed dropped to 6mph. More to do with engine oil cooling than downforce, it was advisable on early models to raise it when stuck in traffic in hot weather. Pressing that button prevented overheating. (LAT)

## Porsche 911 Carrera 2 & Carrera 4 (964)
### 1988–93

**ENGINE:**
Six-cylinder horizontally opposed, air-cooled; aluminium-alloy crankcase, cylinders and heads; rear-mounted

| | |
|---|---|
| Bore x stroke | 100.0 x 76.4mm |
| Capacity | 3,600cc |
| Valve actuation | sohc per bank |
| Compression ratio | 11.3:1 |
| Induction | Bosch DME |
| Power | 248bhp (DIN) at 6,100rpm |
| Maximum torque | 228lb ft at 4,800rpm |

**TRANSMISSION:**
Rear-wheel drive (Carrera 2) or four-wheel drive (Carrera 4); manual five-speed gearbox; four-speed Tiptronic optional on Carrera 2 from late 1991

**SUSPENSION:**
*Front:* Independent by MacPherson strut with light alloy lower wishbones and coil springs; dual-tube gas dampers; anti-roll bar
*Rear:* Independent by MacPherson struts with semi-trailing arms, coil springs; dual-tube gas dampers; anti-roll bar

**STEERING:**
Rack-and-pinion, power-assisted

**BRAKES:**
*Front:* Disc, ventilated (11.7in)
*Rear:* Disc, ventilated (11.8in)
Four-pot callipers; servo assistance
ABS standard from 1990 model year

**WHEELS/TYRES:**
Light alloy wheels, 6J front and 8J rear; magnesium wheels from 1992 model year
Tyres 205/55 ZR 16 front and 225/50 ZR 16 rear; optional from 1992 model year are 7J front rims and 8J rear, with tyres 205/50 ZR 17 front and 225/40 ZR 17 rear

**BODYWORK:**
Steel monocoque
Coupé 2+2, Targa or Cabriolet
Turbo-look body introduced for Carrera 2 Cabriolet from 1992 model year

**DIMENSIONS:**

| | |
|---|---|
| Length | 13ft 11.8in |
| Wheelbase | 7ft 5.5in |
| Track, front | 4ft 6.3in |
| Track, rear | 4ft 6in |
| Width | 5ft 5in |
| Height | 4ft 4in |

**WEIGHT:**
Carrera 4 Coupé: 28.7cwt (1,460kg)

**PERFORMANCE:**
(Source: *Autocar & Motor*)

| | |
|---|---|
| Max speed | 158mph/156mph |
| 0–60mph | 5.1sec/5.2sec |
| Standing quarter-mile | 13.6sec/13.9sec |

(manual Coupé)

**PRICE IN UK INCLUDING TAX WHEN NEW:**
(December 1989)

| | |
|---|---|
| Carrera 2 Coupé: | £41,505 |
| Carrera 2 Targa: | £43,450 |
| Carrera 2 Cabriolet: | £46,699 |
| Carrera 4 Coupé: | £47,699 |
| Carrera 4 Targa: | £49,644 |
| Carrera 4 Cabriolet: | £52,893 |

**NUMBER BUILT:**

| | |
|---|---|
| Carrera 2 Coupé: | 18,219 |
| Carrera 2 Targa: | 3,534 |
| Carrera 2 Cabriolet: | 11,013 |
| Carrera 2 Speedster: | 930 |
| Carrera 4 Coupé: | 13,353 |
| Carrera 4 Targa: | 1,329 |
| Carrera 4 Cabriolet: | 4,802 |

*Notes:*

(1) In 1992 and 1993 model years, 702 Turbo-look Carrera 2 Cabriolets also built – claimed top speed 158mph and 0–62mph in 5.7sec for manual, with 156mph and 6.6sec for Tiptronic

(2) In 1992 and 1993 model years, 15 Turbo-look Carrera 2 Speedsters also built

(3) 911 – yes, that's the number – Carrera 4 Turbo-look Coupés built 1992–93, commemorating 30 years of the 911, plus a further 174 non-commemorative Turbo-look Coupés

## Porsche 911 Carrera RS
### 1991–92

As Carrera 2 except:

**ENGINE:**

| | |
|---|---|
| Power | 256bhp (DIN) at 6,100rpm |
| Maximum torque | 232lb ft at 4,800rpm |

**BRAKES:**
Ventilated and drilled discs, 12.7in front from the 911 turbo/11.8in rear, as used in contemporary Carrera Cup racing

**WHEELS/TYRES:**
Light magnesium alloy wheels, 7.5J front and 9J rear
Tyres Bridgestone Expedia, 205/50 ZR 17 front and 255/40 ZR 17 rear

**DIMENSIONS:**

| | |
|---|---|
| Length | 13ft 11.3in |
| Wheelbase | 7ft 5.4in |
| Track, front | 4ft 8.4in |
| Track, rear | 4ft 10.7in |
| Width | 5ft 9.8in |
| Height | 4ft 3.5in |

**WEIGHT:**
23.5cwt (1,195kg)

**PERFORMANCE:**
(Source: *Autocar & Motor*)

| | |
|---|---|
| Max speed | 161mph |
| 0–60mph | 4.9sec |
| Standing quarter-mile | 13.4sec |

**PRICE IN UK INCLUDING TAX WHEN NEW:**
Coupé: £63,544 (October 1991)

**NUMBER BUILT:**
Coupé: 2,282

**Additionally:**
(1) 290 N/GT versions, totally stripped inside for racing, with roll cages
(2) 90 3.8-litre 300bhp cars, stripped for lightness but with softer suspension, apparently built by racing department in 1992–93
(3) 701 247PS RS cars, built for US

## Porsche 911 Carrera/ Carrera 4 (993)
### 1993–97/1994–97

**ENGINE:**
Six-cylinder horizontally opposed, air-cooled; aluminium-alloy crankcase, cylinders and heads; rear-mounted

| | |
|---|---|
| Bore x stroke | 100.0 x 76.4mm |
| Capacity | 3,600cc |
| Valve actuation | sohc per bank |
| Compression ratio | 11.3:1 |
| Induction | Bosch DME with sequential multi-point injection |
| Power | 272bhp at 6,100rpm* |
| Maximum torque | 252lb ft at 5,000rpm** |

*Raised to 285bhp with variable cam timing for 1996 model year; from late 1994 285bhp or 299bhp performance kits available
** UK market figure; 243lb ft in certain other markets

**TRANSMISSION:**
Rear-wheel drive (Carrera) or four-wheel drive (Carrera 4); manual six-speed gearbox; optional four-speed Tiptronic automatic

**SUSPENSION:**
*Front:* Independent by MacPherson struts, light-alloy lower wishbones and coil springs; double-acting gas dampers; anti-roll bar
*Rear:* Independent by light-alloy multi-link system and coil springs; double-acting gas dampers; anti-roll bar

**STEERING:**
Rack-and-pinion; power-assisted

**BRAKES:**
*Front:* Disc, ventilated (12.0in)
*Rear:* Disc, ventilated (11.8in)
ABS; servo assistance ▶

► **WHEELS/TYRES:**
Light alloy wheels, 7J front and 9J rear
Tyres 205/55 ZR 16 front and 245/45 ZR 17 rear;
optional 205/50 ZR 17 front and 255/40 ZR 17
rear

**BODYWORK:**
Steel monocoque
Coupé 2+2, Cabriolet, Targa (from 1996 model
year)
Carrera S, available from the 1997 model year,
had turbo body but with normal electrically-
extending rear spoiler

**DIMENSIONS:**

| | |
|---|---|
| Length | 13ft 11.1in |
| Wheelbase | 7ft 5.5in |
| Track, front | 4ft 7.3in |
| Track, rear | 4ft 8.8in |
| Width | 5ft 8.3in |
| Height | 4ft 3.2in (with sports suspension, 4ft 2.6in) |

**WEIGHT:**
Carrera Coupé: 27.0cwt (1,370kg)
Carrera Cabriolet: 26.4cwt (1,340kg)
Carrerra 4 Coupé: 28.0cwt (1,420kg)

**PERFORMANCE:**
(Source: *Autocar & Motor*/ Porsche)

| | |
|---|---|
| Max speed | 160mph/167mph |
| 0–60mph/0–62mph | 5.2sec/5.6sec |
| Standing quarter-mile | 13.8sec/not quoted |

**PRICE IN UK INCLUDING TAX WHEN NEW:**
Carrera Coupé: £53,995 (March 1994)
Carrera Cabriolet: £58,995 (June 1994)
Carrera Targa: £64,250 (January 1996)
Carrera 4 Coupé: £58,245 (January 1995)
Carrera 4 Cabriolet: £63,245
(January 1995)

**NUMBER BUILT:**
Carrera Coupé (272bhp): 14,541
Carrera Cabriolet (272bhp): 7,730
Carrera Coupé (285bhp): 8,586
Carrera Cabriolet (285bhp): 7,759
Carrera Targa (285bhp): 4,538
Carrera S Coupé: 3,714
Carrera 4 Coupé (272bhp): 2,884
Carrera 4 Cabriolet (272bhp): 1,284
Carrera 4 Coupé (285bhp): 1,860
Carrera 4 Cabriolet (285bhp): 1,138
Carrera 4S Coupé: 6,948

# Porsche 911 Carrera RS (993)

### 1994–96

As Carrera (993) except:

**ENGINE:**

| | |
|---|---|
| Bore x stroke | 102.0 x 76.4mm |
| Capacity | 3,746cc |
| Induction | Variable-length tracts |
| Power | 300bhp at 6,500rpm |
| Maximum torque | 262lb ft at 5,400rpm |

**TRANSMISSION:**
No Tiptronic option; fifth and sixth gears
lowered on Clubsport model

**BRAKES:**
*Front/rear:* Disc, ventilated (12.7in)

**WHEELS/TYRES:**
Wheels 8J front and 10J rear
Tyres 225/40 ZR 18 front and 265/35 ZR 18 rear

**BODYWORK:**
Aluminium bonnet, thinner rear and side glass,
less insulation and other deletions of luxury
items; rare Clubsport version has bigger front
spoiler and adjustable rear wing, plus rollcage
and full competition equipment. Coupé only

got deeply into racing our Carrera 2, I was asked to go for a drive with a customer who had bought one and wasn't really enjoy driving it. The Porsche sales people made the assumption, which had been correct for decades in such cases, that he needed to be shown how to drive a 911 properly. It was a well-known scenario, going right back even to 356 days at AFN.

So I duly met up with this chap and, well, things did not turn out quite as the AFN team had expected. The man I met was educated, thoughtful, highly intelligent, obviously very successful in business, and he had perfect manners. He was also an extremely good driver. Fast, safe, confident and no hooligan, he measured up to the very image of the perfect 911 owner.

We got on well as I sat in the passenger seat and watched him driving his car with exemplary skill. He easily passed my personal, informal and unspoken driving test, and with distinction. Although he drove fairly quickly, I felt totally confident as a passenger – something I don't normally enjoy very much at any speed – and I said as much to him. That was his cue

to let out his deeper feelings about his new car.

'When I was much younger,' he said, 'I had a secondhand 911SC which I really enjoyed driving. Then I got married, got on in business and ran a series of four-door saloon cars. Now I am in a position to own a car like this, and I have bought it mainly for driving pleasure, but it just doesn't feel the same as my old 911. Maybe it's just that I've got older; perhaps you can show me what I'm doing wrong.'

'You're not doing anything wrong,' I said. 'This is a different kind of car, superior and more advanced in many ways, and certainly safer in an accident. Nobody would thank me for saying this but, between you and me, if you want the traditional 911 driving experience, I have to be honest and say that what you need is a traditional 911.'

We talked it over in detail for another hour, and to my surprise he ended up happy with his new car. It turned out that his real worry had been that he himself had lost something over the years, not that there was anything wrong with his Porsche. He feared that he had become an old man who

couldn't drive a sports car properly any more. He drove away relieved and satisfied when I assured him, in all honesty, that wasn't the case.

But the Carrera 2 story is one with a happy ending: it wasn't long into the 1990s before the engineers at Porsche realised what was going on and started building that deeply satisfying driving experience back into new 911s. I have always suspected that around 1990 they knew they were selling cars to hordes of new customers who bore no resemblance to the informed enthusiasts of earlier days. Porsches, we were told, had become an essential fashion accessory for young men who wore loud braces and collected gigantic bonus payments in the City.

*The author and the AFN Porsche Carrera 2, winning a production car race at a wet Silverstone in September 1990. The heavy Carrera 2 did beat the older and much lighter 911s but it took some subtle chassis development with handling guru Rhoddy Harvey-Bailey and a special braking technique to do it.* (Chris Harvey)

DIMENSIONS:
Height                4ft 2in
WEIGHT:
25.0cwt (1,270kg)
PERFORMANCE:
(Source: Porsche)
Max speed            172mph
0–62mph              5.0sec
PRICE IN UK INCLUDING TAX WHEN NEW:
RS Coupé: £68,495 (January 1995)
Clubsport ('RSR' in UK): £74,795 (January 1995)
NUMBER BUILT:
Standard: 1,014
Clubsport: 227

# Porsche 911 GT 2 (993)
## 1994–1998

As Carrera (993) except:
ENGINE:
Compression ratio    8.0:1
Induction            Twin turbos, twin
                     intercoolers

Power              430bhp at 5,750rpm
                   450bhp at 6,000rpm*
Maximum torque     398lb ft at 4,500rpm
                   431lb ft at 4,500rpm*
* For 1998 model year
TRANSMISSION:
Turbo gear ratios
BRAKES:
Turbo-spec
WHEELS/TYRES:
Light alloy wheels, 9J front and 11J rear
Tyres 235/45 ZR 18 front and 285/35 ZR 18 rear
BODYWORK:
Aluminium bonnet and doors, thinner side and
rear glass, special front spoiler and side skirts,
flared polyurethane wings, plastic engine
lid/adjustable rear wing
Coupé only
DIMENSIONS:
Track, front        4ft 10.1in
Track, rear         5ft 1in
Width               6ft 1in
Height              4ft 2in

WEIGHT:
25.5cwt (1,295kg)
PERFORMANCE:
(Source: Porsche Cars)
Max speed           183mph
(430bhp)/186mph (450bhp)
0–62mph             4.4sec (430bhp)/
                    4.1sec approx
                    (450bhp)
PRICE IN UK INCLUDING TAX WHEN NEW:
Special order only
1995 factory price (430bhp): DM 268,000
1998 factory price (450bhp): DM 287,500
NUMBER BUILT:
430bhp cars: 172
450bhp cars: 21

*Notes:*
(1) Probably 16 of the 430bhp cars were to
Clubsport spec, ie stripped for racing and with
roll cages.
(2) 450bhp cars seem to have steel doors – some
say factory ran out of aluminium ones, but
maybe that's just a rumour!

These people tended to buy the Carrera 4 because it was several thousand pounds more expensive than a Carrera 2. To them, that meant it had to be a 'better' car. How stupid can you get? In fact, on normal roads – wet or dry – the Carrera 2 was invariably quicker than a '4' on the straight and, whatever anyone else might tell you, considerably quicker through the corners as well. And it was more pleasing to drive. Even the 0–60mph time was quicker with a 2 than a 4.

Meanwhile, I had to race that Carrera 2. Apart from the brakes, which needed to be warmed and cooled carefully at all times in racing to avoid heat damage, with never any stamping on the pedal, it wasn't that hard to drive fairly quickly. The frustrating thing was that the production model was set up to be ultra-safe and keep the average driver out of trouble. Consistently, and predictably, it refused to attack race circuit corners as I wanted it too, as if it were saying to me 'Oh, no, let's not go there. Let's just back away

into this nice, safe, compromise.'

The trouble was that despite its 250bhp 3.6-litre engine, its 158mph top speed and its 0–60mph time of 5.1 seconds, I knew it was going to have a job on any circuit beating those 2.7-litre 911RSLs from way back in Porsche's past. By then those great classics were 17 years old but were still racing in some numbers, and very effectively. In fact, steady race development had made them quicker than ever. I knew that because it was only a couple of years since I'd been racing one myself. They were still winners.

The main problem was weight. Those old cars were getting on for 400kg lighter than the Carrera 2, giving the new model a huge penalty to overcome. If that number doesn't seem to mean much, think of it this way: 400kg is nearly 8cwt, or equivalent to five fairly big blokes.

But it wasn't just the weight. The Carrera 2's roadholding was not good enough for racing. The team refused to believe me when I told them that

unpalatable fact. They promptly went off to Snetterton without telling me, put another driver in the car and asked him to try it. At the end of a long day, he was still a second slower than my best time and he completed the job by crashing it and wrecking a front wing. He had made my point for me rather nicely, I felt.

The fact that we did win most of the races was down to some extremely clever development work by a specialist engineer. Yes, once again, I called in the guru, Rhoddy Harvey-Bailey, who had sorted the 928 S4 SE racer for us so very effectively. This time I got permission to enlist his help at an early stage. When I explained my problems with the Carrera 2 to him, his principal tweak was to stiffen up the spring-steel blade that forms part of the semi-trailing-arm rear-wheel location. With that blade almost rigid, the car stopped giving up like a wet rag at the first hint of serious cornering force, and started behaving itself. Grip improved enormously, the responses were sharper and we were in

*Opposite top: A Cabriolet version of the 964 was launched for the 1990 model year, in both Carrera 2 and 4 forms – while the Tiptronic gearbox was available on the Carrera 2 only. A Targa body was also introduced at that time, with the same transmission options. (LAT)*

*Opposite bottom: This 911 had a long name and needed a big cheque – £73,106, plus £1,000 of extras, in late 1991. The 'Porsche 911 Carrera 2 Tiptronic Turbo-Look Cabriolet' was tested then by the author's brother, Peter Dron, former editor of Fast Lane magazine. Fantastic brakes and dry-road grip were marred by the knobbly ride and blunted performance – not to mention the eye-watering price and people shouting 'Poser. Get a real turbo, mate!' (LAT)*

*Right: Based on the Carrera 2, the Speedster was introduced in October 1992 and the factory expected to make about 3,000 of them in the following year. Only about 930 were sold so it remains a rare car, especially in right-hand-drive form. Despite the steeply raked screen, no claims of increased top speed were made for this unusual-looking model. (LAT)*

Above: The famous RS name was revived for the 964-based Carrera in late 1991. Although the car was great on a smooth track, its ultra-stiff suspension, harsh ride, terrible tyre noise and scary behaviour on bumpy roads came as a shock. A worthy attempt to revive the lightweight, pure driver's car, it was just too raw. Still, this guy doesn't seem too scared of it, does he? (LAT)

Left: The stripped-out cabin of the lightweight Carrera RS of the 1992 model year had these impressive-looking Recaro seats but, rare in a 911, few people found the driving position in this model comfortable. This RS cost £15,000 more than a standard Carrera 2. (LAT)

Opposite: The Anniversary 911 of 1993. A batch of the last Carrera 4 Coupés made in that year celebrated the 30th birthday of the 911, using the Turbo-Look wide body with the small, electrically raised rear spoiler. There were 911 cars built, the badge on the engine cover being an underlined 911 in titanium. (LAT)

business. Rhoddy showed how bright he is by getting to the root of the problem very quickly.

But, no, I'm afraid those early Carrera 4s and 2s were incredibly dull cars in standard trim, to me at least. Something needed to happen and it did, eventually, after a bit of a false start that was the RS of 1992.

With the new Carrera 2s and 4s in production, there was still a strong feeling as we entered the 1990s that the 911 had put on weight and gone soft, becoming a range of easy-to-drive cars suited to those get-rich-quick City kids who could not drive well, or even to old boys who were no longer bothered about the keen edge of high-performance driving.

It soon became obvious that there were engineers in the factory who were itching to put this right. They had their way, it seems, for the RS name was revived and we hacks of the Press came to try the latest incarnation of this great name in late 1991. It was a shocking disappointment, at least when it came to normal road use.

It seemed that the old magic touch had been lost. As we all know, if one model had created the 911 legend, it had been the original 1973 2.7 Carrera

RS. Intended to be an homologation special, it had turned out to be a sensational success, increasingly revered as one of the greatest road cars ever made.

Nearly two decades on, much of the same formula seemed to have been applied to the latest car to bear the Carrera RS name: soundproofing was omitted, heavy underbody protection was reduced, air conditioning and lots of electric gadgetry for seats and windows was left out. Thinner glass and lightweight trim were used, and overall weight was reduced by ten per cent. The stiff suspension, based on Carrera Cup racers, was lowered by 1.5in and had little travel, and fatter wheels were fitted, while power from the 3.6-litre flat-six was raised by 10bhp to 260bhp.

The result was a car that worked on a perfectly smooth circuit but was something of a nightmare to drive really fast on normal roads. It had a harsh ride, dreadful booming resonance from the tyres and on bumpy, cambered roads it leapt around alarmingly. The brakes were tremendously powerful but the way the car snaked around when they were used hard put even the best experts off

driving the reborn RS anywhere near its limits. To be fair, it was probably better on smooth German roads than on the undulating olde worlde surfaces still found, and at that time steadily crumbling away, in much of Britain.

It didn't help that the price was £15,000 higher than that of a standard Carrera 2, nor that the corrosion warranty was cut from ten years to three. As a road car it may not have been a success, but for anyone today looking for a serious car for fast and exciting times on track days, a 1992 Carrera RS might well fit the bill at very much the right price. Those who have them expressly for that purpose defend them passionately, praising the bulletproof engine and transmission, the relatively low weight, and the rewarding challenge of the handling on a modern race circuit.

No doubt they are right. At the time, I couldn't see it but there was light at the end of the tunnel even then. Looking back now, the point was that the brainy young guys at the factory had tried to get things back on track: the quest for a pure driving experience had been resumed at Porsche. All right, that 1992 RS was too extreme but it was at least a return to the great ideal,

Above: Late in 1993, yet another new incarnation of the 911 was unveiled and it was immediately obvious that the beautifully restyled and cleverly modified '993' was a really great car. Safe handling had been retained but the steering feel, the handling, the superb brakes and the six-speed gearshift made this 168mph machine something special. (LAT)

Left: Admirably clear instrumentation within the 993 version of the 911 – this happens to be a Targa. Porsche has generally been careful to preserve a traditional look within its 911 and although some press criticism has been levelled at the minor controls down the years customers have tended to like the cockpit. Anyway, when your speedo reads to 180mph, you need to be able to read the dials at a glance, and that's easy in a 911. (LAT)

albeit a painful one. The 'real' 911 was back. Better still, some genuine star cars were just around the corner.

They arrived in the summer of 1993, when we saw what was billed as the very last expression of the 911 theme. The new 911 seen at the 1993 Frankfurt show had wider wings and a sleeker look to its styling. This was the much-altered Carrera, known as the Type 993, and it was a huge improvement over the 964 that it replaced. It was suggested then that in 1996 the traditional rear-engined 911 would be replaced by the Type 996, a mid-engined car apparently. Well, that's what they seemed to imply and we all fell in line, believed what we were told and assumed it would be so.

Meanwhile, this 993, this so-called 'interim, last of the line' 911, was a

mighty impressive machine. Porsche finally gave up on the semi-trailing-arm rear suspension, recognising that they had developed that arrangement as far as it could go. It was replaced with a subframe-mounted, multi-link design that had the effect of an advanced double-wishbone system.

Applied only to the rear-wheel-drive Carrera at first, a major advantage of the new design was increased comfort. Road noise was greatly reduced and the ride was improved. With engine output raised from 250bhp to 272bhp, a stunningly fast car became even quicker, too.

A brand new six-speed manual gearbox was another improvement. At the same time, there was good news for those choosing the modern four-speed Tiptronic transmission. Although

*Peter Robinson, European Editor of* Autocar & Motor, *testing the new 911 Carrera Cabriolet in March 1994. He remarked that if the latest 911 had anything else to prove, then the Cabriolet took care of that. Personally, I remember that the lack of a roof appeared to have no negative effect on the handling whatsoever. Robinson was right, as usual!* (Autocar & Motor/LAT)

the Tiptronic concept always had strong appeal, particularly in the clever way it avoided unwanted changes in gear, early versions had been spoilt for me by the lack of smoothness on changing down. There was always a slight jerk that never happened with a well-driven manual car. Rapid improvements were made in the software and I suspect these were

*A 911 Targa that actually looked great, some said for the first time. With three glass elements, this neat design was based on the 993 Cabriolet body structure. It was available in rear-wheel drive only. (LAT)*

steadily introduced whenever they became available, without announcements being made every time. Certainly, by 1993, Tiptronic downchanges were a whole lot smoother than they had been.

The 911's looks were also updated in this new Carrera, the main changes being that the latest 'ellipsoidal' headlamps were mounted lower than before and the wheelarches slightly flared to accept Carrera Cup wheels. Bosch ABS5 anti-lock brakes were adopted, the interior was tidied up and the screenwipers improved.

From the driver's point of view, the biggest change by far was in the feel of the car. Not only was this version of the 911 easier to drive, it was also far more pleasing to drive fast. Grip was improved but, more important, so were the sense of balance, the high-speed stability and the crispness of the steering response. The new design had enabled Porsche to raise the gearing of

the rack-and-pinion so that only 2.5 turns took it from lock to lock.

Porsche had been through some shaky times in the previous few years, what with a world recession and the problems of trying to sell a range of front-engined models that, whatever their merits, not enough people had wanted to buy. Sales – previously good for the 924/944 and disappointing for the 928 – had dropped to perilously low levels, as indeed they had for the 911. But the financial world was beginning to recover as this new Carrera was launched, and it was so conspicuously good that the production lines at Porsche soon began to look more healthy.

Once again, a brilliant update of the traditional rear-engined car had saved the day. The new man at the top knew what he was doing and where the company was going: Wendelin Wiedeking had joined Porsche AG in 1991 and been appointed Chief Executive in 1993. A long and hard haul lay ahead for him, dragging the company back into a position of strength, but he managed it.

Next to get the new treatment would be the 911 Cabriolet, followed within a couple of years by the Carrera 4 and

turbo models. Demand for the old Targa style of 911 had become minimal, thanks to the Cabriolet, so Targas were to be quietly dropped for a short time, but Speedsters would still be made in limited numbers. The 993 Cabriolet, it must be said, was a stunningly good car to drive, thanks largely to its extraordinarily stiff shell. The lack of a roof appeared to have no negative effect on the handling whatsoever.

Even so, a completely new Targa top was on the way: from late 1995 a brilliantly designed Targa with sliding-glass roof was available, giving a great feeling of open-air motoring. Versatile and practical, it did not compromise the car's looks as previous Targas had. Well, I never thought the old ones looked that great, but that's just my opinion.

Meanwhile the Carrera 4, which of course got the benefit of the 993 treatment in its turn, also came right in a very big way, but for different reasons. All the difference in the world was made to the standard Carrera 4 in late 1994 when the mechanical central differential was replaced with a viscous coupling. That got rid of the dead understeer under power, allowing it to handle like a good rear-wheel-drive car. Porsche cars have always been constantly under improvement but that one change removed any serious criticism of the Carrera 4, at a stroke.

Mind you, I did hear a very strong rumour from a German colleague that the factory had been so confident of the benefits of that central viscous coupling that the test department didn't even bother to head into the high mountains that summer to carry out their traditional annual proving programme. Apparently they know places that are so high that snow-covered roads can be found even in August.

Anyway, they skipped it that time, so the legend goes, and when customers with their brand-new Carrera 4s started arriving in the Alpine ski resorts that winter, they found there wasn't enough drive to the front wheels. In hillstarts on steep slopes,

there they sat with the rear wheels spinning and the front wheels doing nothing. My informant, the sort of guy who finds out these secret things, added that there were a few red faces around the factory that winter, but that the problem was quickly, quietly and easily cured.

As the years went by, there were as usual many more improvements. Power steering and ABS were made standard and there was also the Speedster version, which looked just as weird to me, I'm afraid, as the old 356 Speedster had four decades earlier. The main point, however, was that Porsche cars were very much back on track by then. They had become deeply rewarding to drive once more.

Nowhere was this more true than with the next RS version. Early in 1996 I had my next encounter with yet another brand-new example. It was one of five 911 models I tried during a

two-day trip to Germany. Things had come on hugely for the RS by then. The looks had changed a little since the early 1990s, including more modern headlights, more effective frontal aerodynamics and a more purposeful rear wing.

On the face of it, you still paid more for less, which some people will never understand. You could almost hear them saying, 'Wind-up windows? Hardly any quicker than the standard Carrera? And you pay more?'

There was some truth in that. For £9,500 more than the basic 911

*This time they got it right. The 911 Carrera RS built through the 1995–96 model years was a superb car to enjoy driving fast. Just over 1,000 were built, plus 227 of the RS Clubsport version, seen here, which was distinguished by this prominent rear spoiler. (LAT)*

Carrera's price of almost £59,000, the RS really did have wind-up windows, and smart webbing-loop doorpulls that weighed almost nothing. There was no air conditioning, no central locking and less soundproofing; but there were high-sided lightweight front seats, thinner glass, an alloy front luggage lid and 300bhp instead of 285bhp.

That's where much of the extra money went, but there was more to it than that: this RS was far more than a Carrera with some pricey bits taken off. It was built as an RS from the ground up and this time they'd got it right. Forced to choose one of those five new 911s back in 1996 – well, even an impoverished hack can dream – the RS would have been the one. With the possible exception of air conditioning, I wouldn't have missed any of the luxury items.

At 1,270kg, or 25cwt, the RS weighed 100kg less than the ordinary Carrera, a significant difference that helped to provide finer, faster responses. The difference wasn't night and day but for those who appreciate such things, it was clear, and important. Porsche engineers know this: they feel it themselves, and that's why the RS had returned.

And it felt so right: it's probably enough to say that by 1996 the RS had excellent power steering which was light enough, yet positive and informative. Like the contemporary GT 2, however, it had a curiously hard-rimmed steering wheel that was beautiful to look at and good to use; but you needed gloves to cover any serious distance on twisty roads.

Despite that, this RS was not hard work: far from snaking, darting and weaving around on normal roads, it was stable, lively, reassuring and very quick. Also in the best tradition, the seats looked spartan but I found them great to sit in for hours on end. Shortly after that trip to Germany, I spent a whole day in another new RS at Donington, being paid to give rides to guests of a magazine. It was a full day's work but, even at the close of play, I could not fault the seat. Nor the car, come to that. I loved it.

There simply were no signs of stress or strain in it or in me. From the feel of that car at five o'clock that evening, when the chequered flag came out and the circuit was closed, it might as well have been parked up for the duration. But that's always been typical of 911s.

Understandably, there was a bit more noise inside that RS as well as a bit more 'go' than you got with the standard car. But the noise was enjoyable rather than tiring, and the ride was surprisingly good. By 1996, anyone with a bit of competition driving experience would have found the RS an easygoing everyday road car that could respond instantly to a change in the driver's mood and deliver great satisfaction. It felt alive and responsive and, unlike the 1992 RS, it was a delight to drive on any normal road surface, even our broken-down old British ones. Oh dear, by the end I really wanted to keep that car.

A big part of the fun for me that day was the presence of a charming German chap who was representing well-known independent Porsche tuning specialist, RUF, and he too was giving similar 'taxi-rides' for the same guests in a hugely powerful modified 911. He impressed them by driving sideways all day long. Driving calmly very close to full-race speed, I lapped him over and over again, all day long. His response was to go even more sideways, in clouds of tyre smoke, but that just made him even slower.

A delightful character, our guests were impressed by him and found it hard to believe that 'my' standard RS was cruising past him so easily, even in the corners. By lunchtime, he needed a new set of tyres but the tyres of the RS I had driven were still fine at the end of the whole day.

Once again, the RS had proved that less really can be more. The leaner, meaner RS had become an enthusiast's dream. It had that rare but oh-so-desirable lightweight feel and quicksilver responses. Although only slightly quicker than the standard Carrera in a straight line, its extra alertness was a defining factor. It was one serious driving machine. But it really was a practical everyday car, too.

What of the other 911s in 1996,

apart from the RS? When sent to Germany on that two-day trip early that year, I was lucky enough to drive five of the latest models. The turbo and the GT 2 tested on that memorable trip are covered elsewhere but my recollections of the 911 Carrera and the 4S are relevant here.

The 171mph, rear-wheel-drive Carrera may have been the most popular and the least expensive of that group of 911s but it was still every inch a supercar. Against the others, the suspension was a little softer, so there was a hint of roll, dive and squat. But just a hint. It communicated its intentions lucidly and was a reassuring car to drive in wet or dry weather. Grip was excellent and I was reminded of just how well Porsche had tamed that once errant 911 tail.

That 1996 Carrera was safe and fun at the same time, and you didn't have to be a hero to drive it swiftly. Its race-bred pedigree shone through so that the superb poise and brilliant braking performance made it something really special to drive on a track. Yet, in the best Porsche tradition, it could be driven to work every day and keep its driver very comfortable. Its 7J/9J x 16in rims were the narrowest tyres of the 911 pack I sampled on that trip but they were still wider than those on most other cars and, just occasionally on some surfaces, that could be felt in the ride.

Talking tyres, I am not one of those who believes wider is always better. In my experience, wider tyres can spoil the feel of a car; the tyre width in this case, however, seemed exactly right. There was a no-nonsense honesty about that standard Carrera that made it tremendously appealing, and – I repeat – it delivered on all fronts as a supercar.

By comparison with the standard rear-wheel drive car I tried on the same day, the 1996 Carrera 4S added considerably to all-weather confidence but lost something in agility, predictably enough. The 'S' in its name meant that the normally aspirated engine was teamed with the turbo's wider body, but without the fixed tail spoiler. And the wheels had solid spokes instead of hollow ones.

# The GT 1

If the 993 GT 2 was something very special, the contemporary GT 1 was in another league again. In the summer of 1996, an extraordinary opportunity came my way. If you have read what I wrote then about the GT 1 (in a long-defunct magazine) I would be astonished, so I feel these forgotten words deserve to live again:

‘ I'd heard that a 911 GT 1 would be running on a quiet day at Hockenheim. So I turn up, wander into the pits and there it is, front body removed, engine still warm from a morning on the track. The garage is all but empty, most of the Porsche people are at lunch. I take my chance to inspect the GT 1 closely.

Although unmistakably a close relative of the 911, it's a lot longer:

17in longer overall and 8.9in longer in the wheelbase than the '964'-type 911, and four inches lower. Yet it weighs only a claimed 1,000kg, 507kg less than a regular turbo.

Lurking at the back of the pit, it has a tough, almost intimidating air about it. Largely black, much of its carbonfibre and Kevlar body unpainted and with adhesive tape applied in strategic places, it's obviously had a hard life so far, yet the fit of every body part is still superb.

Unlike 911 road cars, of course, it's mid-engined. The chassis is built from the steel front bay of a 911 with a special floorpan added behind that and the basic structure completed with a substantial rollcage. Complex subframes hold the 3.2-litre water-cooled flat-six engine and six-speed

transmission to the chassis behind the cockpit. Only the crankshaft and crankcase come from the standard Carrera engine: the rest of the four-cam, 24-valve, single-plug-ignition design is purpose-built for the GT 1.

Opening the driver's door, I'm

*Mid-engined but feeling like a 911 at heart, the 911 GT 1 was exactly what a Le Mans car should be – a racer based on the road car. The chassis was built up from the steel front bay of a 911 bodyshell and the 3.2-litre flat-six retained a Carrera crankshaft and crankcase. To meet the rules, Porsche had to make one road-legal machine: in fact, they made two in 1996 and followed that with 21 customer cars through 1997–98. With Allan McNish as the lead driver, a works GT 1 won the Le Mans 24Hrs in 1998. (Autocar/LAT)*

# The GT 1 (continued)

expecting it to be light... but not that light. There's barely any weight to it, yet it feels rigid and opens and closes with delightful precision. With permission, I try the cockpit for size. Even with the seat a little forward of its end stops, it feels great.

Soon, the GT 1's keepers return from lunch. Another stroke of luck: racing chief Norbert Singer is in charge. Singer was the team boss when Porsche ran 924 GT prototypes at Le Mans back in 1980. I drove one in that race. So, naturally, this is a friendly reunion. What follows is better still. A few laps in the GT 1? I had to ask. No problem. I do my best to stay cool. What a chance!

Singer tells me more about the car. The decision to build the GT 1 race cars was taken last August (1995) but the team had been thinking through the design long before that – not easy given that the car had to be road legal. Not only does the GT 1 meet all EU requirements – from safety, noise and emissions to the area of vision scribed by the wiper – it even has a boot of sorts.

This prototype was built in the winter with the construction of the body being contracted out to a special division of Ford race-car specialists Zakspeed. With the car up and running in March, the 600bhp engine and chassis worked well straight away. A couple of final drive failures were made good and a 36-hour test at the Paul Ricard circuit, normal Porsche procedure before Le Mans, was undertaken with the works drivers.

'We considered fashionable items,' said Singer, 'like a sequential gearchange, a dog 'box and a small three-plate racing clutch but opted for our own tried and tested gearchange, synchromesh and clutch.'

Before stuffing in my earplugs, I ask about the rev limit (8,000rpm, but a technician suggests 7,800rpm today)

and the gearchange (normal six-speed). A regular ignition key works the starter. If this weren't a Porsche I'd be surprised: up to this point, the GT 1 had seemed a pure racer. Tightly belted into the close-fitting seat, my helmet isn't touching the roof, the LCD tacho is easy to read, the pedal layout superb, the steering wheel position ideal and, with the seat right back, there's lots of legroom. I can see forward with an excellent wide angle of view, and the two well-designed exterior mirrors give the complete scene behind. They'd be vibration-free at speed, too. I'm comfortable; ready.

On start-up, the GT 1 is pure Porsche. It makes a lovely deep, reassuring and easy noise that tells of very serious performance without jangling your nerve-endings. I'm amazed the clutch isn't heavier and it's a doddle to select first in the synchromesh 'box. I drive up the pit lane as easily as in any good road car. This is what Le Mans cars should be like: related to road cars in a real way but painstakingly prepared for serious international racing. The GT 1 measures up.

You could forgive a hard-used prototype for feeling knackered but this car feels ready for a 24-hour race now and shoots up the first straight. It drives beautifully.

Disregard the lack of trim and all the special controls and the GT 1 is like a regular Porsche, only much faster and even more direct. It rides well for a race car, the steering is accurate and the handling forgiving. If you can cope with the sheer speed, 30–60mph in 2.1 seconds and 30–100mph in only 4.7 seconds (compared with 2.3 seconds and 7.5 seconds for a standard 911 turbo), it feels very reassuring. The track is damp, caution is needed. Even so, the GT 1 hits 131.4mph down the pits straight on the first lap (so the computer print-out later handed to me says). But ultimate speed isn't the point here. It's to get a feel for the car

in four laps; to drive very fast, but not at the absolute limit.

The GT 1 moves so easily, seems wonderfully effortless despite the mighty acceleration, braking and cornering power. On the damp surface, it's quite easy to flick the tail out under power but the car stays balanced, despite its ferocious potential. Carbon-fibre brakes outperform those of any road car I have driven. The GT 1 pulls up from high speeds in a totally reassuring manner.

This cockpit would be a pleasant workstation for long stints in a 24-hour race: the GT 1 wouldn't wear you out prematurely. With such accurate steering, such a great gearbox and such user-friendly torque characteristics, you could just revel in driving your heart out.

I do a slow lap to cool everything off before pulling in. Norbert Singer opens the door and awaits my reaction. As I yank off my helmet and balaclava I just can't stop grinning, which probably says it all. It's a pure Porsche, the GT 1, right to its heart. A great car – one of the greatest I have ever driven. There is nothing else to say.'

That's what I wrote, a bit breathlessly perhaps, at the time. Apart from prototypes, at least 23 road-legal GT 1s were produced even though the homologation rules of international motor racing would have been satisfied with just one single car. A friend of mine had one of those rare cars for a couple of years and I drove it round the old Nürburgring a few times on recent RMA track days.

Oddly enough, I found it unexpectedly alarming to drive, and after that I politely avoided getting behind its wheel. Something appeared to have been severely compromised because my friend's car tended to pull weirdly on the steering and dart about in corners. If you pushed it at all hard, for no apparent reason it would suddenly try to take a dive off the road and I felt lucky when it did not actually manage to do that.

These customers' road cars, I believe, were not quite identical to the racing 'mule' I had driven before at Hockenheim; certainly they were a fair bit heavier, but I think the problem here was rather more simple. The suspension on this particular GT 1 had been raised so that the owner could get up his drive without grounding it. Right. I see. Also, when I drove that car it was on non-standard tyres – slicks, in fact, for those track days, to save a lot of money. The huge road tyres

originally fitted are very expensive and they wear out fast on a track – but I doubt whether that alone was the crucial issue making that car so nervous. My suspicion was that a return to the factory's ride-height settings would have made a world of difference. The GT 1 is not a road car adapted to racing: it's nothing less than an out-and-out racing car that was adapted for road use. It was an extremely clever interpretation of the GT racing rules, if you like, and I just don't think it likes its racing set-up being played with like that.

*Production GT 1s like this one gave 544bhp, did 0–62mph in a claimed 3.7sec and were electronically limited to 192mph. Of the 23 produced, four were offered for sale in the UK in 1997 at an on-the-road price of £457,075. They met all EU rules on safety, noise and emissions. The factory's 600bhp racing 'mule' I drove at Hockenheim in 1996 had sublime handling but a later 544bhp 'customer' car was alarming on the Nordschleife because it had non-standard tyres, plus a raised ride height so that the owner could get it up his drive! With pure race cars like this, it's important to stick to the correct settings. (Autocar/LAT)*

With the extra weight of the drive to the front wheels, the C4S weighed 1,450kg, or 28.5cwt, making it 80kg heavier than the normal Carrera. Looking at the figures, its performance was slightly slower all round but I have to say that I could not notice any difference in the acceleration subjectively.

There were considerable differences in feel, though. Turn-in wasn't quite so crisp, and the extra weight in the nose was noticeable. For some reason, the brakes on that test car required a particularly light touch but their enormous power and resistance to fade were prodigious.

The C4S was very predictable and progressive in its behaviour and it certainly did not require superhuman skills to drive it quickly. In normal, dry-road conditions, the standard Carrera was still the one to go for because the 4S offered no advantage and certainly no more driving pleasure. However, the four-wheel drive 911 had come on so much by then that I had no hesitation in recommending a 4S to anybody looking for that extra bit of security in bad weather. I think some people bought it mainly for the looks, however.

The C4S, as the latest and best incarnation of the Turbo-Look theme at that time, relied on style, traction and braking for its appeal. Given the normally aspirated engine's relatively modest 286bhp, the Carrera 4 transmission and the turbo's wide tyres and tremendous brakes, it was easily the most 'over-chassised' of the 1996 911s. It was a car that flattered an indifferent driver and, like the Speedster, was one of those additions to the range that broadened the appeal of the 911. That sounds like I'm putting it down. On the contrary: remember, it was still good for at least 170mph.

Somewhat less restrained in its appeal was the flamboyant GT 2. At the Nürburgring, back in 1996, I had my first experience of driving one. After pulling in and switching off, I stayed in the driver's seat for a long time. Then I grabbed my pad. 'An almost perfect combination for the most serious enthusiast,' I noted. 'Here's a car that could put the independent performance kit specialists out of business at a stroke.'

These thoughts, committed to paper immediately after driving the car, fully do it justice. The GT 2 looked sensational, the bodywork modifications being based on sound technical stuff but with a brutal, muscular touch to their styling. More importantly, it was a masterly slap in the face to all pretenders. The specification alone was enough to make you stop and think, but driving it on a track was a revelation. Just for starters, imagine a rear-drive turbo without a catalyst and tweaked to produce a staggering 430bhp,

Extra-wide arches enclosed the fattest wheels available, and this was a car with the power to make full use of those big tyres. It needed them. Completing the image from the outside, the huge and adjustable rear spoiler left no one in any doubt over that amazing car's identity.

The 1996 GT 2 weighed just 1,290kg, or 25.4cwt, a mere 20kg more than the contemporary RS and a massive 210kg less than the turbo of that time. Despite the drag of that big wing – the biggest to date ever fitted to a production 911 – the GT 2 did 184mph and 0–60mph in 3.8 seconds when we tested it. Some others claimed 197mph and 0–60mph in 3.7 seconds. Check these figures against almost anything you like. Maybe you'll find something

Opposite: With the Carrera 4S Coupé, launched in late 1995, customers were offered another variation on the 911 theme: a turbo-style body (without the big wing on the back), the normally aspirated 285bhp engine, four-wheel drive, the six-speed gearbox and a lavish level of standard equipment. It was a very easy car to drive but the wide body made it a little slower than a standard Carrera 4. Top speed was still 168mph, however. (LAT)

Above: A 1998 911 GT 2 Evo, with full racing kit. The standard GT 2 at that time, with an engine based on the GT 1 racer, produced 450bhp and gave a top speed of 186mph. To me, the awesome standard car was a drifter's dream and it made a mockery of lesser machines. These racing versions, producing up to 600bhp, were extremely successful. (Porsche)

Right: Owner and expert Porsche driver Richard Green has not lost control of his 993 GT 2 on this track day. This car, his first GT 2, turned him into a confirmed Porsche addict and he can drive them like this all day long. 'It's absolute magic on the track,' he says. (Richard Green collection)

quicker, maybe you won't. What I'll lay money on is the plain fact that you will never find anything contemporary with that car to match its performance and keep it up day in, day out, without needing huge amounts of attention from a service department. Get it straight: this was one extraordinary motor car. Although feasible as a road car, it was really a well-bred monster looking for a circuit.

Connect the light, responsive feel of the RS with turbo-plus grunt and you're getting the idea of what it was like to drive that GT 2. But, with the best Porsche cars, there's always more

*Richard Green with his latest acquisition, a 1998 '993' 911 GT 2 R Evo, on his way to victory in a race at Hockenheim in 2007. Uprated to 700bhp, given a wider track and fitted with a bigger spoiler, this GT 2 Evo is certainly not road-legal! (Patrick Holzer)*

in the way the parts gel to form an even more remarkable whole. What I mean is this: in skilled hands, the ability of that GT 2 was simply awesome. Making a mockery of lesser cars, it cornered at a ridiculously high level of grip – yet all the time feeding back beautifully resolved information about the road surface to the driver's hands.

However, Porsche took care not to sell that limited production masterpiece to just anyone who walked in off the street. It was an extreme car that was made available only to the favoured few who could not only afford it but also truly appreciate it. If the truth be known, it was probably too addictive as a road car.

But for those special trips – such as dropping in for a few laps of the Nürburgring's Nordschleife – there was nothing to beat it. It was so predictable when driven hard: a

drifter's dream. I was told that in the wet it could spin its wheels in third. I wouldn't doubt that for a moment but it was a car that never gave a moment's anxiety. You could revel in the feel of the thing.

The brake pedal needed a firm push but there was just exactly the right amount of travel and that helped with the precision needed near the limit of grip approaching a corner. The hard-rimmed steering wheel seemed odd until I realised that you were expected to wear gloves to drive such cars over any distance, otherwise your hands would start to be rubbed raw and hurt. Of course. That's just fine and, if you have got this far in the book, I imagine it's fine for you too. We just go and get some gloves, then carry on driving.

At the time, the GT 2 was priced at £135,000 and the verdict was clear: the GT 2 was a proper 911 with the seductive lightweight feel of the RS and

the accelerative slam of a Turbo with afterburners, and that stunning performance came in smoothly and controllably thanks to its sequential turbos. If a more exhilarating road car exists for under £200,000, we all said, wheel it on.

More info on the 993 GT 2 will appear in Chapter 12, in which some extreme versions of it will be compared against the equivalent 996 GT 2. For now, it's enough to say the 993 GT 2 represented one of those sublime peaks in the 911 saga.

Despite the fears some of us had felt only a few years before, Porsche had not lost the plot after all and that's all that needs to be said on that subject. My faith had been utterly restored and I have had no reason to change my mind since then. Those guys in Stuttgart still knew exactly what they were doing, and the brilliant Wendelin Wiedeking was leading them. That was the conclusion at the time, and subsequent experience has proved that the 993 GT 2 is indeed one of the great classic 911s.

I had fallen in love with 911s way back in 1971 when I drove a new 2.4-litre 'S'. My brief run in that GT 2 a quarter of a century later was even more special. True to its roots, this was one street-racer of the highest standing. The last note I jotted down that day said it all: 'My God, these people can make a motor car.'

That was just my reaction from one day with the car, but it's backed up by owners' experiences. One whose opinion and driving I respect is Richard Green, who has probably done more track miles in his own GT 2s than anybody, including I suspect even Porsche's own test drivers. 'It is absolutely magic on the track yet soft enough for the road. It feels softer than a 993 RS, in fact,' says Richard. 'The only modification we have made, and I would recommend it, is to fit the Porsche M-Sport anti-roll bar on the rear. The turn-in response is much better.'

I doubt whether Richard will ever be without a 993 GT 2 now. One of them was his first Porsche and it turned him into a complete Porsche addict. A recent addition to his collection is a

# Buying hints

**1.** Much has been said about how Porsche improved the rust-resisting qualities of new bodyshells in the late 1970s and throughout the 1980s, and it's all absolutely true. So, you might think, when buying a car made in the 1990s, you needn't worry about corrosion. You'd be wrong.

**2.** Though these models do resist rust extremely well, they aren't immune and they're all coming up to a critical age now. Little dings and scrapes can set off isolated corrosion areas and rust can also start in those concealed dirt traps that exist under all cars. There could be hidden rust festering away somewhere, so get an expert to check. Remember, too, that any major accident or panel repair can negate the protection which the galvanised original was able to boast.

**3.** These might be relatively recent models in Porsche's history but the best advice is still to approach buying one as if you're out to obtain a much older classic car. Look at condition, history and evidence of care, and be far less concerned about what the odometer tells you.

**4.** Join the Porsche Club Great Britain, talk to the 964 and 993 register secretaries and go to the right

club events at which you will meet existing owners. Listen to what they have to say about their own cars.

**5.** Once you get to this level of Porsche ownership, every single model offers extremely high performance and a few are genuine supercars. Parts can be expensive. Do check the price of a new clutch, for example, plus the cost of having it fitted. It might make your eyes water. An hour or so spent going through a list of replacement parts you might need in the future, and their current prices, is time well spent.

**6.** Take care to look at all the different models made with the 964 and 993 bodies. There is a huge variety in the driving experience available through these years. Be sure to pick the one that suits you.

**7.** Having got your car, you can tell the world proudly that you have one of the last air-cooled 911s. Fair point, I'd say, but don't swank too much if you haven't actually driven a brand-new, water-cooled 997. They are, I can assure you, really rather good. In fact, never look down on any other Porsche. Snobbery is always taboo in Porsche circles.

superb 1955 356 1500 Coupé: yes, the man is a true connoisseur. One time we were discussing 356s and early 911s, recalling the cast iron weights that used to be added within the front bumpers of short-wheelbase 911s to help the handling 40 years ago.

'Interesting,' he said. 'You know, even the 993 GT 2 handles massively differently when its fuel tank is almost empty. Turning-in in the wet can be interesting with an empty tank – sometimes a sharp little prod of the brake with the left foot can help the nose tuck in to the apex.' Fuel tanks in 911s are of course well to the front of the car.

When driving his 993 GT 2 Clubsport at a circuit near Colmar in very bad wet weather, he took this principle a stage further: 'I improved the handling by filling it up with fuel and putting a trolley jack under the bonnet. Turn-in was excellent despite the very wet circuit – and oversteer was even more 'available' too!'

Only 172 of the 430bhp cars were made, and only 21 with the 450bhp engine. Values are therefore likely to rise in future, especially in Britain because a mere seven right-hand-drive 993 GT 2s came here during the five years in which the model was listed!

# The Boxster

*Cleverly named as a contraction of 'boxer-engined roadster', the Boxster was even more cleverly conceived. Seen here is the concept car unveiled at the Detroit Motor Show in January 1993. Attractive, mid-engined and desirable, it created a pent-up demand for the 'affordable' new Porsche. Production versions were expected to reach the UK in 1995 and cost about £25,000. (LAT)*

A certain amount of nervous apprehension greeted the news that Porsche was to launch a relatively modest mid-engined car that would slot into the market well below the price of the traditional models. Purists might have called it the Porsche 986 but the name 'Boxster', a nice contraction of 'boxer-engined roadster' was universally accepted. With plenty of competition from the likes of the new Mercedes-Benz SLK known to be coming up at roughly the same time, and the legendary 911 on the verge of major change, Porsche had to get this one right.

Previous attempts to create a new model that was not a 911, for all their undoubted technical merit, had not always made the grade. We were living in a different age in the 1990s and it just would not do to produce

something as basic as the original 924 that had been launched 20 years before. Much was at stake over the Boxster's commercial prospects. It had been costly to develop such a high-quality new model and the opposition was stronger than ever. But the top Porsche people knew they had a good car on their hands, in fact they were confident it was an excellent car. The question was whether that would be enough to see it through.

Porsche had made some very fine cars in the past that had nonetheless not sold in sufficient numbers. Not all had been welcomed by traditionally minded enthusiasts of the marque, let alone the different breed of buyer Porsche needed to attract to get the company running to full capacity. Memories of the 968 were still fresh. So Porsche took care to get its market research and the design right with this one. Shown as a rather flamboyant concept at the Detroit show in 1993, production of the more practical, real world Boxster model began in 1996.

At the time, some said it had been too long since Detroit, meaning that the market's patience might be wearing thin. Others said the Boxster might be much cheaper than a 911 but it was still far too expensive for what it was. They were all wrong. With this entry-level Porsche, unlike some others that had gone before, the crucial

difference was that from the very start the mid-engined Boxster was a pure Porsche, not something that could be seen as a compromised mish-mash. The look, the sound and the quality of construction were all true to the marque and the handling was quite exceptional. The Boxster also offered open-top motoring truly at the touch of a switch. Even the most conservative 911 diehard had to praise it: the Boxster was truly and very obviously worthy of its Porsche badge and the entire first-year allocation to the UK was sold out immediately.

Its new water-cooled flat-six Porsche

*Above: When the new Boxster did start to arrive in the UK, at the very end of 1996, the entire allocation for 1997 sold out instantly. Close enough to the original concept, it also had just enough power and it measured up as a 'proper' Porsche. Most of all, it handled very well and was fun to drive. The price, £33,950, disappointed some people but proved no handicap to sales. By then, you see, new 911s started at £61,395... (LAT)*

*Below: Boxster 2.7 dash, in late 1999, showing the prominent rev counter. The centre console became standard in the 2.7 but the leather trim in this car was an option costing £2,490. (LAT)*

*Above: The first Boxster Tiptronics in 1997 had five-speed gearboxes and shift buttons in the steering wheel. They were super-smooth in city traffic but performance was marginally blunted and the Tiptronic 'brain' could sometimes override the driver's commands inappropriately. Most enthusiasts preferred the manual models. (LAT)*

*Below: The standard Boxster got a timely boost when engine capacity was raised by 207cc for the 2000 model year. Mid-range acceleration and sporting feel were significantly improved. Top speed rose from 139mph to 149mph. This 'family snap' shows the author at the wheel of an early Boxster 2.7. (Author's collection)*

engine was almost completely hidden in the centre of the car. Driving an early example in 1996, I felt that the engine was just powerful enough for the Boxster's place in the market but, and this seemed far more important, the point was that it responded absolutely as a Porsche should, sounding especially purposeful from 5,500rpm and revving easily. A 3-litre 250bhp engine was said to be on the way but many of us felt there was no need to wait for that. The original Boxster, with its 2,480cc engine, was a gem.

It's easy to think of the Boxster as a small car. Somehow I have always seen

it that way myself but the fact is that it came in slightly longer than the 911, believe it or not. Once inside, the driving position is ideal for anyone of up to 6ft and Boxsters have also always been more than acceptable for much taller drivers. In that early left-hand-drive test car, I found my right leg movement slightly restricted but I adapted to that easily enough and there's been never been any such problem for me on right-hand-drive cars.

The first Boxster interiors bore the unmistakable stamp of Porsche. Back in 1993, the original Detroit concept car had been given an extravagant interior that was, frankly, a bit over the top. Porsche stated quite openly that it would be toned down for production and, when it came to the real thing, the designers took an unashamedly modern approach, resisting the temptation of a fashionable retro look. A theme of eccentric broken circles was chosen for the major instruments, which looked good and were easy to read. Perhaps the minor switchgear on the console was somewhat uninspired. Some people reckoned it failed in that respect alone to set the Boxster apart from many of the better Japanese cars, but it seemed fine to me. The quality of that interior was excellent: undeniably attractive, it was comfortable and everything was easy to operate.

Without exception, I believe, every journalist driving those first Boxsters raved about the handling, roadholding and ride. How right they were. One of the most confidence-inspiring cars, it displayed exemplary poise, grip and feel under all conditions. At high speed it felt extremely stable, although the steering was a bit dead when travelling straight ahead. In corners the feel was just superb, the response being instant and incredibly reassuring. The tightest hairpin bends, however, did demand a fair bit of wheel twirling but that was no great problem. The excellent brakes felt appropriately firm and secure at the pedal, and the latest anti-lock electronics gave the shortest possible stopping distances in poor conditions.

Its well-sorted mid-engined layout probably gave the Boxster a decisive edge against its rivals. Quite apart from the sporting feel of the car, and its desirable image, it was a winner on luggage accommodation. Whereas front-engined, two-seater convertibles can be compromised on boot space, the Boxster had a reasonable boot in the back and then there was a deep, great well up front too. Nor did the space available change with the hood neatly power-stowed away – an operation achieved faster than on any other car in those days, it was claimed. Open or closed, occupants were well protected: with the hood down on a cold autumn day, I found the powerful heater removed all discomfort, and I hate the cold with a passion. With the hood up, wind noise was not even noticed below 110mph.

Beyond all that practical stuff, however, the Boxster was a car that made you enjoy driving. In every way it was the success that Porsche had dreamt of and the company must have been delighted in the first three years to learn that 55,705 people found the original model sufficiently irresistible to go out and buy it. Had it flopped, it could have taken the company, Porsche AG, with it. The situation was that serious.

# Porsche Boxster 2.5/2.7/S
## 1996–2002

**ENGINE:**
Six-cylinder horizontally opposed, alloy heads and blocks, water-cooled; mid-mounted

| | |
|---|---|
| Bore x stroke | 85.5mm x 72.0mm |
| | 85.5mm x 78.0mm |
| | 93.0mm x 78.0mm |
| Capacity | 2,480cc/2,687cc/3,179cc |
| Valve actuation | Variable timing, dohc per bank, four valves per cylinder |
| Compression ratio | 11.0:1/10.8:1 |
| Induction | Bosch Motronic |
| Power | 204bhp at 6,000rpm |
| | 220bhp at 6,400rpm |
| | 252bhp at 6,250rpm |
| Maximum torque | 181lb ft at 4,500rpm |
| | 192lb ft at 4,750rpm |
| | 225lb ft at 4,500rpm |

**TRANSMISSION:**
Rear-wheel drive; five-speed (2.5/2.7) or six-speed (S) manual gearbox; optional five-speed Tiptronic

**SUSPENSION:**
*Front and rear:* Independent by struts, longitudinal and transverse arms, and coil springs; double-acting gas dampers; anti-roll bar

**STEERING:**
Rack-and-pinion, power-assisted

**BRAKES:**
*Front:* Disc, ventilated (11.7in on 2.5/2.7 and cross-drilled 12.5in on S)
*Rear:* Disc, ventilated (11.5in on 2.5/2.7 and cross-drilled 11.8in on S)
Four-pot callipers; ABS; servo assistance

**WHEELS/TYRES:**
Cast alloy wheels, 6J front and 7J rear (2.5/2.7) or 7J front and 8.5J rear (S)
Tyres 205/55 ZR 16 front and 225/50 ZR 16 rear (2.5/2.7) or 205/50 ZR 17 front and 255/40 ZR 17 rear (S)
Wider 17in or 18in rims optional, depending on year (always 18in on S)

**BODYWORK:**
Monocoque, mainly steel construction
Two-door two-seat roadster

**DIMENSIONS:**
| | |
|---|---|
| Length | 14ft 1.9in |
| Wheelbase | 7ft 11.1in |
| Track, front | 4ft 9.3in |
| Track, rear | 4ft 11.4in |
| Width | 6ft 4in (including mirrors) |
| Height | 4ft 2.8in |

**WEIGHT:**
2.5: 24.5cwt (1,242kg)
2.7: 24.6cwt (1,250kg)
S: 25.5cwt (1,295kg)

**PERFORMANCE:**
(Source: *Autocar*)
| | |
|---|---|
| Max speed | 139mph (136mph Tiptronic)/ 149mph/161mph |
| 0–60mph | 6.5sec (7.3sec Tiptronic)/ 6.4sec/6.0sec |
| Standing quarter-mile | 15.6sec (15.5sec Tiptronic)/ 14.9sec/14.3sec |

**PRICE IN UK INCLUDING TAX WHEN NEW:**
2.5 Manual: £34,095 (January 1997)
2.5 Tiptronic S: £36,695 (January 1997)
2.7: £34,232 (November 1999)
S: £42,161 (July 1999)

**NUMBER BUILT:**
2.5: 55,705
2.7: 51,284
S: 46,945

# Porsche Boxster/Boxster S
## 2002–2005

As 1999 2.7 except:

**ENGINE:**
| | |
|---|---|
| Compression ratio | 11.0:1 |
| Power | 228bhp at 6,300rpm |
| | 260bhp at 6,200rpm |
| | 236bhp at 6,400rpm* |
| | 266bhp at 6,200rpm* |
| Maximum torque | 192lb ft at 4,700rpm |
| | 229lb ft at 4,600rpm |
| | 199lb ft at 4,700–6,000rpm* |
| | 229lb ft at 4,600rpm* |

* From late 2003

**DIMENSIONS:**
| | |
|---|---|
| Length | 14ft 2.4in |
| Track, front | 4ft 10.7in |
| Track, rear | 5ft 0.4in |
| Width | 6ft 4.2in (including mirrors) |
| Height | 4ft 3in |

**WEIGHT:**
25.1cwt (1,275kg)/26.0cwt (1,320kg)
(2003 models weigh 20kg more)

**PERFORMANCE**
(228bhp Boxster/260bhp Boxster S):
(Source: *Autocar*/Porsche)
| | |
|---|---|
| Max speed | 155mph/164mph (165mph with 266bhp) |
| 0–60mph/0–62mph | 6.3sec/5.7sec |
| Standing quarter-mile | 14.8sec/not quoted |

**PRICE IN UK INCLUDING TAX WHEN NEW:**
Boxster: £31,140 (October 2002)
Boxster S: £38,150 (October 2002)

**NUMBER BUILT:**
Boxster: 19,289
Boxster S: 11,415
Boxster S '50 Years 550' limited edition: 1,953

They need not have worried. From the start, the mid-engined Boxster had been seen and accepted as a pure Porsche. And, somehow, it had that magic touch. Without being too ostentatious, it looked and felt like the car of a person who had succeeded in life, and was something in which to arrive anywhere with a discreet sense of pride. Never mind the fact that some observers had been quite rude about it in the early days, even down to mentioning 'headlights like runny fried eggs' and making jibes about its supposedly ample rear end. Others saw something of the 550 sports-

*To look at, the Boxster S was distinguished by an extra vent under the front number plate and by its uprated brakes with red callipers. The leap in performance given by the 3.2-litre, 252bhp engine was much more noticeable, lifting top speed to 161mph. The S, which went on sale in the UK at £42,161 in October 1999, felt closer to the Carrera in character but Porsche took good care to keep its 911 that bit quicker. (LAT)*

racing Porsches of the mid-1950s in its styling, and commented favourably to that effect. The people in the market to buy it, however, loved the Boxster – and they are always the only ones who really matter.

As we know very well now, its success must have come as a huge relief to the top people at the factory. In planning it, they had wanted to produce a car they could sell for not much more than £20,000 but the over-budget development costs made that impossible. At around £35,000 when it first went on sale in the UK, it was certainly not cheap but it could be seen quite legitimately as an entry-level Porsche even if its price was a hell of long way above the affordable level they had intended to achieve.

Money had been saved where possible, using a modified 911 floorpan and suspension, but in truth the final result was a very different product, effectively a completely new car, right down to its engine which on paper was based firmly on Porsche's tradition but which in reality was all-new.

That original 2.5-litre, water-cooled, flat-six engine produced a very adequate 204bhp at 6,000rpm and that was more than enough at the time. The top speed was 139mph, with 0–60mph achieved in 6.5 seconds. The Boxster also had a smooth, fast and positive five-speed manual gearchange, with well-chosen ratios. The early car was always a pleasure to drive. It could lope along with the lusty, deep-breathing engine eating the miles easily but it could also respond rewardingly when driven with more verve.

That 3-litre version, promised from the start, had prepared us for more excitement to come in the future but it seems the Boxster's terrific initial success enabled Porsche to embark on a rather more ambitious programme of developments. That became clear when the latest Boxster models were unveiled three years later. Subtle tweaks to the chassis sharpened up an already excellent driving experience

On the one hand, by lengthening the stroke, there was an upgrade to 2.7 litres for the basic car, the manual

version having shorter gearing for better performance in the two highest gears while the Tiptronic ratios remained unchanged. This engine gave the standard Boxster a mean top speed of at least 149mph, and minor improvements since then have pushed it comfortably over the 150mph mark. That welcome upgrade to 2.7 litres improved the appeal of the basic Boxster in late 1999, especially as the price increase was held down. That 2000 model year 2.7 only cost just over £100 more than the 2.5 had on the model's debut some three years earlier. No-one complained about that, of course, and discourteous remarks about the price declined to almost nothing, but some of the options were a different matter. Paying nearly £2,500 for leather upholstery in a two-seater did seem a bit steep, I suppose.

On the other hand, there was also the sensational new Boxster S, which actually displaced 3,179cc. Launched a few months before the 2.7, it cost about £8,000 more than the standard car when it went on sale in 1999. But power was raised to over 250bhp, with

top speed up to just over 160mph, and that placed the 'S' neatly between the standard Boxster and 911 Carrera in terms of performance.

Although very much from the same family, the bigger capacity of the Boxster S engine was achieved by lengthening both bore and stroke. The flat torque curve of this version gave a huge increase in thrust from as low as 2,000rpm. Despite that, the 'S' was also given a strong six-speed gearbox, based on that from the 911, and again with a superb gearchange.

It had bigger 18in wheels as standard – 7J front and 8.5J rear – and even wider options were available, but little needed to be done to the chassis, which was easily up to the job of handling the bigger engine. The springs and dampers were stiffened a little but that was it. The competition, always envious and keen to topple Porsche off its perch, of course, was pressing as hard as it could. Yet, despite an increased number of attractive rivals, the Boxster S offered such a fine and balanced dynamic experience on the road that most people agreed it was

*The second-generation Boxster, launched in late 2004, had subtly improved style but evolutionary changes under the skin ran deeper, resulting in sharper handling and better performance. The 2005 model year Boxster S seen here came with a six-speed manual gearbox or the much-improved, optional five-speed Tiptronic S. (LAT)*

easily able to hold its class-leading position.

Porsche had given special attention to the interior of the Boxster S, improving the feel of quality and the looks over those of the original car. That was probably a very wise move in an image-conscious market but I must admit it meant little to me. What should matter even more, in my view at least, is the driving experience. Here the Boxster S really did deliver. A great sports car had matured into something very special indeed.

Producing the Boxster had been a very big gamble for Porsche, but nothing else would do. Early in 1996 it seemed that the chips were down across the board, that the Boxster's

costs had spiralled out of control and that its launch timing had slipped dangerously. It really was a time for steady nerves at the top. As things turned out, they got it right hadsomely and reaped the hard-earned rewards of well-deserved success. So oftcn in the past, Porsche Cars had fallen back on the 911 to keep afloat through hard times. The simple fact is that, this time, this brilliant car saved the company at a particularly tricky time in its history.

Since then, the Boxster has become steadily more high-tech, sharing much with the latest 911s. For the 2001 model year, for example, all Boxsters got drive-by-wire throttles that were necessary for its new 911-style Porsche Stability Management package. It has also got steadily faster but through all that nothing has detracted from its status as a great, everyday sports car.

The second-generation Boxster, or Type 987, introduced for 2005, brought more style, less drag, more grip, more speed and no loss of character in Porsche's least expensive model.

Also launched for 2005, the Cayman S may have been based on the Boxster's floorpan but it's in fact a very different sort of car, aimed at the serious driver. First of all, the remarkably high torsional stiffness of its coupé bodyshell gives it a different feel from the admirably stiff Boxster. It's smaller than the current 911 and is more nimble as a result. On taking the first corner in a Cayman S during a brief drive in 2005, it seemed to ring some bells in my head. Obviously a pure Porsche, something about it reminded me somehow of the greatest 911s of many years ago, only with much more grip and much more sophisticated handling. In short, I took an instant and very strong liking to the Cayman.

There's no need to take my word for that, though. A few months after it was launched, I spent a day at Goodwood with Richard Attwood, who famously drove a works 917 to Porsche's first outright Le Mans win back in 1970. He was at Goodwood to try a 40-year-old classic 904/6 racer but he arrived at

the wheel of a Cayman S and I had to ask him what he thought of it.

'It's a rorty car,' said Attwood, 'you can hear the engine and, unlike so many modern cars, it gives the driver a great feeling of direct engagement with the road and the world outside. It's more raw, if you like, as a driving experience than so many other cars today, which tend to be just too bland and too quiet inside. The handling is superb and the active damping makes it feels incredibly stable under all conditions. But the Cayman is also very usable and there's plenty of space inside.'

That's a reliable, expert opinion if ever there were one. My own short drive in a 3.4-litre, 295bhp, 171mph Cayman S was enough to put a happy grin on my face. It seemed such an appropriate evocation of everything in Porsche's glorious past. Added to its raw appeal, the Boxster-based cockpit design was extraordinarily good. I could have stayed in there for hours, enjoying its great character and prodigious performance, but I was dragged out, reluctantly, in the end.

# The 911, Types 996 and 997

*Journalist and Cresta Run rider Colin Goodwin took this left-hand-drive Carrera 4 to St Moritz in early 1999, soon after the Type 996 911 was launched. A Carrera 4 can be supremely good in these road conditions but Colin agrees with me that winter tyres remain essential. As Autocar agony uncle, Colin writes the entertaining and informative 'Ask Goodwin' column every week. (Autocar/LAT)*

Yet another huge change for the 911 came in 1997. Porsche's policy of regular, bold modernisation had kept this extraordinary chain of rear-engined sports cars at a peak of desirability for four decades. Sometimes it has involved, as here, a total redesign. This time, though, most Porsche enthusiasts were delighted and even a bit astonished by the latest road cars. What surprised them was that, despite almost universally gloomy expectations, the integrity of the 911 had been retained. Just about everybody had thought that when we finally had to face a bigger, heavier car with a new water-cooled engine, the

chapter on real 911s would close for all time. Only a few years before, there had been strong hints that the replacement would be mid-engined. As so often before, Porsche designers yet again confounded their critics by successfully updating the true 911 theme.

Strictly speaking, the new 911 that appeared in 1997 was the 'Type 996' but again the 911 name was retained in the market place for the usual sound reasons. Creating this new version cannot have been an easy task. The demands for increased passenger protection in accidents, ever-tightening emissions regulations and drive-by noise considerations, plus the need to reduce fuel consumption, are merely some of the real challenges that keep any motor manufacturer under constant pressure.

When the task at hand involves redesigning a sacred item such as the Porsche 911, and retaining its character, all I can say is that there are times when I'm glad I'm not a designer with an empty screen facing me on a computer. Apart from a touch of genius, you would need real nerve to tackle a project like that. The job was probably even tougher than the move from 356 to 911 had been in the early 1960s, yet it had to be done. Get such a thing wrong and it would blight the rest of your life.

What they produced in 1997 was a thoroughly modern expression of the classic Porsche theme, complete with that water-cooled, flat-six engine placed in a 911 for the first time. Water-cooling the cylinders not only helped the engineers to get the new model through those stricter drive-by noise regulations, it also enabled them to extract more performance per litre from the otherwise traditional layout, without compromising reliability.

Although the 1997 911 Carrera was considerably bigger than the previous model – 185mm (7.3in) longer and 30mm (1.2in) wider – and although it had a smaller engine – 3,387cc instead of the by then familiar 3.6-litre unit – it was actually faster. More power – 296bhp at 6,800rpm in 1997 – plus a sleeker body and a 50kg reduction in

*Above: Introduced for the 1998 model year, the '996' retained the distinctive look of previous 911s but was in fact completely different. Considerably bigger yet 50kg lighter than the 993, body strength was increased by its high-strength steel and modern construction techniques. The 300bhp, 3.4-litre flat-six engine was water-cooled. (LAT)*

*Below: November 2001, and the author is about to sample the latest Carrera. Improvements for the 2002 model year included a revised nose and turbo headlamps. More significant was an increase in engine size to 3.6 litres, giving 320bhp and a flatter torque curve. Top speed rose to 177mph. (Frederic Manby)*

# Porsche 911 Carrera/Carrera 4 (996)

### 1997–2001

## ENGINE:
Six-cylinder horizontally opposed, water-cooled; aluminium-alloy crankcase, cylinders and heads; rear-mounted

| | |
|---|---|
| Bore x stroke | 96.0mm x 78.0mm |
| Capacity | 3,387cc |
| Valve actuation | dohc per bank, four valves per cylinder, VarioCam |
| Compression ratio | 11.3:1 |
| Induction | DME engine management |
| Power | 300bhp at 6,800rpm |
| Maximum torque | 258lb ft at 4,600rpm |

Performance kit gave 320bhp at 6,800rpm and 258lb ft of torque at 4,600rpm

## TRANSMISSION:
Rear-wheel drive (Carrera) or four-wheel drive (Carrera 4); manual six-speed gearbox; optional five-speed Tiptronic automatic

## SUSPENSION:
*Front:* Independent by MacPherson struts, 'disconnected' light-alloy locating links using elastic rubber bushes, and coil springs; double-acting gas dampers; anti-roll bar
*Rear:* Independent by light-alloy multi-link system and coil springs; single-tube gas dampers; anti-roll bar

## STEERING:
Rack-and-pinion, power-assisted

## BRAKES:
*Front:* Disc, ventilated (12.5in)
*Rear:* Disc, ventilated (11.8in)
Cross-drilled discs with four-pot callipers; servo assistance; ABS

## WHEELS/TYRES:
Alloy wheels, 7J front and 9J rear
Tyres 205 or 225/50 ZR 17 front and 255/40 ZR 17 rear; optionally 7.5J front and 10J rear wheels, with tyres 225/40 ZR 18 front and 265/35 ZR 18 rear

## BODYWORK:
Steel monocoque
Coupé 2+2 or Cabriolet

## DIMENSIONS:

| | |
|---|---|
| Length | 14ft 6.4in |
| Wheelbase | 7ft 8.5in |
| Track, front | 4ft 9.3in |
| Track, rear | 4ft 11in |
| Width | 5ft 9.5in (inc mirrors) |
| Height | 4ft 3.4in |

## WEIGHT:
Carrera Coupé: 26.0cwt (1,320kg)
Carrera 4 Coupé: 26.5cwt (1,375kg)

## PERFORMANCE:
(Source: *Autocar*)

| | |
|---|---|
| Max speed | 173mph/164mph |
| 0–60mph | 4.6sec/4.8sec |
| Standing quarter-mile | 13.0sec/13.3sec |

## PRICE IN UK INCLUDING TAX WHEN NEW:
Carrera Coupé: £64,800 (June 1998)
Carrera Coupé Tiptronic: £68,100 (June 1998)
Carrera Cabriolet: £71,450 (June 1998)
Carrera Cabriolet Tiptronic: £74,750 (June 1998)
Carrera 4 Coupé: £68,100 (January 1999)
Carrera 4 Coupé Tiptronic: £71,300 (January 1999)
Carrera 4 Cabriolet: £74,800 (January 1999)
Carrera 4 Cabriolet Tiptronic: £78,100 (January 1999)

## NUMBER BUILT:
Carrera Coupé: 31,135
Carrera Cabriolet: 23,598
Carrera 4 Coupé: 12,643
Carrera 4 Cabriolet: 9,411

Additionally, in 2001–02, limited run of 911 'Millennium' Carrera 4 Coupés, with special trim and 'ChromaFlair' paint, containing a light-interference pigment producing a colour change when viewed from different angles

# Porsche 911 Carrera/Carrera 4 (996)

### 2001–05

As earlier Carrera except:

## ENGINE:

| | |
|---|---|
| Bore x stroke | 96.0 x 82.8mm |
| Capacity | 3,596cc |
| Compression ratio | 11.3:1 |
| Power | 320bhp at 6,800rpm |
| | 345bhp at 6,800rpm* |
| Maximum torque | 273lb ft at 4,250rpm |
| | 273lb ft at 4,250rpm* |

* With performance kit

## BODYWORK:
Newly-introduced Targa with three-part glass roof, opening rear window

## DIMENSIONS:

| | |
|---|---|
| Track, front | 4ft 9.7in |
| Width | 5ft 9.7in (inc mirrors) |

## WEIGHT:
Carrera Coupé: 26.5cwt (1,345kg)
Carrera Cabriolet: 27.0cwt (1,370kg)
Carrera Targa: 27.9cwt (1,415kg)
Carrera 4 Coupé: 27.7cwt (1,405kg)
Carrera 4 Cabriolet: 29.7cwt (1,510kg)

## PERFORMANCE:
(Source: *Autocar*)

| | |
|---|---|
| Max speed | 177mph/164mph |
| 0–60mph | 4.6sec/4.8sec |
| Standing quarter-mile | 12.9sec/13.3sec |

*Left: Carrera 4 engine as seen in an early production 996 in late 1998. Testers appreciated the improved behaviour of this new model and felt that it was by far the best Carrera 4 yet. (LAT)*

*Opposite: The instruments and controls of the new 996 attracted universal praise. It could only be a 911 in there but everything was so much tidier. A few diehards might have regretted the move from floor-hinged pedals but had to admit that the more conventional new design was excellent. (Autocar/ LAT)*

Carrera 2 with 345bhp performance kit:
(Source: Porsche)

| | |
|---|---|
| Max speed | 180mph |
| 0–62mph | 4.9sec |

**PRICE IN UK INCLUDING TAX WHEN NEW:**
Carrera Coupé: £55,950 (December 2001)
Carrera Cabriolet: £62,000 (December 2001)
Carrera Targa: £61,730 (January 2004)
Carrera 4 Coupé: £68,000 (January 1999)
Carrera 4 Coupé Tiptronic: £71,300 (January 1999)
Carrera 4 Cabriolet: £74,800 (January 1999)
Carrera 4 Cabriolet Tiptronic: £78,100 (January 1999)

**NUMBER BUILT:**
Carrera Coupé: 6,621
Carrera Cabriolet: 7,524
Carrera Targa: 2,693
Carrera 4 Coupé: 12,643
Carrera 4 Cabriolet: 9,411

Additionally 1,963 special-edition 345bhp Carrera Coupés in 2004 model year, celebrating 40 years of the 911 – 180mph and 0–62mph in 4.9sec claimed – and 911 'Millennium' special-edition Carrera 4 Coupés, with special trim and ChromaFlair paint, in 2001–02

# Porsche 911 Carrera 4S (996)
## 2001–05

As contemporary Carrera 4 except:
**BRAKES:**
*Front/rear:* Discs now 13.0in (otherwise as Carrera 4)
Ceramic discs (13.8in front/rear) with six-pot front and four-pot rear callipers optional from late 2002

**WHEELS/TYRES:**
Wheels 8J front and 11J rear
Tyres 225/40 ZR 18 front and 295/30 ZR 18 rear

**BODYWORK:**
Turbo-style body, with normal Carrera electrically extending rear spoiler; Cabriolet added early 2003

**DIMENSIONS:**
| | |
|---|---|
| Length | 14ft 6.6in |
| Wheelbase | 7ft 8.5in |
| Track, front | 4ft 10in |
| Track, rear | 5ft 0.2in |
| Width | 6ft 0in (inc mirrors) |
| Height | 4ft 3in |

**WEIGHT:**
Coupé: 28.9cwt (1,470kg)
Cabriolet: 30.8cwt (1,565kg)

**PERFORMANCE:**
(Source: Porsche)
| | |
|---|---|
| Max speed | 174mph |
| 0–62mph | 5.1sec (Cabriolet, 5.3sec) |

**PRICE IN UK INCLUDING TAX WHEN NEW:**
Coupé: £62,260 (January 2002)
Cabriolet: £70,135 (August 2003)

**NUMBER BUILT:**
Carrera 4S Coupé: 17,298
Carrera 4S Cabriolet: 5,757

# Porsche 911 GT 3
## 1998–2001/2003–2005

As Carrera except:
**ENGINE:**
| | |
|---|---|
| Bore x stroke | 100.0 x 76.4mm |
| Capacity | 3,600cc |
| Compression ratio | 11.7:1 |
| Power | 360bhp at 7,200rpm |
| | 381bhp at 7,400rpm |
| Maximum torque | 273lb ft at 5,000rpm |
| | 284lb ft at 5,000rpm |

**TRANSMISSION:**
Altered gear ratios (some higher, some lower) for six-speed manual (ratios can be changed to suit specific requirements); no Tiptronic option

**SUSPENSION:**
Special front wishbones; stiffened and lowered 1.2in

**BRAKES:**
1998–2001: Cross-drilled discs (13.0in) with four-pot callipers
2003–2005: Discs 13.8in front and 13.0in rear, with option of ceramic discs (13.8in front/rear, cross-drilled, ventilated) using six-pot front and four-pot rear callipers

**WHEELS/TYRES:**
Wheels 8J front and 10J rear (1998–2001)/ 8.5J front and 11J rear (2003–2005)
Tyres 225/40 ZR 18 front and 285/30 ZR 18 rear

**BODYWORK:**
Coupé only

**DIMENSIONS:**
| | |
|---|---|
| Length | 14ft 6.4in/14ft 6.6in |
| Wheelbase | 7ft 8.5in/7ft 8.7in |
| Track, front | 4ft 10.1in/4ft 10.5in |
| Track, rear | 4ft 10.9in/4ft 10.9in |
| Width | 5ft 9.5in/5ft 9.7in (inc mirrors) |
| Height | 4ft 2in/4ft 2.2in |

**WEIGHT:**
26.6cwt (1,350kg)/27.2cwt (1,380kg)

**PERFORMANCE:**
(Source: *Autocar*/Porsche)
| | |
|---|---|
| Max speed | 188mph/190mph |
| 0–60mph/0–62mph | 4.8sec/4.5sec |
| Standing quarter-mile | 13.2sec/not quoted |

**PRICE IN UK INCLUDING TAX WHEN NEW:**
£76,500 (August 1999)
£72,750 (November 2003)

**NUMBER BUILT:**
1998–2001: 1,868
2003–2005: 2,589

200 GT 3 RS Coupés produced for homologation purposes in 2003–05; basically street-legal racers

weight over the previous model saw to that.

This was the biggest change ever in the 911 story and, perhaps for that reason, the more exotic among the old 993 models, such as the turbo, the 'S' models, the Targa and the GT 2, remained in production alongside the new 996 well into 1998. However, in the UK the transition was probably more defined than that suggests as the 993 and 996 appeared in the British price lists together only in the first week of February 1998.

Although some people suggested at first that the bigger water-cooled model lacked the raw appeal of most of the

# Porsche 911 GT 2 (996)
## 2000–02/2003–05

As Carrera except:

**ENGINE:**

| | |
|---|---|
| Induction | Twin turbos, twin intercoolers |
| Compression ratio | 9.4:1 |
| Power | 462bhp at 5,700rpm/ 483bhp at 5,700rpm |
| Maximum torque | 457lb ft at 3,500–4,500rpm/ 472lb ft at 3,500–4,500rpm |

**SUSPENSION:**

Special front wishbones; adjustable ride height, toe-in, camber and anti-roll bars; stiffened and lowered 0.8in (20mm)

**BRAKES:**

*Front/rear:* Ceramic disc (13.8in)
Six-pot front and four-pot rear callipers

**WHEELS/TYRES:**

Wheels 8.5J front and 12J rear
Tyres 235/40 ZR 18 front and 315/30 ZR 18 rear

**BODYWORK:**

Based on Turbo; Clubsport model had partly demountable rollcage, racing seats, six-point driver's seatbelt, fire extinguisher and battery kill switch. Coupé only

**DIMENSIONS:**

| | |
|---|---|
| Track, front | 4ft 10.9in |
| Track, rear | 4ft 11.8in |
| Height | 4ft 2.2in |

**WEIGHT:**

28.4cwt (1,440kg)/28.0cwt (1,420kg)

**PERFORMANCE:**

(Source: *Autocar*/Porsche)

| | |
|---|---|
| Max speed | 196mph*/198mph* |
| 0–60mph/0–62mph | 3.9sec/4.0sec* |
| Standing quarter-mile | 12.8sec/not quoted |

*Porsche figures

**PRICE IN UK INCLUDING TAX WHEN NEW:**

£116,000 (August 2001)
£116,180 (April 2003)

**NUMBER BUILT:**

2000–02: 963
2003–05: 325

---

earlier 911s, those critics seemed to change their tune quickly when the 996 was rapidly recognised as a technical masterpiece. Inside the car, there was more space and the water-cooled engine still sounded right. The new engine definitely delivered the required performance, with 173mph available in sixth gear and a 0–60mph time of well under five seconds.

It was also a masterpiece of styling and aerodynamics: making it slightly bigger made it possible to slope the screen back a further five degrees and that helped to achieve a remarkable drag coefficient of 0.30. The first time I saw the old and the new parked together, I was surprised to note that the previous model looked almost dumpy by comparison – thanks to its more upright screen, I suppose.

Roadholding and braking in the 996 were quite outstanding but – inevitably, perhaps – the handling was a far cry from the distant days of 356-style sideways fun. It was still possible, and safe, to get the tail out, but it was quite difficult to get the car fully wound up. Most of the time it would understeer mildly but the important thing was that it did remain a supremely satisfying car to drive, at least on the road.

Back at the end of the 1980s, the then-new Carrera 2 had depressed me because it actively prevented enthusiasts from enjoying fast motoring. That car had been safe but it was also just plain dull, at first anyway.

Porsche got over that in due course, turning the 911 back into a real driver's car through the early 1990s, but it had been a painful path, I suspect.

Oddly enough, devoted 911 fans seemed to have little to say against the early Carrera 2 yet they screamed blue murder before the water-cooled jobs came along in 1997. It was an interesting reaction based on prejudice and I think all of them have long since accepted that they were totally wrong, and are delighted to admit it now.

Yes, the new car was more comfortable, almost a bit too plush inside perhaps, and it was very pleasant for long-distance grand touring, all of which suggested 'GT' rather than 'sports car'. That's all fair comment, but to my mind a radical and necessary update had been carried through with such accomplished flair that the finished product was quite irresistible. Just think about it for a minute: after every such major change, whether to the 356 or to the 911 in their many guises, it has always taken time to return to that fully-engaging feel that we associate with the rear-engined Porsche car. For example, the definitive 2.7 RS did not arrive until a decade after the 911 had replaced the 356. Following its introduction, the 996 approached a similar peak in just the same way, although this time it was a rather quicker process.

As soon as it appeared, the 996 saw constant development, including the predictable widening of the range into Cabriolet and Targa body styles, plus the turbos, GT 2s and GT 3s and so on. There has been so much choice within the 911 range in recent years that I have often wondered whether every customer selects the correct model with sufficient care. Certainly with the 996 it would have been very easy to make an apparently logical choice only to end up with something you didn't expect.

This point is well-illustrated by a trip I took in a 996 Carrera 4S Coupé to Austria a few years ago. The excuse was that I needed to drive a modern model for the purposes of writing this book! I also admit that borrowing that 4S provided a stylish way to travel to my skiing holiday. The 1,912 miles of the round trip were covered at an overall average speed of 65mph, including a lot of tootling around once I got there, with an overall fuel consumption of 25.5mpg. The car used only half a litre of oil.

Reading my original notes on that car, I see that the first thing I jotted down was, 'What a fabulous engine – the noise inside was surely devised by the marketing department. It sounds perfect, it's so smooth and easy to drive and it packs one hell of a punch.'

That said, the very idea behind the Carrera 4S concept did confuse me a bit at first but I think I worked it out in the end. Apart from showing off, the notion behind taking that particular car to Austria was that four-wheel drive would be a Good Thing for the mountain roads in winter; to take advantage of that transmission, however, I still wanted to fit winter tyres because they make an enormous difference to any car on ice and snow. For that part of the Austrian Tyrol, though, the Porsche GB people said I wouldn't need winter tyres and they declined to fit them. That surprised me as I remembered plenty of snow on those roads from my frequent trips there in the past.

They were right in a way: there's much more traffic there now, plenty of efficient snow-ploughing and a changing climate has meant there's less snow in that area these days than there used be. In short, the skiing was great but the roads were dry, though I still think I was a bit lucky there. One day I did a long round trip to visit Gmünd – for obvious reasons, that just had to be done while I was there – and I found clean tarmac all the way from Kitzbühel and back.

The car park at our local ski-lift, however, was packed with snow and

the interesting thing was that the four-wheel-drive Carrera was completely useless on it. No exaggeration, the car park was almost level but, on wide and low-profile summer tyres, the 4S wouldn't even climb the very gentle incline to get out of the higher end of it. To leave, it was strictly downhill only.

OK, so what's the point of this devastatingly quick four-wheel-drive car if it won't do that, then? What was that particular package really for? If you have your mind set on the admirable scheme of buying any new Porsche today, you really do need to choose the model and its specification more carefully than ever before. There's a good reason for everything available in the range and it takes some research to make the right choices. That particular version of the 911 had the big wheels to go with its wide, turbo-style body, plus a special interior with hard, deep-bucket sports seats in the racing style.

With such extreme seats, it's not that easy to get in but they are great in that they do give plenty of support in all the right places. After three or four hours

at the wheel, parts of my body did feel a bit stiff for a time but many hours further on I still felt unexpectedly comfortable because the design was so good. On balance, however, normal seats would have been better for general motoring, if only because those sports seats made it incredibly hard to get large items into the back of the car. Who considers that sort of thing in advance? It never occurred to me, anyway. Those seats would have been ideal for circuit driving days, I realised, and that's when I began to think really hard about what that particular 911 was meant to be.

It had tremendous traction anywhere without snow under its wheels and, when braking and cornering, the grip and handling on wet or dry roads made it pretty well foolproof. It would be

*All automatic, up or down in 20 seconds, and fully retracting under a hard cover with nothing to clip down by hand – the 911 Carrera Cabriolet version of the 996, with its very neat new design of soft-top, went on sale in April 1998. (LAT)*

*Given a typical circuit, the quickest road car available in 2001–02 was surely the latest 911 GT 2, costing UK buyers about £118,000. This, the '996' GT 2, did tend to understeer in the wet and it lacked feel when compared with outstanding previous 911s. However, with its extraordinary roadholding, 457bhp engine and 196mph top speed, what could live with it? Nothing, really, except perhaps a GT 2 Clubsport. (LAT)*

hard to get into real trouble with a 996 Carrera 4S, which was a very easy to drive well. Cars that flatter the driver that much when driven hard are often a bit dull, yet there was something very satisfying about driving that 4S.

Eventually, I worked out what it was. Mr Average could have taken that 4S on a track day, sat in his racing seat all day long around Spa and come away feeling like Jacky Ickx. It was incredibly quick, it sounded right and you could make it go seriously fast in complete safety. Experts, however, have always appreciated the slightly more demanding 911s rather

more because they always deliver more at the extremes.

The ride of that 4S was superb on most roads but it was badly caught out on some surfaces: its wide wheels tramlined a bit in truck grooves, for instance, and tyre noise was high on concrete roads. None of that's a great problem in this sort of car; the only disappointing thing I did notice was that the wipers weren't absolutely perfect in clearing the screen above 150mph. Perfection in that area, I recalled, was a most noticeable feature of the very first 911 I drove way back in 1971.

We got back from the Austrian Tyrol in record time: the 712 miles to Calais were covered in 9 hours and 20 minutes, including all stops, without breaking speed limits in a silly way. 'That wasn't exactly arduous,' said my passenger, who normally finds long car journeys tiresome. 'I thought it would be exhausting.' She was astonished to be informed that we had touched 167mph at one unrestricted point while she had been sleeping peacefully

in the dark. It was the fastest she'd ever been, by a long way, a notable grand-touring experience, and she didn't even wake up when it happened.

The 996 GT 3 and the twin-turbo GT 2, of course, were then the cars for a more hardcore take on Porsche motoring. At one stage in writing this book I thought I was going to have to admit it straight out: I had never driven a 996 GT 3 and I was running out of time. Fortunately, a completely unexpected opportunity came up late in 2004 when I was asked to take on the tough job of spending an afternoon taking members of the Goodwood Road Racing Club on 'taxi rides', one by one, round the Spa Grand Prix circuit in a current GT 3. That will do nicely, I thought. The club members were there, enjoying an exclusive visit and driving their own cars as well. I had already seen enough of the GT 3, close-up in action, to say that, if I had the money, I would have bought one. This was my chance to see if I was right about that.

That afternoon at Spa confirmed

most of my thoughts but what I hadn't expected was its performance up that long engine-sapping hill after the daunting Eau Rouge and Radillon corners. The GT 3 was even faster than I'd expected and had no problem in pulling a genuine 150mph up there before I had to brake for Les Combes. It did it time and time again throughout the afternoon, happily maintaining its consistent, very high performance without showing a hint of the effort involved. The brakes remained incredible in their stopping power and I think every GRRC member I drove round there was also properly impressed by the cornering speeds.

Apart from the astonishing performance up Spa's long, steep hill, that GT 3 surprised me in another respect. It felt and sounded like a true Porsche in almost every way but it handled almost like a normal car, if you see what I mean: thanks to modern rubber and the chassis set-up of the 996, I didn't need to hang the tail out nearly as far as I would have done with a much older 911. I'm not a sideways cowboy by nature, but I was used to a bit more opposite-lock than that in a 911 when on a circuit. It liked to drift on to the slightest trace of oversteer at times, the GT 3 of 2004, but not much. Still, it was devilishly quick.

It was extremely safe in its handling but a little inconsistent in that I could never predict exactly how much the tail would move – but such differences were tiny, almost insignificant, and the fact that it was a bit 'edgy' in its balance was not something any of the passengers picked up when I asked them what they thought after their rides.

Even so, that lack of absolute predictability was a characteristic that made it slightly less engaging than most older 911s, but, if you are into 911s, please just accept that it still represented to me a magnificent point in the long story of the car. How often we had expected 911 production to end altogether yet there it still was, 41 years after the first 911 appeared, belting round Spa with 381bhp driving its back wheels. If perfection wasn't quite reached in the 996 GT 3, it came damned close and the driver was

always well aware that it was pure 911 from stem to stern.

Something extra was expected of the more extreme GT 2 of those days, however, and here again I rely on the experience of Richard Green, an owner with an extreme addiction to the Porsche ethos and whose judgement I have come to trust completely. Over the years he has built up a collection of great Porsches, the oldest being a 1955 356 Pre-A and, as this book goes to print, his latest acquisition is a 700bhp 1998 '993' 911 GT 2 R Evo circuit car in which he is winning races in Germany.

Richard's road-legal cars include one 993 GT 2 CS and two of the rare 450bhp 993 GT 2s and, as a matter of interest, he says that he cannot really feel much difference in power on the road. It may well be right, he says, that the latter 20 cars got steel doors when the factory ran out of aluminium ones. One day, he'll get out his magnet and check that!

Meanwhile, as someone who owns some of the fastest Porsches ever made and who uses them to the limit on circuits frequently, he gave me an interesting anecdote about ceramic brakes a couple of years back. He agrees that they do work fantastically well and we all thought that they would last almost for ever, at least for so long that we could forget them. Apparently,

he and some of his friends soon found that they could wear them out surprisingly quickly, after only 30,000 miles in some cases. At £4,000 a corner to replace them, this is a serious matter and Richard told me that a significant number of owners reverted to conventional steel discs just to save money.

But back to the 996: although Richard still rates the 993 GT 2 as one of the greatest 911s of all time, he also owned a 996 GT 2 CS for a year or two and it has to be said that he was never so happy with that later car. Richard found he couldn't commit his 996 GT 2 to corners in the same that he could with any of his 993 GT 2s: 'The steering response is very sharp but in fast corners it gets twitchy. The fact that it's very overweight doesn't help, I think: you just can't tell exactly what it's going to do next.' Its handling was obviously similar to that of the 996 GT 3 I drove and while that's probably fine for a GT 3, it just wasn't good enough

*The GT 3 went on sale in May 1999. Only 40 were available to UK buyers with £76,500 to spend. Based on the 996 Carrera 4 body, the rear-wheel-drive GT 3's 360bhp engine gave it a top speed of 188mph. Serious enthusiasts preferred this engaging car to the faster, more expensive GT 2 alternative that appeared alongside just over a year later. (LAT)*

*Above: True to tradition, the new '997' model launched in 2004 looked like a good old 911, if a little wider, but was 80 per cent new in its parts. There were big improvements in handling, ride and refinement. The 177mph base model, with its 3.6-litre 325bhp engine, was very attractively priced at £58,390. (LAT)*

*Below: The 3.8-litre Carrera S of late 2004 shared all the improvements found in the new 997 base model but was a little more powerful at 350bhp, a little faster at 182mph and a little more expensive at £65,000. A tricky choice! (LAT)*

for the GT 2 in which I think the problem was probably more extreme. Although I never drove a 996 GT 2 myself, I do trust Richard's assessment.

It was a heavy car, that GT2 and, oddly enough, it wasn't stripped down anywhere near as much as the 993 GT2 CS was. 'In fact,' says Richard, 'the only changes over a standard car are the bolted-in rollcage, the full harness for the driver and fire extinguisher. So, oddly enough, the CS version of the 996 actually weighs more than the standard car because they put in more

than they took out. That's another reason I don't like them, on track at least. On the road they are deceptively quick, and stable in a straight line. Once, I was in the passenger seat being driven by an engineer. He ran over a fairly large dead animal lying in the road – possibly a badger – at close to 190mph and it trashed the lower lip of the spoiler – but the car didn't budge an inch!' Without doubt, he was right about the 996 GT 2, and he has sold that car since then.

However, I do have faith in Porsche's never-ending ability to sort their cars properly and I have observed a particular cycle of events over and over again: a totally new model is released and perhaps the extreme versions don't quite have that full touch of magic in their handling, but only at first. I did suggest then that Porsche would get those finer points back on track in due course, for the simple reason that they have always managed to achieve that in the past.

The feel and handling of the basic 996-type Carrera road car, good from the start, were improved steadily from its launch in 1997 onwards, and by the 2004 model year there were more distinct 911 models available than at any time in the past – some 15 variations in all, from the basic Carrera Coupé to the GT 2 Clubsport, with special performance packages available for them all.

*Right: The current 911 GT 3 in March 2008, at Rockingham Motor Speedway with the author. Arguably the supreme road-usable track-day car of its time, this version of the GT 3 sold out quickly in the UK. A magnificently awesome machine, some say it must be the last of its kind but how often have we heard that before? Don't be fooled! (Matt Howell)*

*Below: Universally applauded for its outstanding qualities, the '997' 911 GT 3 RS is an exciting yet user-friendly machine of extreme performance. Note the special finish of Richard Green's example here. He was the first to ask the factory to deliver in white with black script and black wheels, which wasn't an option then. He took delivery in April 2007. (Richard Green collection)*

The 997, launched in late 2004, brings us up to date. Again, far from being a mere facelift, this was another almost all-new 911 and it now seems clear that the major changes corrected an underlying problem in the handling of the 996. Whether or not that's true, the 997 chassis set-up is superb in all its forms, principally it seems as a result of a wider track and body.

The current 911 really is hard to fault in any of its different forms. In recent road tests the extreme GT 3 version has received the greatest praise from those who might have been its sternest critics had anything been not quite right. Supremely accomplished, blindingly quick and beautifully balanced when driven hard, it's also astonishingly good value for money in this rather exalted bracket of the market. My friend, Richard Green, who probably seems like your friend too by now if you have been reading this book closely, has naturally acquired a new GT 3 and he rates it very highly indeed. If he says it's good, it's excellent.

For those who feel that the 911 has perhaps grown a little too large now, I would disagree but immediately point out that Porsche also offers the Cayman S, covered elsewhere in the book, which encapsulates everything they have learnt over the years in an equally brilliant but smaller package. Having covered all the cars from the very beginning in the course of writing this book, it's more than pleasing to be able to state honestly that Porsche's product line-up has never been better than it is today.

# Epilogue

I f you have got this far in the book you must be as much of a Porsche nut as I am. Maybe also a few readers have been converted to the cause along the way. But, either way, the Porsche name is revered by the likes of us, and not for idle reasons. Porsche has taken its place at the top of the tree for us by means of its own excellence. What's more, the company has imposed on all its rivals what might once have seemed a radical concept: that of reliability in high-performance motoring.

*Carreras through the ages: looking back on three great cars from the 1960s, 1970s and 1980s reminds us of the pleasure that the long line of classic rear-engined Porsches has brought to road driving over the decades since its beginnings in 1948. (LAT)*

The incredible 911, of course, has been the mainstay product, but there were many attempts to branch out and repeat that success in other areas, none of which was truly successful until the Boxster of the mid-1990s. Since then, the Cayenne and Cayman, of course, have also proved extremely successful.

Porsche cars have changed over the decades, obviously, but the character of Porsche itself has remained remarkably consistent all along. The achievement of Ferry Porsche in building his company on the firm

foundations laid by his father was outstanding. With the last air-cooled 911 still in production, Ferry Porsche retired in 1993 and died in March 1998, 50 years after the first Porsche had been constructed by him and his dedicated team at Gmünd.

Despite all the problems he faced in establishing a business immediately after the Second World War and, later on, the sometimes painful process of turning a family business into a major company, Ferry Porsche had the vision, the energy, the management skills and polished personal style to emerge from it all in triumph.

That's not to say that all Porsche cars have been great – no-one can deny that there has been the odd lemon in this basket of peaches – but in my biased view a Porsche lemon is usually better than any product of most rivals.

Over the years, Porsche has produced an extraordinary number of wonderful cars, and even one or two superb machines that have not, oddly enough, been recognised as such by the buying public. Sometimes, way back in the past, I think Porsche created certain new models just because they liked the idea of them.

That may have been a valid business method of testing the market in its

time, but no manufacturer can afford to take such a risk today. There's no doubt that Porsche is much more proficient on the marketing front now. Take the Cayenne, which is well outside the scope of this book but must be mentioned in passing here because it has proved such a big success. It seems pretty obvious that Porsche people looked up the driveways of typical 911 owners and spotted that there was a Range Rover or something like it parked there as well. There was a ready-made market of existing Porsche owners just waiting to be offered a really high performance alternative sports utility vehicle. It wasn't guesswork. Long before the first new Cayenne reached a showroom, the company had more than a shrewd idea of how well it would sell and who would buy it.

In one way, Porsche has been in constant change from the start, always moving ahead of the times, always energetic, intelligent and alert to the importance of what it is doing. More often than not, Porsche has been a leader of the motor industry and that's a position which stemmed from the attitude of the company's founder and, even more perhaps, from that of his psychologically more rounded son, Ferry.

Making cars is not an easy way to

*The magnificent Carrera GT, first seen as a motor show concept car at Geneva in September 2000, is a mid-engined V10 of 5,733cc, giving 604bhp at 8,000rpm. Based on racing technology, this very drivable supercar has a top speed of 205mph. Production ran to 1,282 cars, ending in May 2006. (LAT)*

succeed in business and nobody in that game faces an easy future in the 21st century. So many failed in the last century by trying to make money instead of trying to make good cars, cars that were so good that people really wanted to buy them. That spark must be there to stop it going horribly quiet in the showrooms. That has been part of Porsche's secret from the start, simple as that: Porsche's exceptionally good cars have always been the products of genuine enthusiasts in a tireless quest for perfection. That's why people have bought them, not because of clever advertising campaigns or anything like that.

At the same time, some things at Porsche never change. There has always been a magical atmosphere about the place – an atmosphere of enterprise, discipline, technical mastery and, surprising to most non-

*Porsche must have looked up the drives of their wealthiest customers and seen a Range Rover parked next to every new 911! True or not, the company has hit a rich vein with the world's supreme SUV, the Cayenne, since late 2002. This is an early, 165mph Cayenne turbo, with world champion rally ace Walter Röhrl at the wheel. (LAT)*

Germans, a sense of fun. When you're in with Porsche, as I was in a very small way at one time, it's rather like going to your parents' house for a visit. It's a real family atmosphere.

For the superstars, it's all on a different level. Years ago, Jacky Ickx was treated like a god. You could feel something change in the air as he walked past the Porsche works team's pits at Le Mans, even when he wasn't driving one of the factory's cars in the race. Today, I'm sure he would still be fêted as a Porsche-driving superstar of the past even if something of that quasi-religious devotion must surely have evaporated by now. In more recent times, Derek Bell enjoyed similar status.

Such things come and go, even at Porsche. What has endured, however, is an absolute dedication to an ideal, the desire to produce the best drivers' cars relevant to any given age of

motoring. More often than not, the people at Porsche have got that right – though not always at the first attempt. Despite the odd, forgivable error of judgement down the years, Porsche has never lost the ability to pull it off nearly every time. Long may that last.

Crystal-gazing at possible cars of the future is not the purpose of this book and, anyway, that game has proved a first-class way for writers down the ages to make fools of themselves. Back in 1906 Charles Jarrott wrote in a famous book that cars couldn't possibly get any faster or any better. Cars have got somewhat quicker since then, whatever he said, so all I will say is that it seems highly unlikely to me that Porsche or anybody else will be selling 300mph road cars in the years to come. The ultimate in speed isn't everything but an exquisite quality in what a car is like to drive, and its day-to-day reliability, are things that matter more to me. Today's Porsche range meets those criteria as never before and, of course, they're also extremely fast cars.

The introduction of the very engaging Cayman intrigued me and if I were allowed one wish for a future addition to the Porsche range it would be for an even smaller sports coupé, based on a modern interpretation of

the mid-engined 550 theme. With everything Porsche has learnt in the past 60 years, they could produce something stunning of under 2 litres, possibly even as light and compact as a 356, with astonishing fuel consumption for the performance. There might be faster, far cheaper rivals to this entry-level Porsche of my dreams, but they would be like drinking decent plonk instead of a truly fine wine. Dare I suggest it might even have a flat-four engine? No, that must probably remain my absurd, private little fantasy. The people running Porsche today understand marketing far better than I ever will but, as for the rest of us, who really knows what will happen in the years ahead?

My homage to Porsche and all those decades of wonderful cars is done. Whenever I get back into a 911, whether it's brand new, like the latest fabulous GT 3 that I drove for a week as this book was about to go to press, or one of the finest classics, I'm reminded that this incredible car has always been what the rest must try to match. This is it: the real thing, how a car should go and how a car should be built. As I drive off I still say to myself every time, 'My God, these people know how to make a motor car.'

# Acknowledgements

My personal thoughts on Porsche cars have appeared here and any errors are down to me. That said, I am extremely grateful to a host of people consulted over the years it took to complete this book.

Many journalistic colleagues who appear in the photographs were kind enough to tell me their memories of the cars, including Roger Bell, Richard Bensted-Smith, Stuart Bladon, Michael Bowler, Richard Bremner, Gordon Bruce, Charles Bulmer, Anthony Curtis, Peter Dron, Andrew Frankel, Colin Goodwin, Rex Greenslade, John Miles, Jeremy Sinek and David Vivian.

From Porsche Cars Great Britain Limited, John Aldington granted several interviews before his untimely death. From the modern organisation in Reading, Andrew Davis and Nick Perry were good enough to give access to the right cars and information.

The friendly and efficient Porsche Club Great Britain, in particular former AFN stalwart and ex-racer Steve Kevlin, always answered my questions usefully and promptly.

Interviews, freely given, with such luminaries as Richard Attwood, Vic Elford and the late Denis Jenkinson were much appreciated.

Countless hours were put in cheerfully by Porsche specialists, most of all Josh Sadler of Autofarm and Andy Prill of Maxted-Page & Prill, as I pestered them for facts.

Finding all the photographs would have been a nightmare without my friends at LAT, especially the indefatigable Kathy Ager. Dieter Gross of the Porsche Historisches Archiv was equally helpful. The staff of *Classic Cars* magazine, notably Editor Phil Bell and Archivist Tony Turner, were most generous with their assistance in finding photographs. Special thanks must go, too, to photographers Jeff Bloxham and Mike Valente for permission to use their work.

Without the generosity of countless hundreds of Porsche owners who have allowed me to drive or race their precious cars, this book would not have been possible at all. Special thanks are due here to Richard Green, a dedicated Porsche enthusiast and collector.

Finally, while I have a horrible feeling that I must have left out somebody important, I do have to acknowledge the kindness, the encouragement, the unfailing good humour and, above all, the extraordinary patience of Mark Hughes, the Books Division Editorial Director at Haynes Publishing. I must admit it did take rather a long time.

*Above: Porsche specialist Andy Prill of Maxted-Page & Prill Ltd, at his workshop premises near Halstead in rural Essex. Andy's immensely detailed knowledge of the 356 was invaluable to the author in the preparation of this book. (Author)*

*Below: Nobody knows more about early 911s than Autofarm founder and proprietor Josh Sadler, seen here judging cars at the 'Porsches at the Castle' event in 2007. The author leaned heavily on Josh for advice on 911s of all ages, and is very grateful for his help. (Author)*

# Further reading

For further background information I am grateful to the following writers:

*Porsche, Excellence Was Expected*
(Automobile Quarterly) Karl Ludvigsen
*Porsche Data Book* (Haynes) Marc
Bongers
*Porsche Boxster Story* (Haynes) Paul Frère
*Porsche 911, Volumes I & II* (MRP)
Michael Cotton
*Porsche 356* (Osprey) Denis Jenkinson
*Original Porsche 356* (Motorbooks)
Laurence Meredith
*Huschke von Hanstein, the Racing Baron*
(Könemann) Tobias Aichele

Plus: Generations of road-test writers on the two magazines variously known as *Autocar, The Autocar, Autocar & Motor, The Motor* and *Motor*.

# Clubs

*Porsche Club Great Britain*
www.porscheclubgb.com

*Porsche Club of America*
www.pca.org

# Index